LEAPING FROM THE BURNING TRAIN

LEAPING FROM THE BURNING TRAIN

A Poet's Journey of Faith

JEANNE MURRAY WALKER

SL/NT
BOOKS

LEAPING FROM THE BURNING TRAIN
A Poet's Journey of Faith

Copyright © 2023 Jeanne Murray Walker. All rights reserved. Except for brief quotations in critical publications or reviews, no part of this book may be reproduced in any manner without prior written permission from the publisher. Write: Permissions, Slant Books P.O. Box 60295, Seattle, WA 98160.

Slant Books
P.O. Box 60295
Seattle, WA 98160

www.slantbooks.org

Cataloguing-in-Publication data:

Names: Walker, Jeanne Murray.

Title: Leaping from the burning train: a poet's journey of faith / Jeanne Murray Walker.

Description: Seattle, WA: Slant Books, 2023

Identifiers: ISBN 978-1-63982-145-7 (hardcover) | ISBN 978-1-63982-144-0 (paperback) | ISBN 978-1-63982-146-4 (ebook)

Subjects: LCSH: Autobiography | Autobiography--Religious aspects | Imagination--Religious aspects--Christianity | Fundamentalism--United States

For Helen Siml deVette

Contents

Prologue | ix

1 Leaping from the Burning Train | 1

2 Buying the Cross at Bible Camp | 20

3 Saving and Getting Saved | 34

4 My Dead Brother Teaches Me to Travel | 55

5 Shakespeare Asks to Meet My Mother | 76

6 Writing as a Subversive Activity | 92

7 Saving Images | 107

8 Like Postcards from a Friend | 126

9 How to Read a Poem | 139

10 Diary of a Rehearsal | 157

11 The Communion of Saints | 173

12 Christmas: The View from Prison | 188

13 Deeper than Memory | 197

Acknowledgments | 217

Prologue

THIS IS A BOOK ABOUT a girl who left home without quite meaning to. It began willy-nilly one night while I was sitting in bed in Lincoln, Nebraska, writing out algebra equations and listening to a DJ on the radio. I was sixteen. Until then I lived in the chrysalis spun by my parents and their close friends. Weekdays I attended a Christian school started by my father. And then there was church. Every time the janitor turned on the lights, we were there: Sunday School, church, prayer meetings, young peoples' meetings, vacation Bible school, mother-daughter banquets, midnight vigils, revivals, car washes. I eschewed makeup, fell in love with the approved boys, handed out tracts in the neighborhood, and spouted my parents' invective against Adlai Stevenson.

That fateful night, listening to "The Purple People Eater," an improbable thought pierced and held me. *Suppose none of this is true?* I had the sense, suddenly, that I was glancing out between stones in the walls of a fortress. It wasn't just that I saw the vast meadow outside or that the meadow looked tantalizingly fresh and green and worth exploring. I saw for the first time that I was living inside a fortress.

Most Sundays of my life I had listened with my family to the evangelist Billy Graham argue on his radio show, *The Hour of Decision,* that the destiny of my eternal soul would depend upon the choice I made about whether to accept Jesus as my savior. It never occurred to me to question that. When I saw this way of thinking about the world was not the only reasonable alternative, I understood that, indeed, I had a choice to make. I had never before comprehended that a single decision could change everything—the people I befriended, the way I dressed, what I ate, who I married. Nor did I understand that the notion of choice involved far more than whether a person ought to steal candy on a Tuesday afternoon from the corner store. I had to choose whether to stay in the fortress or to leave.

About three years later, I left.

This book tells the story of that leaving and the particular path that led me out of the fortress: the language of poetry. It is also, as I discovered in writing it, a book about returning home—or, to put it a different way, about the journey I had to travel in order to preserve the heart of the faith we all clung to so fiercely in my childhood.

It is a story fraught with grief and confusion and astonishment. I went to college and graduate school, where I felt painfully out of place (though I found, to my surprise, that my knowledge of the King James Bible made me more comfortable with sixteenth-century texts than most other students). I encountered writers whose voices felt so familiar I might have heard them before I was born. Eventually, I started writing myself. People who read my books began writing to me. And I began to work in the theater, a pleasure long forbidden by fundamentalism. This book reveals the joy and desperation I felt with each step away from my snug fundamentalist home.

At the same time, I hope this book also reveals the love and respect I feel for "my people." We called our parents' friends *Aunt* and *Uncle*. We knew that if you got a bad diagnosis in the morning, by evening the phone chain would spread the word and your phone would start to ring. You could feel people all over your city thinking of you. When my father died, my people brought hams and scalloped potatoes and Jell-O. The women loved to cook, and we ate together at the drop of a hat. People visited us when we were sick. They stayed till the doctor got there and held our hands and prayed for healing. Even the poorest of us donated to those who lost their jobs. If we cast our bread upon the waters, we believed, it would return to us. We shared a comforting, coded dialect, and the grown-ups were dependable as granite.

Prologue

Many of the core fundamentalist beliefs are still what I affirm. T.S. Eliot's lines from *Four Quartets* have been quoted so often they've become something of a cliché but I can truly say that in writing this book the end of my "exploring" has been to arrive where I started "and know the place for the first time."

Historians and theologians have produced brilliant studies of the American Protestant fundamentalism within which I was raised. Rather than attempt a summary of that tradition's origins and tenets, I will stick with what I know and what I can render: the stories and memories of my childhood and the community that nurtured me.

What I will note here is that over the decades I became increasingly aware—with a shock of recognition—that certain strains of American Protestantism bore similarities to other fundamentalist movements around the world, including ultra-orthodox Judaism, portions of the Islamic tradition, and the rise of highly politicized secular ideologies. The dark side of fundamentalism—and of the literalism that is required to sustain it—can be seen everywhere these days, and not just in religious circles.

Which is why I hope my story can be seen as more than one person's idiosyncratic narrative. The particulars of this narrative are mine, but many other people have faced similar choices, considered the same quandaries, wavered, stumbled, struggled, and finally made a decision. It is the narrative of an individual torn between birthright fundamentalism and a more capacious world, someone who, through sustained attention to the imaginative language of metaphor and symbol, allusion and ambiguity, came to inhabit a wider and more vibrant sense of the world—and of God as its creator and redeemer.

1

Leaping from the Burning Train

A FRIEND OF MINE HAS a burn scar, like a violet, asymmetrical puddle on the left side of her face. When we were in college, she bought a cheap seat on a train that took two days to snake across Europe from Paris to Hungary. Awaking from a snooze in the late afternoon, in the haze of dusk, she thought she saw red flames. The passengers around her were reading, playing cards, sleeping, talking lazily.

She had a little discussion with herself. Because really, what do you do? Clear your throat and make an announcement? Discuss the likelihood of its being fire with the gentleman sitting next to you? Yank the emergency cord? And what if you're wrong? Usually when you think you've seen a fire, you haven't. It's the sun setting like a smear in the window several seats ahead of you.

As she was thinking about this, she smelled smoke. Feeling a wall of heat move up the aisle, she yelled, "Stop the train!" And then someone else called out, in what she remembers as German. There was a pandemonium of voices in different languages. People lunged toward the front of the car. A stocky man and woman stopped and began arguing in the aisle, pushing and shoving one another, screaming words she didn't understand. Behind them everyone jammed the passage, thrusting, heaving, desperate to get to the doors, unable to move forward. Panic-stricken, the clot of people who couldn't move pushed someone down. Several people fell. My friend couldn't see what happened to them.

She wrenched herself up and wedged herself into the stream of people in the aisle. A woman, whose big straw hat tilted at a bizarrely jaunty angle, stabbed her with a red umbrella. Eventually, she reached the door. The train was rocking crazily, the fields were racing by, green and blurry. People behind her shouted and pressed against her. In the car ahead, some were hurling themselves through the open door. She couldn't see where they landed or what happened to them.

My friend leapt from the open door. She balled herself up and rolled into a silent ditch filled with flowers, which she tells me she recalls with manic clarity. Opening her eyes, she saw delicate, slender purple iris, pink lilies with tiger faces. At the bottom of the gully stood a group of tall, prickly-looking scarlet cone flowers. In the field on the other side of the ditch, she could see squat little green plants set in rows across the ashy black soil. Far above her, the clouds traveled on in the absurd blue sky, and in the vast silence, she heard the iterated chirp of a single bird. She lay there for a long time. Eventually, two firemen picked her up tenderly and moved her to a stretcher. There were a lot of fatalities on the train. It took over six months for her to recover enough to come back to classes.

What I know about her—what little anyone can know about a friend, the one-tenth of the iceberg you see sailing above the surface—is funny and garrulous. She tells about the fire as if it happened to another woman a long time ago. When I saw her recently at a conference, I reminded her of the train story.

Eventually, we drifted into a discussion of politics. She mentioned that Jim Lehrer, at the end of his *NewsHour*, was still screening the faces of American servicemen killed in Iraq and Afghanistan. The first time I saw those pictures of faces, I told her, I was stunned that instead of hearing the info-news chatter typical on most other stations, we watched the pictures go by in total silence. We talked about the rising cost of health care, and the bad jobs numbers, and we narrated the tragedies of some our unemployed friends, who had given up on finding new jobs. We worried in 2008 about whether we would ever be in a position to retire, given the recent catastrophic loss of our retirement funds. And then our discussion moved to Iran, which then was defiantly insisting on developing nuclear energy, and to the shocking changes in weather all over the globe. On the East Coast, we had just suffered a series of blizzards which closed schools and stopped business for days at a time and which, we agreed, were symptoms of global warming.

The two of us spoke about this quickly, in code, speeding up feverishly as we became more certain that we still agreed with one another. We were worried and angry. We held the Other Side responsible. We referred to George Bush, to his lies about WMDs, to his incompetence after Hurricane Katrina, to his laws rescinding constitutional protections against wiretapping, to tax cuts to the superrich. We ticked down our lists. And then we had to leave for other appointments.

Later that day, I felt haunted by a peculiar emptiness as I realized that we had not really talked, that we had simply rehearsed a script. What about her marriage, her children, her career as a lawyer, her personal discoveries and changes? I began to feel bereft. We had substituted political speech for our own experience. The truth is, I was beginning to feel the bankruptcy of name-calling and re-circling the same angry, despairing political accusations in the company of friends who agree with me.

Fast forward. It's months later, late August 2009, and I'm writing during the blistering dog days of summer. Our glorious basil, which has grown waist-high, needs to be cut for pesto. The hedges need trimming again. Afternoons are so hot that when I step through the door of my study onto the patio, I feel like a candle, melting. My shirt is damp in ten minutes. Most of our neighborhood has cleared out and friends are off on vacation. Senators and U.S. Representatives are back in their districts talking about the health care bill. We have a different President now and a different set of policies. A different set of citizens opposes his policies than the citizens who opposed George Bush's. These people have been showing up around the country to disrupt and drown out town hall-style discussions. Some of them arrived at a meeting in Colorado yesterday carrying guns. "They" are the political Right, and they include a fair number of Christian fundamentalists.

You might say the engine of civil conversation, which should be moving America into the future, is on fire. Meanwhile, those of us on the train are screaming and pushing one another down. Much about this country needs to be fixed—the economy, our environment, health care, our fear of terrorism, racial inequality, education, and our troubled cities. Without solutions to some of these problems, our future as a nation looks dim. In fact, our future on the planet appears to be in jeopardy. But we have trouble reaching a solution because we can't talk to one another. Neither can our representatives in Washington. We are a deeply and disastrously divided nation.

Several weeks before George W. Bush ordered the attack on Iraq to bring about *regime change*, as he called it, my husband and I marched against the war. Sort of. We were in Paris. It was February 14th. The early evening was chilly and because the Metro was undergoing repairs, the stations were cluttered with scaffolding. We were going to celebrate Valentine's Day with a special dinner at Le Petit Prince, where we had first dined a decade ago. We emerged from the underground around 5:00 p.m. to glimpse a river of French men and women, young and old, pouring down Boulevard de la Mutualité. People walked, rode bicycles, waved flags from the backs of trucks. They wore scarves and berets and layers of sweaters. Slender, beautiful young people defied the cold wind by leaving their shirts open. Ragtag dudes hoisted bed sheets with slogans. Pregnant women sang. Professor-like figures trudged along in full length coats reading books. A child wearing mittens led a puppy on a red leash.

The first time I protested a war, I was twenty. Mike Burton, the editor of our campus newspaper at Wheaton College, joined me in the lunch line. He had just come from reading modern philosophy, and as I ordered a hamburger, he quietly effervesced about Heidegger. Then he slipped me a copy of *TIME* magazine opened to a picture of an American soldier's astonished face, snapped by a photographer at the very moment the young fighter took a bullet to the stomach. The caption reported that the soldier was twenty. I was shocked at how young he was: my age.

I glanced at the close-up, stepped out of line, and, feeling I might throw up, wandered off to the ladies' room. When I returned to the lunchroom, Mike, who was by nature courtly and generous, apologized but nevertheless went on to make a case against the war. The authorities—President Johnson, Dean Rusk, Robert McNamara—and our administration at Wheaton—argued that if we pulled out of Vietnam the country would turn Communist. If Vietnam turned Communist, a string of other countries in the region would follow suit. This was known as the Domino Theory. Michael had been arguing against it quietly for a year. I paid for my cheeseburger, then scraped it into the trash, listening while he turned the fire hose of his powerful logic on me. Shaken as I was, I hung on for dear life to my skepticism. How could any of us know? We weren't there in Vietnam. And we didn't possess the statistics.

I was the dutiful child of a father who died early and a mother who had heroically taken on both parenting roles. I needed to believe the parent is right. The child who rocks the boat sinks the ship. I believed that if a parent makes a mistake, at least she might have an idea about how to fix it. How could McNamara, who was reputed to be a genius, who had been head of Ford, who had access to so much information, be mistaken? How could any of us who had not run the world guess its complications?

Like many students at Wheaton at the time, however, I was reading philosophy, taking what I understood of it to heart, struggling to comprehend the stunning, recent deaths of my father and my brother. Like many of my friends at the school, I was beginning to see that I had a responsibility to behave ethically in the world. Reading Sartre and Kierkegaard and Camus, talking about them until late at night, some of us began trying to act, not as a person "should," but as we said, "authentically." I wanted to take my freedom as an individual seriously, to feel each moment honestly as it passed. The immediacy of that young soldier's expression became a catalyst for me. I began to question why he had to die. I no longer felt so certain that people who had started the war were right.

The year before that, as president of my freshman class, I was expected to appear in a routine ROTC ceremony to review the cadets. The truth is, as I thought about the event, I was mainly preoccupied with what to wear. The morning dawned, cool and crisp and full of blue sky, as only the Midwest can be. I had bought a white suit with gold buttons. I could ill afford to buy new clothes, but I justified the price by thinking of the occasion as a responsibility. The suit with its gold braid looked vaguely military to me. For two weeks, I kept it hanging on the handle of my closet door, so I could admire it. That morning after taking a shower, I tore off the sheltering plastic and put it on for the first time. I pulled on white gloves. I stood in front of the mirror looking like a million dollars.

Then reluctantly, I began to pay attention to the war inside me. I knew some of my friends believed our support of the Saigon government was immoral. I went to the refrigerator and gnawed on raw carrots for a while, then paced my room, wracking my brain about whether I should go through with the ceremony. I phoned a friend and told her I felt torn between opposing duties. I had been summoned by the college administration, and I wanted to fulfill my responsibilities as class president. On the other hand, I had been horrified several weeks before when one of my close friends had shipped out to fight in Vietnam. On the other, *other* hand, I knew my distress at his leaving wasn't proof the war was wrong. My friend on the phone was kind enough to take me seriously, to ask sympathetic questions.

What I did not confess to her, or even to myself, was that I loved the idea of standing at attention on a reviewing stand, looking spiffy in my white suit as the wind blew gently through my hair. I probably did not quite understand that the ceremony involved role-playing that did not require the presence of any particular individual. If I had declined to review the troops, our administrators would quickly have substituted one of the other freshman class officers. But I loved the notion that they had personally summoned me. After a long, tortured, semi-honest debate with my friend, I said goodbye, put the phone down, and dashed off to review the troops.

Would it have made a real difference if I hadn't?

To me, it would have.

To students at the school or the wider world? I doubt it.

The Vietnam War drove a wedge between the generations in my family because both sides were absolutely sure they were right. Several times a year, I visited my mother, who after ten years of surviving as a widow, had married my stepfather and gone to live with him in Dallas. During the day, my mother and I gallivanted around to museums and stores, never mentioning politics, but one night at dinner, my stepfather, who was usually mild-mannered, generous, began ranting against the spoiled, presumptuous, out-of-control youth who were taking over buildings on campuses. He had been watching TV.

I got up from their dining room table, pretending to clear the plates, and walked around their kitchen, fuming. I wanted to scream, so I stuffed a red plaid dish towel into my mouth. In truth, at the time, I wasn't sure about the war. But my parents' staunch, unflinching refusal to think or to investigate, to consider alternatives, drove me nuts.

For years we stood on opposite sides and glowered at one another. We spoke to each other about the war in prefabricated, ready-made slabs of language that we had probably picked up from political rallies or television or our separate churches. After that, the subject of the war flared up only occasionally, but for years it lay beneath the surface of our visits, the implacable conflict that defied resolution or even civil discussion.

Why? What was at stake? I can only answer for myself. If I'd had a real conversation with my parents, they might have won because, in my heart of hearts, I wasn't as sure of my own position as I pretended to be. And my definition as a member of my generation—rather than theirs—rested, in part, on my stance on the Vietnam War. What was at stake for me in holding my position against my parents was dignity, what the Spanish speakers in Lima, Peru, where I traveled the next year (in an effort to gain some independence) called *dignidad*—self-respect, a sense of my own nobility as a human being. Like most children, I needed to define myself as separate from my parents, which I did in some arbitrary ways. But this didn't feel arbitrary; it felt like a matter of morality.

As it turned out, I was right about the war, but I was, perhaps, as much at fault as my mother. I disdained her for her opinion, and I am sure she never felt contempt toward me for mine. The scorn I felt for the other side helped me to barricade myself against real discussion. What I'd have risked by having a real conversation with my parents was that if they had convinced me, I would have needed to change. To change would have meant to stop being the self I recognized. I did not want to stop being myself.

My fundamentalist parents were always driven by anxiety about change. I realize now, as I did not at twenty-three, that my mother had a history that pre-disposed her to see the Vietnam War as she did. She was a teenager during the Depression when her parents lost a good bit of their farmland. In 1933, she taught twenty-two kids in a one-room schoolhouse in rural Minnesota for $60 a month. My father, during the war, dropped out of college. After they married, they wanted something they could count on at any cost, something that would not change. No wonder they joined the fundamentalist movement.

Any form of gambling or card-playing became a symbol of the kind of financial and moral risk my fundamentalist parents abhorred. Shortly after they were married, they spent a blowout weekend at the cabin of some friends on Lake Miltona, a resort community close to Parkers Prairie, where my father served as postmaster before he took over the general store from his father. Apparently, during that weekend, which later became notorious in our family stories, a number of couples my parents' age had celebrated the mild June weather by drinking and dancing and playing cards on the shore of the lake. My father had grown up with these people in Parkers, and his with-it childhood friends now socialized as couples. He had brought his farm wife home to the town, and she had, apparently, passed the test and joined his group. They'd been swimming, the women in their flowered World War II bathing suits with pleated skirts, the men daring one another to take off their shorts and skinny dip. For Saturday night dinner, they splurged on butter and eggs and meat, and they told ribald jokes and bet a small bit on card games. The next day they skipped church, lingering at the beach until late in the afternoon.

That Sunday night, as my parents drove back to town, they talked about the money they had lost, which was not much, but which they needed to pay the rent, and about the drinking and the way they had unaccountably abandoned caution to join the loose lifestyle of my father's group. Later that night, in a solemn ritual that my mother could still describe when she was eighty, they climbed downstairs together to the wood-fire furnace, opened the door to the red-hot coals, tossed their playing cards into the iron jaws, and watched the flames eagerly leap up to devour the pack. After that, my parents never allowed cards in the house, and they renounced parties at the beach and alcohol of all kinds.

My parents' need for certainty also manifested itself in the concept of personal "reputation." My father, in particular, drilled into his children that however we felt about our duties, we needed to follow through on what we had promised. Our whims would come and go, but in a small town like Parkers Prairie, and in the small world of the fundamentalist subculture, people had long memories and character counted.

One day in the autumn, a high school kid, the son of my parents' friends, asked to borrow my father's hunting decoys. He took them out on the lake over the weekend. When my father ran into the kid at the hardware store a week later, he enthusiastically described using them to bag a couple of ducks.

My father came home puzzled. The kid had said nothing about bringing the decoys back. When he didn't return them the following week, my parents convened a family discussion over a dinner of scalloped potatoes and ham. What should they do? My older brother suggested that my father should buy more decoys.

"They're expensive," my father said. "They have to be ordered from Minneapolis."

"For how much?" my brother asked. He was older and he knew more about money than I did.

"Hmmm. More than your bike."

"Well, ask for them back, then."

"I shouldn't have to do that."

"Why?"

"He borrowed them. He should know enough to bring them back. It's been three months and I'd like to go hunting before we get a lot of snow."

At this point, my mother pitched in with the story about how, when she was a young wife, she had borrowed a cake pan from my father's aunt, a short, stout beloved woman named Aunt Joe. When my mother failed to return it the next day, Aunt Joe marched the two blocks to our house, rang the doorbell, demanded it back, and read my mother the riot act for not promptly returning what she had borrowed. The rule was you don't merely return a borrowed pan. You return it promptly and you fill it with a gift of candy or freshly baked bread or canned peaches.

We kids stirred our potatoes around on our plates and blinked at the seriousness of not returning property we had borrowed.

"Why don't you talk to Morris?" my mother suggested. Morris was the father of the teenager who had borrowed the decoys.

"Don't you figure he's got enough to worry about?" Morris had six children and he was struggling to keep his farmland.

In the end, my father spoke to the kid—weeks later—who told him that the decoys had floated away. Just disappeared. Poof. As if that were enough to convince my father that the score was settled. This story became famous in our family. *Remember the decoys*, our parents would say to us. It became a marker, warning us that we needed to build a reputation for reliability.

My parents' love of stability and permanence may have been what made my father design and build two houses for us with his own hands. He knew the plumbing was reliable because he had put it in himself. He could depend on the electrical system because he had wired the house. The first house he built was in Minnesota. The second was in Lincoln, Nebraska, where my parents moved us so my mother could find a job. And so we could be close to the *Back to the Bible* broadcast, an early fundamentalist radio show produced in Lincoln. And so, after my father (who was terminally ill) died, we kids could save money by living at home while we attended the University of Nebraska. That was my parents' idea. None of us went to school there. But we could have. What my parents wanted was insurance. If we needed it, the university was close by.

I watched my father build our second house. On a spring day when the fledgling leaves were budding on our tiny dogwoods, I stood beside him at the edge of our new lot line on the outskirts of Lincoln and watched an earth-moving machine slowly roll onto our land. The din of the machine made us plug our ears. I could feel vibrations in my feet. As its jaws bit cleanly through the grass, I understood that the way to start building a house is simply to subtract earth.

For months afterward, whenever I wasn't in school or doing my homework, I was helping to raise the walls of our house. My father let me practice pounding nails until every time I whammed the head three times, the shaft flew straight in. Every time the hammer hit home, I felt closure. There. That's done. That will never come out. I still hear the clang of my handsome father's pounding, and I can feel the rhythmic swing of his freckled right arm as he nailed the raw studs in place. His straight reddish hair fell over his forehead as he pounded. He was *going to die, going to die, going to die.* For himself, he wasn't afraid. He wanted to finish this house before he left us. I suspect he wanted to anchor the studs of that house to the foundation of the universe.

My father was not afraid to die because he felt convinced of the one most essential and final thing. With absolute certainty, he believed that to be absent from us was to be present with the Lord. We would all be reunited. Both my parents repeated that often as a fact. As a result, they faced his death with bravery that—especially since I've been a parent—seems inconceivable to me. My father never became an invalid. He was looking for adventure until the week before he died.

The certainty that buoyed my father was esteemed among my fundamentalist people and it was strengthened by hymns and the fundamentalist culture, which was set apart from the secular world. We sang about blessed assurance. We lustily harmonized, *I'm a child of the King*, and *When the roll is called up yonder, I'll be there*. These convictions, of course, obligated us to feel happy. We kids sang *Jesus wants me for a sunbeam*, and *I've got the joy, joy, joy, joy down in my heart!* Our private dialect and potlucks and prayer chains and Christian school reinforced the certainty my fundamentalist parents so prized. We lived in a feedback loop.

Above all, our language set us apart from the mainstream culture. We were washed in the blood of the Lamb. We bore witness to the faith and let our lights shine before men. We wanted to fully surrender to the Lord. Jesus knocked patiently at the doors of our hearts. We repeated the same words and images until we knew—we *knew*—the world through those images. My parents tended to live the way they talked. We said grace before meals. Before long car trips, we bowed our heads and prayed for safety. My parents quite clearly loved one another, and they got along famously. I had no inkling then, of course, that their fervent beliefs and language could be called an ideology. I thought it was just obviously and simply the truth.

Years after my father died, when I was in my twenties and visiting my mother in Dallas, she had the dial tuned to a radio preacher, as she often did all day. She loved to feel awash in the music and language of fundamentalism, which by then had started driving me bonkers. We were making turkey sandwiches for lunch. The preacher was praying. *Oh Lord, shower your blessings right now on our radio audience. And we just thank you that you have adopted us as your sons!* I was reflecting on why the Lord never seemed to adopt any daughters when, out of the blue, my mother remarked, "He's a godly man."

"How can you tell?" I asked.

She looked at me strangely as if I should know. "His language."

I had never before heard my mother comment on language. I had never realized that she understood so clearly her own linguistic choices. *There's a code*, she was warning me. *Follow the code I've taught you.* I knew she thought that when I went off to graduate school I was sailing in dangerous waters. By then, I was reading *Moby Dick* and Spenser's *Faerie Queene* and the difficult, radiant poems of Emily Dickinson. I had already apprenticed myself to these masters. I was, indeed, sailing in fresh waters—beyond shallow fundamentalist clichés, out into the deep, ferocious ocean of the English language. To me, the waters felt not dangerous but heady and freeing.

My mother was right. There is a code. The idiom my parents spoke was a language of fundamentalist protest against modernism and consumerism. Back then, it was the dialect of people who had almost no power. Many of the fundamentalists I knew had little control over politics and they tended to be lower middle class. Their echo-chamber language tended to be limited to religious ideas. But with the political mobilization of the fundamentalist right in the middle of the twentieth century, the dialect of fundamentalism became a language of power, and it took on a new dimension: politics.

Ideological language, whether it's the language of religion or of politics, deals in prefabricated slabs of words. A phrase can frame and define a whole issue. The phrases are often metaphorical. The metaphor makes an argument that may not be surfaced, that smuggles a hidden assumption into the conversation.

Language is endlessly shifting, of course, so specific examples become outdated before a book like this is through the publishing process. But consider idioms like *death panels*, or *the war on terror,* or *government takeover of health care*, or *socialized medicine*. These phrases imply whole ideas. Take *death panels*, for example. This term, which Sarah Palin concocted, argues that the authorities under the new health care bill—those who decide which medical procedures can be reimbursed and which can't—are going to pull the plug on your loved ones. Of course, insurance companies, who are currently the "deciders," may pull the plug. But the term *death panels* banishes discussion about these questions. It puts the rabbit in the hat. It obscures problems and questions with a clever phrase.

The political right is not alone in its use of ideological language. The left refers to itself as *the progressives* and refers to conservatives as *the lunatic fringe*. It frames its own agenda as *tax relief* and its proponents chant *Yes we can!* Of course, prefabricated, ideological language is nothing new, but it increasingly takes the place of discussion, not only on the streets, but in Washington. Both the liberals and the conservatives—whatever those words mean anymore—both Republicans and Democrats hire linguists to shape language. They scheme ways to distort political issues in favor of their points of view. They repeat the new cliches until they seem natural. They imprison us in points of view before we open our mouths. And since by and large we listen to news that confirms our biases, we lock ourselves ever more firmly into our prejudices.

Given that we're together on a train—and the train is on fire—we could use some discussion. But what language can we use? What assumptions do we both agree on to start with? Those of Glenn Beck or those of Rachel Maddow? Talking politics with someone on the opposite side is scary. The effort to get past all the manufactured phrases takes reflection. The risk of offending is great. So instead of talking, we just push one another down in the aisle of the train.

Or maybe it's not our separate languages that keep us from talking. Maybe it's the fear that drove me during my discussions with my parents about the Vietnam War. I had a compulsive need to think of myself as correct. I didn't want to risk having to admit to them that they were right and I was wrong. And I was afraid to change. If I really listened to their point of view, if I gave them a chance to convince me, I would not leave their house as the same person. I would cease to recognize myself.

I don't know about you, but most of the time I feel a great need for certainty. In that way, I am not unlike my parents. I would like everything around me to be safe and predictable. Until I'm bored. Then I would like only small changes—only the ones I want. Among other things, I love to feel certain of my political positions, for example, that street people can be cleaned up and made productive and that it's possible to create a healthcare system that doesn't exclude fifty million Americans. So why should I talk with anyone who disagrees, especially since I don't really know how that kind of talk might go. I have my own prefabricated language and they have theirs. Hate speech is the business of some of them who write blogs and host talk shows. But I know the people who tune in to hear those personalities might be less doctrinaire, more capable of compassion and empathy than the speakers are. I just don't know many of them. I have opinions about them, but generally, I'm afraid to talk to them. I don't even know where to start. *Hi. What a cute dachshund! Is he yours?* Anything more complicated—like discussing the coming election—and I'm out of my depth.

And besides, I've spent many years now *not* talking to "them."

But here's the rub. There's a difference between *knowing* I'm right and actually *being* right. My parents knew they were right about the Vietnam War. They were absolutely certain. They were so certain that after a while, they didn't entertain discussion about the war. Feeling certain about something doesn't guarantee that you're right. It just prevents any connection with the other side. As I have said, in the argument about the Vietnam War, I was even less well-behaved than my parents because I *wasn't* certain the war was wrong, but I pretended I was.

Certainty is one of the fundamentalist values I don't believe is possible anymore. I say that with sadness. Who doesn't long to be certain? But unfortunately, because we're human, there's a limit to how certain we can be of anything. At least, that's what I believe when I'm not climbing the wall with anxiety. I understand how important *blessed assurance* was to my father and mother, who knew my father was dying and wanted to be positive that we kids would be safe and that we would all be reunited. I think my parents were right. We'll all be reunited. But how can I know for sure? The only way of knowing that is through faith.

I nominate faith to take the place of certainty. The problem is faith is scary, at least for me. For the last several decades, I have spent a fair amount of time in London. I worship sometimes at St. Paul's, one of London's magnificent cathedrals. A few weeks ago, I was sitting on a wooden chair in the nave with six hundred other people, listening to a boys' choir. Their treble soared through white marble columns to the dome three hundred and fifty feet above us. At the end of the service, the procession of robed clergy filed up the center aisle toward the rear. Our triumphant voices sang *All Hail the Power of Jesus' Name,* rising to mingle with sunlight from the balcony windows.

After the service, I decided to change my perspective from the vast and exalted and holy marble expanse of the nave to the more dangerous tower. I decided to climb to the top of the dome. I've decided that many times, and I've always backed out. This time I promised my students; I swore to them and to myself that I would follow through.

The stairs are shabby and cramped. Five hundred and thirty rickety wooden steps circle around and around, leading to a platform where a person can get a birds-eye view of the city. I feel alternately nauseated and exhilarated. My legs tremble with animal terror. Several times I decide to turn back. But I'm enclosed in a small circular passage. There's no room to turn around and walk down. And the steps aren't solid, either. When I look through the steps, I can see the whole precipitous, dizzying way to the bottom.

Abandoning certainty in favor of faith feels like climbing those five hundred plus steps. But those steps have taken hundreds of thousands of pilgrims to the top of the dome, and, so far as I know, they have always held.

There's a fire in the train, sweeping towards us from the car ahead. The air is looking shimmery with heat, and the hair on my arms is singed, and I would like to say bad people are pushing and shoving in the aisles. But I'm pushing and shoving, too. My own shouting is preventing me from hearing anyone who disagrees with me. And when I think about it, I feel like I'm going to be sick. Because I don't know what to do to stop us from attacking one another—even to stop myself. It seems to me that the impasse between factions in this country might be permanent. The standoff has been so long in the making it seems impossible to resolve.

Then I go to a theater conference, and a tall, skinny graduate student named James with cowlicky red hair gets up and tells us he'll be talking about the parable of the Good Samaritan. I feel myself nodding toward boredom. Everybody knows that one. It's about doing good to your neighbor. Except James—who, it turns out, is a smart cookie—has already counted on us knowing that way of looking at the story, so he isn't focusing on being nice to the Samaritan. The story about the good Samaritan is one most of us know.

James is talking about the setup for the parable. Although there are about twenty of us in the room, somehow, he speaks as if to each of us personally. He holds a piece of chalk in his left hand and occasionally marks a blackboard. He hooks his finger in a belt loop while he tells how Jesus went to the Temple so he could talk to his political opponents. After a Pharisee spotted him and asked him a smart-aleck question to put him down, James says, Jesus must have wanted to attack, just like we do when we've strayed off our own turf. Just like I feel when I have to do more than repeat my favorite positions to people who agree with me.

James's point is that Jesus didn't repeat his same old positions. Instead, he told a story. That story got everyone in the Temple involved in the messy, complicated aspects of being human. It got their minds off ideology and confronted them with their own bodies, with sickness, death, and their regular need for assistance. Sitting there listening to James that day, I thought, *Ah ha! This is the way to talk to people I disagree with. Everyone loves a story.*

I'm reminded that I once went to a nursing home to teach a poetry workshop. The wiry, energetic director informed me that she had invited a special needs class at the local high school to join us. This freaked me out slightly because I knew the age differences in the audience would be so huge. I wondered how I'd ever find something that would work for both groups. Soon the students arrived. The young women in the group were showing a lot of low-cut black and purple lingerie. Many of their orifices were be-ringed with metal, and the entire bodies of several of the men were covered with tattoos. The white-haired nursing home residents, who were wearing carpet slippers and cheap flowered cotton dresses with zippers up the front, watched coldly as the students trooped in. Each group sat in its own little enclave with a no man's land of empty chairs between them.

It was a disaster. I began to grasp that the hour would be a catastrophe. But I asked them all to close their eyes and picture the house where they had lived when they were ten. Obediently they closed their eyes. Suppose they were walking up the front sidewalk, I said. What did they smell? The greenness of grass as a father mowed the lawn? A mother cooking spaghetti sauce in the kitchen? What did they hear? Quarreling? Someone practicing scales? A record playing the Beatles? What did they see? The assignment was to write for twenty minutes as fast as they could—everything they felt and sensed.

They didn't want to stop, but eventually, I asked for volunteers to read the images aloud. Every single one of them read. They didn't weep. Not openly. Well, not the high school students, at least. But a surprising number of them ended the session with smudged mascara. And they all lingered afterward to talk to one another. The wiry director, who knew what she was doing, as it turned out, broke out cookies and coffee.

All the preconceived notions we had in our heads about one another got short-circuited by those stories. Ironically, I, who was being paid to run the workshop, also moved beyond my own limitations for a while when one of the participants asked me to remember my own home. It was our stories—our own images and emotions—that gave us a way of talking to one another.

Poetry and music and other kinds of images circumvent our ideological language, and they can forge connections too. I am remembering what happened in Sarajevo after they closed the opera. It had been shelled until the frightened patrons stopped coming. The singers and many orchestra members, who had been braving gunfire, disbanded. Some of them pawned their instruments to buy food. They barricaded themselves in their houses. Sporadic gunshots from soldiers reminded them they had no power. Music had been their only power, and their music had been shut down by guns.

Then one day, the army shot to death twenty-two citizens of Sarajevo while they were standing in a bread line. The next day Vedran Smailovic took his cello to the town square, anchored it in the dirt, and began playing. For days after that, he walked out to the square alone in clear sight of the gunmen and sat down, arranged his cello, and played the Bruch, the Dvorak, the Elgar. He played for twenty-two days, one day for each of the twenty-two citizens who had been murdered.

No one fired at him.

He played music. That's all. Drawing horsehair across catgut, he let loose the unearthly music of the great cello concertos. The long, rich notes echoed against the buildings and resonated in the central square. Maybe to some people, it was the sound of this truth: guns are not stronger than music.

At any rate, he offered what he had, and so did the kids and the old people at the nursing home. The language of personal stories and the various languages of art short-circuit politics, replacing ideology with experience. Both provide ways for us to connect with people from the other side.

I aspire to write a truth that is stronger than guns. I want to plow the locked and infertile soil of our politicized, abused English language. I want to find new and fair and striking ways to tell what I know. What I am trying to say by telling my own story is this: we can quarry our own lives for images instead of buying the ready-made ones from political and religious operatives. And we can be aware, as we talk, that we might be wrong. We might even keep a sense of humor and revel in the fact that we still have something to learn. Risk is scary, but along with it come possibilities that are worth celebrating.

Think of it. We might find ways to talk to one another.

My friend said that, as the noise of the tracks jolted her feet and hammered her ears, she realized that she was more likely to die if she stayed on that train than if she jumped. She thought she would never make it down the blocked aisle. People were shouting, and pushing, and savaging one another. Some passengers burned to death. But she made it to the open door. The wind sucked her orange scarf away.

And then she leapt.

2

Buying the Cross at Bible Camp

THE NECKLACE RESTS IN a small box on one of the sales tables in the camp canteen. It's a cross about the width of a table knife, the height of a Popsicle stick, made of milky greenish plastic, and affixed to a rawhide string. I stand at the edge of the table staring at the necklace. I keep myself very still. I can feel my eyes blink and my heartbeat in my wrists, which dangle at my sides. In the stifling Nebraska summer afternoon, a trickle of sweat runs down my stomach. I cannot believe how beautiful the cross is. A little placard explains that it glows in the dark.

Glancing significantly at the grownup tending the cash register, so he understands that I am not stealing, I remove the cross from its box. I stoop and thrust it into the shadows under the table. It emits a minty light, which is entirely inexplicable since the necklace doesn't contain any light bulb or battery. Shining beneath the table, it appears to be cutting into the darkness with its clear edges.

It is not raining, but mist clouds my eyes. I want this cross the way a person wants health. At Temple Baptist Church, where my family belongs, we believe it's wrong to keep images like this cross. Our sanctuary is plain, and we don't have religious symbols in our houses either. So, though I have been taught, as a Protestant, to disdain religious imagery, I have never held a crucifix or looked at one carefully, and my aching love for this simple fluorescent cross is as astonishing as it is powerful. The trouble is, it costs two dollars, and two dollars is the entire amount wadded up in the small red plastic coin purse back in my cabin. It is the amount my father handed me just before I got into Audrey Jones's car yesterday and, for the first time, drove away from my family home.

During weeks of dreaming about being at camp, I imagined buying soft drinks and cookies during breaks, wandering nonchalantly through the canteen with my hands in my pockets, perusing the items carefully, weighing alternatives. It feels lovely now, the possibility of putting my hand out to touch something, knowing that I could either choose that or move on to something else, knowing that I can touch something entirely different tomorrow, and it could be mine too.

Yesterday I was careful not to spend any of the two dollars. I just looked. What I have left is enough to buy something in the morning and in the afternoon every day for the rest of the week. If I give the man at the cash register my whole two dollars now, I will have to stop coming to the canteen, because I couldn't bear seeing the crafts and candy and soda pop and books and bookmarks and plaques without being able to buy something.

So I make my feet walk out of the canteen past the cross, into the brilliant sunshine. My feet are sweaty in my tennis shoes. They don't want to leave. Lifting them is as hard for me as lifting the heavy flatiron at my grandmother's house in Pipestone, Minnesota, the thing she sets on the wood stove so it will heat up and she can press her dresses.

Church camp introduced me to the fabulous idea of life without my parents. No one would force me to pick the peas, or eat my slimy kohlrabi, or dry the ugly dishes, or go to bed while it was still light. Six whole days of freedom stretched before me like a veritable midway of circus rides. I could swim whenever I wanted, including after lunch. My reading reveries wouldn't be interrupted by my mother telling me to go outside and get fresh air. I could get by eating nothing but cookies and stay up all night.

The Monday we set out for camp, my mother had to leave for work at seven. I was already up and dressed. I sat on my parents' bed, watching her pull on her white nylons and adjust the seams. She powdered her chest above her bra and stepped into her nurse's uniform. My father handed her the lunch he had packed for her, and then we walked behind her to the car. Her nylons made a reassuring swishing sound as she walked, but when she turned around to say goodbye, her face registered inclement weather. She hugged me for several seconds longer than normal, then got into the car and twisted the key in the ignition. The starter motor turned over, but she idled in the driveway, rolled down the window, stuck her head out, and said, *Don't forget your sweater*. She backed the car a few feet, then stopped. *Give her a little money*, she said to my father. He pulled out his wallet and handed me two dollars. *You'll be okay,* she told me, flicking her head quickly. Then she hastily backed out. I felt delighted that she was going to miss me. It gave me a sense of power.

My father helped me fold and pack my nicest dresses in our tan suitcase because I wanted to look wonderful at camp. He had a heart condition, as my parents called it, which is why he'd sold his general store in Parkers Prairie, Minnesota and moved us to Lincoln, Nebraska, where my mother could get work. In our new city, he enthusiastically bought the family groceries, tended us kids, and sewed small cheesecloth bags of herbs for his savory vegetable soup. That fall, he had poured all his extra oomph into starting the Lincoln Christian School in our church basement. As I watched my familiar sandy-haired father latch the suitcase with his freckled hands and buckle a belt around it, I began to feel slightly queasy. I walked downstairs, carefully gripping the handrail, and outside to my favorite spot at the side of our house by the tiger lilies. Closing my eyes, I tried to recover the reckless pleasure of being without any parents for a week, but I felt as if I were standing in a violently rocking boat. I was seasick, and the waves, pulling me farther from the shore, were not about to stop. I was going to camp.

That afternoon, I could feel how tenuously the bunch of authorities ruled over us campers. There was a director named Pastor Ray, who looked slightly goofy in his tight rayon shirt and brown pants. A few parental volunteers stood around Pastor Ray, and a squadron of gangly kids worked behind folding tables. They looked about the age of the high schoolers I knew from church. We were standing in a clearing in the woods. Cabins were scattered around the edge of the clearing. Above their doors, on posters, fat, cloud-shaped magic marker letters spelled out: *The Purple Dragons, The Holy Ghosts,* and *Nancy's Storm Troopers.* One was called *Cabin Six.* I feared I might be assigned to Cabin Six, which must have something wrong with it.

Our counselors shoved one another, hooting and laughing as they checked off our names, allotted us sheets and pillows, and handed us our schedules. They ebbed and flowed like water, losing track of us briefly, retreating, whispering, buzzing, swarming in a group, then remembering their jobs, returning to their posts. I didn't know anyone except Audrey Jones, the friend of our family who had driven me to camp with her daughter Marilyn. She was talking with the other parent-volunteers. Other campers went off with their friends, laughing and talking, holding their assignment sheets. I was on my own, and I was literally struck dumb by the high jinks of the counselors, unable to picture any appropriate way to interrupt them to ask which line I should join. I stood in the longest line behind one of the tables, hoping I was right. When I got to the front, I faced a tousle-haired high school boy and asked for my schedule. My words sounded far away and disconnected from me, like the voice of a ventriloquist.

Accepting the schedule and my cabin assignment and the whole unwieldy welcome packet, I juggled it with my suitcase to the edge of the clearing, where I stopped and put everything down in the brown pine needles. Then I stooped over and picked up the documents one at a time. I examined each, trying to decipher some code explaining what I should do next. Surreptitiously I watched other campers in hopes of guessing what the other girls were doing, but many of them were entirely without suitcases, rushing impulsively into one another's arms or screaming with laughter as they crossed the clearing in small gangs. That day, and truthfully every day after that, I watched with stupefied bewilderment as the other girls performed simple actions such as introducing themselves, or telling jokes, or playing volleyball, or testifying. Many of them did these things with such grace and elegance that I believed I had stumbled into a place where every one of the campers except me was destined to become Miss America.

Once I figured out how to read the camp schedule, it looked fine. Later I realized it was something Pastor Ray could show our parents if they had any questions. It started with reveille, ran through breakfast, hymn sing, Bible study, lunch, quiet time, sports, crafts, free time, dinner, revival meeting, and campfire. It ended with taps. I didn't know what any of these things were. I discovered the next day. But in practice, the drumbeat of this schedule turned out to be more irregular than it appeared on paper. Above it, I could always hear the soaring descant, the melody, the troubled, throbbing, torrid libretto of our counselors' personal lives.

It's Wednesday, after lunch. I have gotten through two days and we're resting on our bunks in our cool, dark cabin. We can hear the sighing of the pines outside, and a little breeze blows through the screened windows. Our counselor Nancy checks the door to make sure no one is eavesdropping, then motions us campers to gather on the bunks around hers. She confides in her hoarse, sensual voice, that the Lord is leading her toward John. John has big shoulders and a beard. He buries the camp garbage and builds the bonfires. Yesterday I saw John holding hands with Maureen. I am astonished. Does Nancy really think that God wants John to break Maureen's heart? My parents are intensely loyal to one another, and it is just beginning to occur to me that people actually jilt and get jilted.

As a mosquito buzzes in the humid early afternoon air, we sit, hushed. I am stunned by the magnitude of Nancy's confidence in us, waiting for her to unburden herself further. Nancy fishes in her purse and draws out a new lipstick. She breaks the seal and screws out its tongue. Then she passes it around, permitting us to test it on one another's lips. I am puzzled because I have been taught that wearing makeup leads to false pride. It seems peculiar to me that a counselor at Bible Camp is pushing lipstick, but I've never held a tube of lipstick, and, when I get my hands on it, I feel a flutter in my stomach. I pass it to the girl on my left. Before we resume Quiet Time, Nancy makes us hold up both hands, palms out, and swear to secrecy. She plans to put a frog in John's bed tonight. As an afterthought she makes us swear that we will not get into mischief while she is busy with the frog.

The amount of time our camp counselors spent climbing around in the Alps of teenage love damaged their judgment. Maureen soon realized that Nancy's objective was to gain the attention of Maureen's boyfriend. Under Maureen's direction, her girls bolted our cabin door from the outside. When a brown-haired girl named Gwendolyn, the only camper quieter than me, got up in the night to go to the bathroom, she couldn't open the door. I awoke to bumping and whispers. Gwendolyn was wiping the floor with her pajama top.

In our morning Bible study, the counselors took turns giving testimonies about the Beatitudes (blessed are the meek, blessed are the poor in spirit), but cabin loyalty led to a system of tribal vengeance. Nancy organized us. During the revival service one evening, we propped a plastic pitcher filled with pancake syrup on Maureen's cabin door so it would fall on whoever opened it first. We threw sheets over our heads at midnight and waited for Maureen's girls. We hovered in silence among the ghostly trees by the dark, spooky path to the bathroom, not far from a massive stone we believed marked a grave. One of the girls whispered to me that it denoted the place a former camper was buried, a camper, I thought, who might have been caught in the gears of heartbreak and revenge. Trotting down the path to the bathroom, passing that stone, I could feel terror welling in my chest like a sparkly fountain, creating a romantic thrill that I now realize I must have nurtured, sometimes taking that path just so I could feel it again.

Other pranks amazed me because they seemed to hover on the periphery of the world I understood as civilized, which is to say Christian, which at that time meant the world of my family and our school. One afternoon a counselor named Nate swam underwater, seizing and biting the leg of one of the fat, unpopular boys. The boy, who thought he had been attacked by a shark, shrieked, and leapt out of the water. He balled up his fists and screamed for a long, long time. He never went swimming again. My conscience was so smitten by watching him sweat on the shore as we swam that I didn't go into the water myself for one whole day.

Then some kids ran one camper's pajamas up the flagpole, so he had to sleep naked. They stole and hid the silverware from the dining hall. Nancy paged through Seventeen magazine in our cabin while we raced around and threw Rice Krispies at one another. She painted our toenails the color of brake lights. She advised us about which boys she thought were cute and hinted at the sultry mysteries of sex. I was so inexperienced that I became a silent observer learning the jokes and gambits of an alien tribe. Meanwhile, the camp director sat in his shirtsleeves in the office, fanning himself and talking on the phone.

I was nine, probably the smallest child at camp, and I had no inkling of the awakening that would befall me in a year or two. For me, the curtain hadn't opened on the opera of adolescence. I didn't even know there *was* an opera. Not that I wasn't passionate. That summer, I lustily sang in four-part harmony "Do Lord" and "Since Jesus Came Into My Heart," praise songs that seem almost pornographic now. I bellowed them with a joyful urgency I didn't quite comprehend.

And chow. I adored chow: fried chicken and mashed potatoes, macaroni and cheese, tapioca pudding, creamed cauliflower, peanut butter cookies, all of it overcooked. But no one was making me eat carrots or liver. We campers stood on the grass in a snaky line, breathing in the aroma of baking bread, singing *Here we sit like birds in the wilderness, birds in the wilderness, waiting to be fed,* until the cooks opened the wide doors, and we could heap our plates with white, starchy, abundant food.

At night we huddled in a circle, mesmerized as the bonfire licked the sky with its yellow and red tongues. I felt like a Neanderthal child: close, folded into her tribe, safe against the enormous, breathing dark. But the truth is, during the day, I walked around camp on the edge of tears, overwhelmed by the terrible facts I was discovering about the world. For one thing, I wasn't sexual yet, and I felt I was living in a strange new country pulsing with an undercurrent of fervent, adolescent sexuality. And then there was the predatory society of the camp. Sometimes I wondered whether everything I had understood at home as normal human behavior was flawed and deviant.

What brought on full-blown homesickness in me was a tactless remark towards the end of the week from some older girl—a sarcasm, some condescension that made me suddenly aware of how young I was, how out of place. The girl might have been Maureen, who by then had surrendered John to our counselor, Nancy. I don't remember. Maureen must have felt humiliated, and she must have hungered for revenge against our cabin. As I look back, I marvel that we felt so gleeful about what must have seemed a catastrophe to Maureen. We were idiotically devoted to the theatrical, wisecracking, gum-chewing Nancy. Me too, even though—or perhaps *because*—I had been raised by steady, serious, understated parents. By contrast, I now realize, my counselor Nancy was not unlike a mental patient who had broken out of a ward and was running the institution.

It's mid-week, and I am brushing my teeth in the primitive, rough-timbered bathroom. Someone—say it's Maureen—is standing beside me at the next sink. She is a willowy high school girl with some power to say what happens at camp. Her long, brown hair curls tastefully fall to her shoulders. When I look up at her, she is watching me, appraising me. The glistening, hard black of her pupils makes my heart hammer in my chest. I work to breathe, flailing like a caught fish in a boat, trying not to betray my alarm.

"Hi," I say through a mouthful of Crest. I have learned that much. You have to greet people in the morning, even if you don't feel like it. Even if you never greet members of your family at home.

She tosses her hair back. "Are you old enough for this camp?" she asks.

"What do you mean?"

"I bet you're not ten!"

"I'm nine."

"Honey, Jesus wants you for a sunbeam."

I'm not sure what this means, so I am unable to contribute a reply to the conversation she has honored me by starting. In our church, they sing "Jesus Wants You for A Sunbeam" at the children's service. The last time I sang it, I was about six. It slowly dawns on me that Maureen must be telling me I am too young to be here. I realize that she's probably been watching me observe and then follow what the older kids do. Maybe, in fact, I seem even more bizarre than I feel. I hear the water gushing from the faucet. Outside there is the sound of tremendous flapping, as if wet sheets are blowing in a gale—a mob of startled crows taking to the air.

Maureen is standing with her toothbrush in her mouth, staring at me, waiting for me to reply. I try to think of something, but my mind is blank and smooth as a bald gray highway going nowhere. I'm breathing fast. I turn and begin brushing my teeth again. She shuts the water off with a flourish and walks out, a gesture that seems to put a period at the end of the long sentence of my childish incompetence. When I am done brushing my teeth, I walk to the canteen and gaze at the cross for a long time.

Although I had been taught that such religious symbols were idolatrous, whenever I looked at or even thought about the glowing greenish piece of plastic, I felt calmer. Sometimes I walked over to the canteen to look at it because I felt it calling me. The minutes I spent staring at the cross were probably the only respite I experienced during that week from the sense that if I didn't continually watch my step, I would become an object of camp-wide ridicule. I was wretched with the self-consciousness of an alien pretending to be a native—except in the presence of that cross, which focused me and filled me with serenity.

Homesickness is a disease that rivets its victim's imagination on home so powerfully that nothing else seems vivid or real. Suddenly, after my conversation with Maureen, I longed to go home. I, who read *The Boxcar Children* and dreamed of the pleasures of being an orphan, now suffered from an imagination entirely filled up with my mother. I pictured her getting into her car the Monday I left for camp. I heard her voice calling my name over and over. I smelled her Tweed perfume and felt her hand lightly on the back of my neck. The very woodsy air I breathed stifled me. I couldn't eat. I cried. I vomited. My head pulsated. I feared talking to anyone in case I might dissolve in tears. I was infected with self-consciousness. I was like a homesick child in a movie who loses weight and slowly dissolves into a landscape. The next day, I stayed in my cabin during Hymn Sing and Bible Study. Pastor Ray didn't notice. Even Nancy didn't notice.

Dutifully I went to craft time, where I lolled in front of bins of Popsicle sticks and clay and yarn strips and paper and sequins and glue and paints. I could not think of a single reason to pick up any of it. I needed to lie down. I wanted to sleep. The counselor in charge cheerfully tried to convince me to braid a lanyard, which I could use as a key chain. He suggested different colors, the bright gold, the royal blue, the forest green. The thing is, I didn't own any keys. "Then give it to your mother," he suggested, and I bolted from the tent.

My mother's friend, Audrey Jones, who had brought me to camp, drove up on the last day to volunteer and noticed that something was wrong with me. She lured me out of my cabin by inviting me to the canteen. She bought me a bottle of Coke and asked me whether I was all right. She meant well, but she was, by nature, blunt and clumsy. She had a habit of wearing anklets with high heels, and she had such a raw-boned, big-jawed, cartoony body that as I sat at the table across from her, all I could think of was how different she was from my elegant, cozy black-haired mother. I knew I was being monstrously ungrateful. But I was unable to stop feeling a mawkish longing that this woman could not satisfy. At the time, I believed she couldn't even understand it. Surely I was wrong. She wanted to understand, at least. But I couldn't explain myself. I had no words. I listened to the rain beating on the canteen's metal siding. We sat together in awkward silence, a generous, concerned adult and the broken child she was trying to help.

I have relied heavily on my memory in describing my camping experience, and memory can be notoriously unreliable. What I recall of that summer may exaggerate our counselors' obsession with sex and vengeance. It's possible I have lumped together several years' worth of my camping adventures into this one awful week. I have only one piece of evidence for what I was feeling. It is a black and white picture taken by a cheap Kodak, a photo which I rescued from my mother's album after she died. I remember exactly what was driving me as Audrey Jones snapped that picture. I am kneeling to cover up my bare legs. I am wearing a dress. Everyone else wore jeans. That snapshot has provided my gateway back into a week of Bible camp in the raw, hot wilds of central Nebraska.

The suffering of one child in the middle of the last century--though it is insignificant compared to Sputnik and the House Un-American Activities Committee, and even the design of the pillbox hat—may, nevertheless, be worth noting. Why did I suffer from such crippling homesickness? Why would nothing but the scent and touch of my mother satisfy me at the age of nine? In fact, I was close to my tenth birthday.

It's surely, in part, a question of genetics and temperament, but maybe my parents' fundamentalism also had something to do with it. The pact they made when they got married—which became our family policy—was to join other fundamentalists and circle the wagons. Imagine the prairie schooners traveling west. At night they pulled around the campfire. They appointed gunslingers to patrol the perimeters to keep out coyotes and wolves and bandits. They knew the dark around them was full of six shooters and fangs. They didn't trust it. They were smart. Many of them got to Colorado or Oregon.

My parents' belief in transcendence was so essential to their understanding of themselves that they needed to preserve it at all costs. They simply denied that there was any other alternative. They divided the human species into two groups: the secular world and people who, like them, were believers. This latter group did not include Catholics or Mormons, for instance, or Presbyterians, whose statements of faith were not precisely like theirs. The "secular world" is like a river, my parents explained to us, which can transport you very quickly to a place you don't want to go. You have two choices. You can be passive as a leaf that the rapids carry to a catastrophic waterfall. Or you can swim against the flow towards something you believe in. For them that meant forging a culture that would seal them off from anyone who couldn't sign their creed.

I know now that every social group must draw its boundaries and fight to defend them, or the group doesn't survive. It would be silly and wrongheaded to claim that fundamentalists are the only people who limit their borders. But my parents' counterculture was so specific, and its borders were so impermeable, that it became a ghetto. They diligently worked to create that enclave: the church, the Christian school, the potlucks, the Christmas pageants, the language code, the literal way of reading, the kinship of believers.

By the age of nine, I had been inculcated with a life-and-death need for belonging. Moreover, I had been taught that my eternal soul depended on it. My training gave me a keen sense of how to behave in a pleasing way among my own people. I had a near-perfect sense for who was in and who was out. Although I had learned manners from my parents, I had no code of behavior to deal with a company of strangers, even strangers of similar faith, whose creed was always bound to be somewhat different. Because I had no experience with deviance, I didn't comprehend that deviant behavior could educate me and set off sparks of joy.

So maybe it's not surprising that I adopted Maureen's view of the child who was too young, too naïve, who wore dresses to camp while other girls wore pedal pushers. I saw myself as deviant and weird. The system my parents devised to save us, by excluding anyone outside our fundamentalist enclave, ended by estranging their child. I had developed an immune system so exquisitely tuned that it turned on itself and began to devour its own identity.

I left the fundamentalist church much later, in part for the very simple reason that, once I figured out how to talk to strangers, I liked so many of them. My parents' view of the world began to seem too simple. I became bound by ties of affection to more and more outliers. I saw how similar we all were, how, despite different customs and cultures, our human quandaries tended to be the same. My parents were smart. Their predictions of what might happen if I stepped outside the enclave were dead right.

I left for good.

That week at camp turned so nasty not merely because I was so young and so desperately needed to belong to a group but because our counselors were also idiotically unprepared to manage a bunch of children. And maybe my parents should have foreseen that.

But I haven't yet explained why they sent me to camp at the age of nine. I'd spent the previous August roving our neighborhood with a juvenile delinquent named Junior. We lurked around the houses, sneaking onto porches, claiming whatever we found. We told each other that we felt justified in taking the stuff because of the "finders keepers" rule. If people left toys and sprinklers outside, we might teach them a lesson so they wouldn't fall prey to even greater thievery.

One afternoon, we pillaged cookie samples from the garage of a Keebler salesman and ate them till we lay like fat ticks on his front lawn. When he rang our doorbell that evening and complained to my mother that I had stolen his samples, she murmured with embarrassment that she was sure I would not have done that. He raised his voice and repeated the accusation, fueled by an anger that made him walk around in small circles on the sidewalk in front of our door. He had a limp, and he talked loudly enough to attract attention from the neighbors. My mother summoned me to the door. "This man says you went into his garage and took his cookies." I could feel her eyes evaluating me. "You wouldn't do that, would you?" I felt sick. I swallowed back the sickness.

"No," I told her.

No.

But my mother was no fool. She knew her children. Bible camp was a way of separating me from Junior. And maybe my parents thought that at Bible camp, I'd experience a programmatic change of heart. As it turns out, that week did set me on a path toward a different life.

On Saturday, before I climbed into Audrey Jones's car for the trip home, I made a final journey to the canteen, to look at the cross. I'd taken that walk many times, even though I had decided early in the week that I couldn't afford to buy the cross. I had already spent too much on candy. Standing there on Saturday morning, I saw that the canteen was having a sale, and the price of the cross had been slashed to a dollar thirty. Noticing that I was eying it, the man at the counter asked me how much money I had. I showed him my dollar ten. He took my money, slipped the cross into a bag, and handed it to me.

I have been homesick since that summer, but never as homesick as I was then, maybe because after that summer, every time I had a chance, I tried to get the knack of talking to strangers until I finally learned how.

On the bumpy ride back with Audrey Jones, I wore the cross, holding it steady in a chute of sunlight that streamed into the car window. I could almost hear the thing gathering whatever light it could into itself. That night, at home in my own bed, I watched it slowly pay out radiance into the darkness. As the day around it failed and night came, the cross grew steadily more articulate, its edges sharpening against the dark. It seemed like a star that had fallen to earth, something a person could navigate by.

3

Saving and Getting Saved

MRS. MEEKS CLUTCHED THE bottom of her white Ban-Lon sweater and tugged it towards the floor. In her high, piping child's voice, she began to recite the minimum requirements to run for President of the United States. "*A person must be a natural born citizen, must be at least thirty-five years old, must have resided in the United States for. . . .*"

My eyes drifted toward the wide classroom windows. It was a gorgeous October, the maples firing their colors in the sun. From the street, I had seen this handsome, new public school building for years, but only in the last month had I discovered within its walls the dark undercurrent of boredom that carried students from one class to another. Here the zip was homogenized out of civics and history and English. These subjects now appeared so tedious that I couldn't remember what had previously seemed interesting about them. So on this afternoon, the fall after I left the Lincoln Christian School, I blocked civics out of my mind and turned to the problem of how to make a friend. One friend, I thought, would be a reasonable number to shoot for.

For several weeks I had surreptitiously watched Julie S., who sat ahead and to the left of me in civics, a girl with a perfectly oval, shiny face, short, thick, light-brown hair and eyelashes so abundant that they cast a shadow on her cheek. In the lunchroom, I had seen her fold and save her brown lunch bags for reuse, and several of her knife-pleated skirts were apparently homemade since the pleats wouldn't stay in—just as my own didn't. Her blouses had simple boy collars, and she avoided extreme colors like red and orange. She wore the kind of clothes a person could keep wearing for a long time without getting sick of them. I was looking for a fundamentalist kid, like me, and what little I knew about Julie suggested that she might be one. She was a good candidate for friendship.

"Class!" Mrs. Meeks cheeped at the top of her tiny voice. "Class! May I have your attention?!" The students stopped passing notes and murmuring across aisles. "Who can tell me the requirements for becoming a senator?" she asked.

No hands.

Mrs. Meeks must have given herself a permanent the night before. Her black hair, which she normally wore in loose curls, looked stiff and wiry as a hairy black poodle. It was a home-style Toni, I guessed. After a recent home perm, I had been cursed with the same nervous, rigid coils. They would take several weeks, I knew, to relax.

"Did you read the chapter?" Mrs. Meeks asked.

We all focused our eyes past her on the blackboard. Julie S. was the only student paying attention to Mrs. Meeks. Her head was tilted slightly upward, and her face glowed, maybe from running to class, but I thought it made her look like a seraph. I wondered what interested Julie about Mrs. Meeks's list of requirements to become a senator. Was she thinking of running for senator someday? But Julie didn't seem dull, and only a very dull person would imagine a girl could hold office. Furthermore, I was an expert at detecting hypocrisy, and it didn't look to me like Julie was faking interest.

I considered the idea of exiting the classroom with Julie after the bell rang, pretending I needed to go whichever direction she took and then asking her what she thought about civics. To pick out Julie as a target this way and develop a plan to befriend her felt manipulative, but because I had arrived at this new school a year after the social groups had formed, I felt left out of jokes, hall discussions, weekend activities, all the delicious adolescent camaraderie around me. I was desperate for a friend, someone who would not find me strange, someone more or less like me.

Then Julie turned around, and I noticed she was wearing an expensive new black and white party dress, which I had seen from the bus in the Miller and Paine window the week before. My heart sank. It seemed at odds with Julie's stolid, radiant face. Provocatively at odds. It was not the kind of thing any of my friends from church or Christian school would wear, this dress with its suggestive, scooped neck, its short skirt, and its splashy, brindled-Guernsey cow pattern. It signaled that Julie was not like me, not at all. I didn't own party dresses, much less wear them to school. Like me, the kids at my old school wore hand-me-downs. Even the ones who ordered from the Sears catalog wore clothes that were drab and mismatched in a way that didn't become fashionable until the first decade of the twenty-first century.

My cheeks flamed, and my hands tingled. I realized I didn't know how to make a friend, because for many years I hadn't needed to. Since second grade, I had been pals with the kids at the Lincoln Christian School. Because my father had helped to found the school and sat on the school board, pretty much everyone knew us. After all our sleepovers and pot-luck dinners, my friends and their parents felt like members of our family. We spoke a kind of dialect to one another, referring off-handedly to God and prayer and the Bible in an idiom I had discovered no one in public school either spoke or comprehended.

After we ran out of grades at the Christian school, my old friends scattered all over the city to attend different public schools. As Lincoln Southeast became a daily reality, my past comrades' importance dwindled in my memory. I called them less often. I couldn't remember exactly what they looked like or what their voices sounded like. As I slumped down in my seat, studying Julie, I felt it was improbable that I would ever again meet anyone I could be friends with.

For months before I started public school, my parents had beseeched me not to join a gang of bad kids. Kids who drank and slept around is how they defined *bad*, but I knew they meant anyone who was not a fundamentalist. They sketched swift, powerful tales of apparently decent kids who would lead me down an evil road. My mother, who by then was a junior high school nurse, informed me that students in her public school used drugs and drank. Girls came into her office complaining of headaches, wilting onto her cot, and after twenty minutes of her kindness, they confessed that they were pregnant. I was not sophisticated, but I realized that it would be physically possible for me to have a baby, and I was haywire with terror at the prospect. It happens fast, my parents told me. One thing leads to another, and before you know it, you own a squalling, red-faced infant. *And don't bring your illegitimate children home to me,* my mother cautioned. Privately I worried that my own baby would be no more loveable than the unattractive children I babysat for.

The landscape of Lincoln Southeast, from which I now needed to pluck a friend, was strewn with what we now call IEDs, delinquents disguised as normal teenagers, like the explosive devices that terrorists hide under trees and in innocuous-looking trash cans. Any of the regular, seemingly decent kids around me at Southeast High School might blow up my morals if I got close to them.

Mrs. Meeks, who had concluded that her fifth period civics class was not going to talk about the requirements for becoming a senator, retreated behind her desk and was now reading aloud from our textbook about the difference between the legislative, the judicial, and the executive branches of government. She took a break to blow her nose and then tucked her hanky back into her sleeve. Her eyes were red-rimmed. The rumor I'd overheard Vonda Kaye VanDike whispering to Sandra Starkey in math class was that Mrs. Meeks had had a baby last year. I began to pity Mrs. Meeks.

Across the street, above the new subdivision, clouds were rolling across the wide Nebraska sky. A bush beside the front door of one split-level house had been clipped to look like a giraffe, or possibly a zebra. I speculated on why anyone would want to humiliate a plant by making it look like an animal. Although my grandfather pruned trees for practical reasons, to make them bear apples or to keep them out of the electrical wires, we didn't have any friends who cut their hedges into shapes. If the goal was beauty, I preferred plants to spread naturally so they looked like green wildfire. But it dawned on me that maybe the point was to show that the family could afford a gardener. I decided that, like Julie, the people who lived in the subdivision across the street must have a lot more money than we did. We didn't know anyone who had money. All our friends were like us: careful, saving, frugal.

That night I dreamed Julie S. had invited me to her house and I was sitting beside her at her aqua Formica kitchen table, nibbling cookies. Julie had found us pastel-tinted plastic glasses in one of the cupboards and poured us lime Kool-Aid. Her mother tripped into the room wearing a low-cut red dress, red velvet heels, and a little heart-shaped purse. She appeared to be going out.

"Oh, hi kids," she chirped, drifting over to us at the table, clutching a bulky bottle of rum in one manicured hand. "You should try this," she urged me. She dashed a little of the transparent liquid in my glass of Kool-Aid, then wobbled backward on her high heels to watch my reaction. Manners dictated that I try some. My parents were teetotalers, so I had never tasted alcohol, and within minutes of the first sip I slumped to the floor, drunk and senseless.

I woke up in the dark of my bedroom with prickles of alarm exploding like tiny Roman candles in my hands and chest. I lay listening to the shade banging softly in the breeze against my window. As my heartbeat slowed, my dread was replaced with dissatisfaction that I didn't know how the dream ended. Lying there, I willed myself to picture an ending.

Perhaps Julie and her mother stuffed my body into a large black rubber bag and handed off the bag to a man who was waiting in a black car at the back of their house. He opened his trunk, lowered me into it, and drove away. The sleek black car exited onto a highway with me in the trunk, the car moving toward the horizon. I tried to envision where he was taking me, but everything around me was dark, as if I were inside a bag, and I couldn't see what happened next.

Around this time, I had begun to question our accepted view that the world was pretty much unremittingly either hostile or treacherous, a view I had gleaned not only from my parents but from fundamentalist books and sermons. Looking back, I realize that I simplified their warnings and overdramatized their opinions, but my people were, indeed, zealous about protecting their children from the world. They wanted to notify us of the dangers to our faith. As I lay in bed reflecting on the image of me crumpled in a body bag, I felt a nagging sense of improbability. How likely was that scenario? True enough, the year before, in Lincoln, Nebraska, Charlie Starkweather had gone on a shooting binge, which ended in eleven cadavers. Still, such violent news was exceptional in our part of the country. And we rarely heard about kidnappings, except in cautionary tales.

I realized that I had no real basis for predicting what people were like. People in our circle were the only ones I knew. In those days, I craved novelty, yes, but I actually needed first-hand, basic personal knowledge to test reality. I'd had some experience outside my family's subculture in grocery stores, for instance, at camp, and around our neighborhood. But each of those encounters, according to my parents, involved risk. Well, I thought, I would just have to take some risks. I had to talk to someone at school soon. Not Julie, maybe, but someone. Who? And how would I decide who? The trouble was, any such dialogue seemed so momentous—I had built this into a life-and-death encounter—that I could not think of any way to begin.

One morning before school, I locked myself in our bathroom, and with a cue tip, I dabbed a red food coloring on my lips. I'd cut the intensity of the scarlet with water. I planned every morning before I went to school to closet myself and stain my lips a bit darker, accustoming my parents to the change so incrementally they wouldn't notice. In the bathrooms at school, I had watched the speed and skill of girls my age drawing on crimson lips without even looking in a mirror. At the Lincoln Christian School, no one, not even the teacher, wore makeup.

So at 7:30 that morning, when my mother called "All aboard" and gathered her height-and-weight charts and grabbed her purse to drive me to school, I flushed the toilet and exited our bathroom, looking, I hoped, innocent. As my mother walked by me to the front door, she glanced at me, but she didn't say a word.

Shortly after that, I began to bargain with my mother to wear my skirts shorter, the way other girls at school did. Mother did not consider the length of a girl's skirt a fashion question but a moral issue. One Saturday morning, she sat on the floor beside a box of straight pins, her legs sticking straight out like a child's, and laid a yardstick against my pink skirt. My mother, the daughter of a dressmaker, also believed that a perfectly even skirt hem spoke volumes about a woman's moral character. I had learned, at such fittings, to stand patiently as a dray horse, just trying to get the job over with.

"Twenty-one inches," my mother intoned, taking a pin out of her mouth, marking my skirt with it. She was measuring with a yardstick from the floor to the bottom of the hem.

"Twenty-four," I negotiated, bargaining for what the other girls wore at my school.

"Twenty-two," my mother countered, smiling. Her amusement, which seemed condescending, annoyed me.

"Everybody at school wears their skirts shorter than me," I argued.

"Well, you're not everybody!"

We settled on twenty-two inches. That is, my mother settled on it. In our house, the children did not do the settling.

One Sunday, after our family had devoured our ritual evening meal of cheeseburgers and potato salad, I returned to my bedroom to finish my grammar homework for the next day. Very soon, my parents trooped into my room. My mother sat on my bed. My father leaned in the doorway. I don't remember exactly what they said, but they addressed me about my accumulating rebellions. Obviously, they had discussed me earlier, privately. They were united and affectionate and pleading. The upshot was that they couldn't comprehend why I didn't save myself grief and just endorse their view of the world.

"You're changing," my father said. "Do you realize that?"

Because I had lived in my family for more than a dozen years, I understood that changing was a bad thing.

"You don't want to do what everyone else does," my father said. "You're not a sheep."

I did not answer. I didn't have any words to explain the truth—that I didn't have any friends at my new school, that I was lonely, that I had begun to suspect the bright line we had drawn between our fundamentalist group and "the world" was in some way false. I weathered this period of my life in an inarticulate stupor.

"Darling, what's going on?" my mother entreated gently.

Silence.

"Do you really think you know more than we do? "she asked.

This sent up flares of anger in my chest.

In fact, I had indeed begun to wonder whether they were right about some things, including their judgment on outsiders. Not that I knew better. I just wondered. But I kept my mouth shut because I had a sense of dignity that did not allow me to admit, certainly not to my parents, how little I knew. Looking back, I realize the great and terrible question was whether I would ever begin making judgments of my own and how I would get information that permitted me to do that.

By Halloween I was trudging so slowly to the bus in the morning that I often missed it. My father frequently had to drive me to school. It took me longer and longer to get dressed. I stopped talking at home and didn't talk at school, either. One night at dinner, my parents asked me what was going on. I stared at the ceiling and envisioned the advice session they'd subject me to if I told them.

"Nothing," I said.

The next afternoon I missed the bus on purpose so I would not be disgraced again by having no one to sit with. Slogging home, I passed by another house whose whole front hedge looked like a sideshow of performing animals.

"Hello," I said to the animals, testing whether my voice still registered sound. The strange noise rising from my throat disappeared into the air like smoke.

Lollygagging got me home around the time darkness was falling. My mother had been driving the streets looking for me. When she pulled into the driveway, she rolled her window down and asked me what I had been doing.

"Thinking," I told her.

"Thinking? You mean you can't think and walk home at the same time?"

"Well, I was tired."

"What were you thinking about?"

"I don't know."

"You don't know what you were thinking?"

"No, I guess not."

"Are you in trouble?" I thought she meant with the authorities, at school, for instance.

"No."

"Really?"

"Really."

"Are you okay?"

"Yeah."

"Okay. Change your clothes. It's time for supper."

I simply could not grasp what was so rapidly happening to me. It felt like I was becoming transparent, non-existent, a blown-out candle.

That night my parents lectured me. They didn't give two hoots for being fashionable and popular. They pooh-poohed the myth of human progress. We weren't all getting better and better. Oh Lord, no. Things had been better in the past. Living for the present, they said, didn't work. My father stood in the kitchen door, his shoulders stooped, his face lined with regret. He gazed out the window silently as if his cornflower blue eyes were glimpsing his teenaged self. He had dropped out of the university and begun carousing, as he put it, and running around with loose girls. By the time he gave up that life, his health was broken. Our family was still suffering because he had thrown away the values his parents had taught him.

The next afternoon I walked home again, remembering how slackly my father's shirt hung on him as he talked. When did that start? Was he losing weight? A shadow of fear for my big strong father passed over me, clipping my breath off. I stopped walking and stood still, holding my side. The trees were flaming against a sky that was growing gray and scaly with clouds. The wind was picking up. It whipped the red and yellow leaves into eddies. I smelled a leaf pile burning on someone's lawn.

I felt haunted by guilt. My mutiny, I realized, was saddening my father and possibly worsening his heart condition. The doctors at the clinic in Temple, Texas had given him three years to live. Didn't I care enough about him to do what he asked me to do? What he said about me was surely right. If my fundamentalist people were characterized by saving and maintaining the past, I was drifting away from my people. And what would I do without them—my family, our friends, the church?

And then I felt a powerful surge of fury. Who did my parents think they were, with their pathetic arguments, appealing to me out of pity for my father and fear of the future? What did they know? They were utterly self-interested and old-fashioned; furthermore, some of the people my parents ran around with were crazy. I needed to find a way out of their pathetic little group! My face burned.

I began running, the houses blurring, the wind tearing at my hair. After blocks and blocks, I stopped with a sharp stitch in my side, thinking furiously that this was the first time in my entire life I had seen the truth. My father had explained to me that his parents were right. How convenient! He said that in hopes that I would think *he* was right about me, just like his parents were right about him! Because now he was the parent. But when he was my age, he had the luxury of doing whatever he wanted.

Well, I thought, I'm doing what I want, too! I have one life, and I will live it the way I decide! After all, I'm not a child. I'm thirteen! Thirteen sounded to me like a massively large number.

My civics and algebra books were becoming heavy. I started trudging along the sidewalk again, hardly more than halfway home. It was almost dark and getting cold fast. My hands felt like rocks. I had no coat to put on. How could I have predicted that morning that I would have to avoid taking the bus home once again because of my embarrassment at having no one to talk to? In my misery, I blamed my loneliness on my parents also.

I wanted to become real again, but I didn't know how, although at some level I must have realized that I would have to seize a moment at school and open my mouth and say something to somebody. If I sounded idiotic because I didn't speak their slang or because I hadn't heard the most up-to-date gossip, so be it. Then I would have to try again with someone else. And I would have to keep trying until I found someone who would take me for myself—whatever kind of creature that was.

I needed someone smart and funny, someone I could give the key to my diary, someone with whom I could fight and make up on a daily basis. A fundamentalist like me. It would have to be a fundamentalist. I had never known anyone except a fundamentalist. But I began to realize that the fundamentalists I had been raised with varied. Some were fat; some were thin. They were variously dumb, smart, funny, serious, good baseball players, bad ones. So how could I detect which of my fellow students was a fundamentalist?

Saved, I thought. We're saved. *And we save things!* My understanding of this intersection of two kinds of salvation, this crossroads of saving, this nexus where we fundamentalists were both saved and saving—this became a turning point in my life.

Fundamentalists saved things, and we got saved.

How could I identify which kids at school had been saved?

I'd have to look for someone who saved things.

Suddenly I saw—in the way an anthropologist sees—how saving things defined my people. We didn't spend afternoons lolling in stores or beside swimming pools in summer, the way I imagined rich people did in Lincoln, Nebraska. We tended gardens. We canned the phantasmagoric abundance of tomatoes and rhubarb. We didn't throw away sour milk; we made pancakes. We covered the smallest dab of leftover potatoes with tinfoil and fried it for breakfast. We stashed the cotton from aspirin bottles. We hoarded deli cartons to box our leftovers. We pasted S & H Green Savings Stamps (awarded for spending money at certain stores) and redeemed them for silverware. We saved everything that could be reused and some things that couldn't. No one forced us to. We took saving for granted.

I ran home, jumped on my bed, burrowed under the covers, and wrote a list. I had learned from my mother that a list can hold the world in place, at least for a while.

Reuse waxed paper
Reuse wrapping paper
Make quilts and rugs from old clothes
Pluck chickens—pillows from feathers
Fix cars. Drive 20 years
Save bacon grease
Darn socks
Fix mechanical pencils, tape together broken glasses
Boil leftover soap for new bars

We saved things, in part, because we didn't have much. A tenth of everything my parents earned, they gave to the Lord. A tithe was the rule. In fact, my parents gave more. They figured that everything they owned actually belonged to God. What was left over, we stretched as far as we could make it go. I could have listed every shirt and dress in my closet. They might as well have been pets. I remembered when and how I acquired them. I could tell you in detail whether they felt stiff or soft or too tight or too loud or mousey. If I lost a glove, I had to wait to get another pair until the next fall. I carefully nursed and tended my one pair of shoes and my pencil case. Our entire electronic paradise consisted of a black and white television with a screen about the size of a *TIME* magazine, a black telephone with a rotary dial, a box camera, a hooded blender, a vacuum cleaner, and a radio. And we were thrilled with our good fortune.

We knew people who went hungry. I knew several kids who didn't have a coat or ten cents for the bus. They were not statistics, or friends of friends, or folks in some section of town we drove through. We talked to and went to Christian school with these people, though we didn't know many of them, and the ones we knew tried to disguise their need. Oh, but we suspected. I could still name their names. Their mothers were widows, and they took in boarders; or their mother had died; or their father had been laid off. They wore shiny, frayed shirts with sleeves that stopped above their wrists. The idea of deprivation made our family clamp down and save even more carefully so we could donate to people who needed help. My parents had no interest in accumulating new stuff.

They preferred the past. My mother drove five hours to be at the farm when the hay rakes and wooden chests and the butter churn from her family farm were put up for auction. She returned home, nervy with triumph, our blue Ford piled full of stuff she had rescued. In those days, it wasn't chic to furnish your house with antiques or to wear handmade clothes. It smacked either of privation or of bad taste. But my mother defiantly furnished our house with nineteenth-century chairs, old glass dishes, and her grandfather's spinning wheel, leftovers her parents had traded in for Danish modern.

Moreover, my mother spurned *au courant* clothes. Handmade was sturdier. And unlike wearing what came off the rack, if you wore homemade clothes, you didn't meet yourself coming and going. As for me, I didn't even comprehend that styles change until I switched to public school. Then suddenly, I was smitten by fashion. Upward-inching hemlines. Puffy sleeves. Voluminous gathered skirts and crinolines. Madras. Seersucker. Waffle cloth. The textures and patterns captivated me. So did the mystery of human form as it could be variously revealed and hidden by fabric stitched into different shapes. The nape of the neck showing this year, the calves the next. I stepped up my babysitting jobs, for twenty-five cents an hour, so I could afford a chic dress in the fall.

About a week after my great moment of insight, I noticed a short girl with a blond pixie cut, white blond, a shade you can't get out of a bottle. She wore tidy, plain, understated skirts and blouses. Her gray-blue eyes were kind. But I recognized irony when I saw it, even though I didn't yet have a name for it. I had begun to experience irony, too. Like me, she knew more than she said.

We fell in step with one another and began talking about classes. Within weeks we were taking turns sitting on her bed or mine, our bedroom doors shut against our parents and siblings. We listened to The Kingston Trio bellow "Hang Down Your Head, Tom Dooley" over and over. We mimicked Vanda Kaye, the star of eighth grade, a squawky-voiced, put-it-out-there girl we both loved and hated. We joined the Pep Club, and our parents drove us to games together. Several times a week we baked chocolate cakes, frosted them with fudge, and guzzled them down as we listened to the Smothers Brothers and laughed ourselves silly. We were both enrolled in college prep, it turned out, but we both took typing, in case we needed something to fall back on. We were girls, after all, and we knew girls usually became secretaries. Between what the two of us were thinking at any given moment, there wasn't space enough to slip a piece of typing paper. Except that she studied less than I did and got better grades.

In retrospect, finding this new friend seemed easy as sunlight falling across the backyard.

Except that she was not the child of fundamentalists.

Her family was Lutheran, a denomination I knew something about because my mother's parents were Lutheran. I was troubled by the peculiar Lutheran custom of reading prayers from a book instead of speaking from the heart. And I was concerned about infant baptism. Sprinkling infants is a heresy, I had been taught. I didn't bring up the details of my best friend's religion to her, though, because I didn't want to jeopardize our friendship. But I began to worry about whether she was saved. I couldn't bear the thought of her spending all eternity in hell. And that is what I had begun to imagine, because I had the feeling that although she wore the kind of clothes I did and had a fundamentalist way of saving things, she didn't have the faintest idea what it meant to invite Jesus into her heart.

By this time, it was summer. The zinnias in our garden had grown violent orange and purple in the hundred-degree heat and big as dinner plates. The corn was taller than my mother, and the tassels emitted a marvelous astringent odor. Tomatoes swelled like balloons.

Every day dozens of them turned from green to streaky yellow to orange to red. We sliced and ate them with basil every night for dinner.

Suddenly school was out, and most days I felt bored. I sprinkled breadcrumbs from our hoard of stale bread on the sidewalk, then lay in the grass watching ants lug huge white tidbits to their holes, as I debated whether to invite my new friend to the revival service the following week, where she might get saved. The low-level rage that perpetually animated me that summer made me scramble up one afternoon, run into our house, and phone her.

Yes, she said. Yes!

I stopped at the sink to gulp a drink of water. I could hear the crickets singing in the heat. I was so happy. The screen door slammed behind me again, and I lay down to watch the ants. I felt confident that my friend, who agreed with me about everything else, with whom I shared everything, would get saved.

I imagined sitting beside her at the revival. We were bowing our heads while we sang the invitation hymn. Then I had the panicked thought that she probably didn't know what an altar call was. My grandparents' Lutheran church didn't have altar calls, and my grandparents never spoke of getting saved. I realized that my Lutheran friend might have agreed to go to the revival without understanding what she was up against. I thought that maybe it was unfair of me to invite her. I didn't want to embarrass her. I didn't want anything awkward between us. I squeezed my eyes shut and rolled over in the grass. I could feel a mosquito biting my arm. I didn't even brush it off. When it finished biting me, I ran inside and picked up the phone. But I couldn't think of a polite way to disinvite her, so I didn't call.

That was Monday. We were going to the revival on Tuesday night.

In late summer, when the air chilled under a harvest moon, the chosen from many of the city's conservative Protestant churches gathered in one enormous downtown stadium to hear an evangelist preach. In a holiday mood, whole families flocked from all corners of the city. Sometimes my parents would arrange to meet family friends at 5:00 p.m. in the sunken garden several blocks from the stadium. My father would carry a picnic basket across the wide, sleepy Midwestern city street while my mother called out cautionary instructions about danger and traffic. We bounded out of the car, laughing and calling to the other children, ecstatic to see our mates, out of our minds with joy at our coming adventure. We streaked around the garden, ignoring printed signs about privacy and contemplation. We pushed one another into the lily pond. We sweated, and our hair would get matted and stuck to our heads. We stuffed cookies into our mouths. Then one of the parents would settle us down, and we would troop obediently into the stadium to hear the evangelist, who got and fixed our attention on whether we were saved.

How the evangelist was chosen and who chose him, I never knew; probably a team of men from the city's fundamentalist churches. The evangelists were charismatic personalities who traveled on the Midwestern revival circuit, splendid-looking young men with good hair and resonant voices, which they could slowly lever up to a shout and then gradually take back down to a whisper. They prowled the stage, lithe as panthers. A few punctuated their messages with gyrating hips. Several years later, as I watched Elvis for the first time, I thought of the evangelists who warbled and thundered and wooed us in that stadium.

The evangelist would stand by himself, one hand clasped in the other, on a platform in front of a 500-voice choir, and peer out at the massive, gathered ranks of us. He was a bullfighter assessing the disposition of the bull. Whatever sins we were hiding, it was his job to stalk them, to speak to our souls, to make us forget our pride and walk down the aisle to the front of the stadium, where flotillas of trained counselors from local churches waited to help us get saved.

I had been saved when I was six, not at a revival service, but during the routine altar call in our white clapboard Baptist church one Sunday morning in Parkers Prairie. I had just grasped the fact that, at the judgment, I would be separated from my family. The sheep go to heaven; the goats go to hell. I pressed my face to my mother's red corduroy dress. My nose prickled. My face felt watery. I didn't know what was happening. I didn't want to go to hell, but I was too scared to walk down the aisle.

My parents took me quietly to the pastor after the service. So I was led to the Lord by a middle-aged minister of the First Baptist Church of Parkers Prairie, Minnesota, Reverend Hosendorf. Like most good pastors, he was built for the long haul, the sort of man who could sit quietly in a rowboat on Lake Miltona for hours with his line in the water. Not that he didn't have strong opinions. At high school football games, he might leap up to yell his objections to the referee. He sported a white goatee, and he savored my mother's egg coffee while he chatted with my parents at our kitchen table. You could count on him to be compassionate and fairly boring.

The night my friend came to the revival with me, the evangelist was anything but boring. As the voltage in the stadium ratcheted up, as he pitched his voice at us, people one by one stopped fanning themselves with the funeral parlor fans. The auditorium lights glared down, the congregation sang "Just as I Am," and, in a voice-over, he gave the invitation to come forward. "God has given you one more chance. Get right with God! Don't wait till tomorrow. Tomorrow you might die. And what excuse will you give the Lord when you're face to face with him?" Because we were running out of verses of the hymn, the Evangelist sent us back to the first, and we began going through them all again.

Far below in the 4,000-person auditorium, the evangelist was a tiny figure, but I felt personally fixed in his sights. I could feel myself melt and run like sap in the spring. My throat constricted as he pled, seemingly directly with me, a suitor for my hand in marriage. He seemed like a lone Christian facing the lions in the Roman Colosseum. We were the lions, a hard-hearted, hardboiled lot. We had heard the dreadful consequences of resisting God many times in every urgent way imaginable. We were experts at defense.

I worried that if someone didn't step out and begin moving down the aisle soon, it would become clear to everyone in the auditorium that the handsome young evangelist had failed. But who could he count on to come forward? Most of us, I guessed, had already stumbled down some aisle or another. And a person only needed to be saved once. His failure was becoming apparent. He asked us to hum the second verse, which revealed that he was losing his grip: after all, humming the second verse sounds the same as humming any other.

As if reading my thoughts, he turned on those of us who were already saved. "Beloved, you may think you're redeemed. But are you *really*? Was your encounter with Jesus authentic? Was it for all eternity? Was it your whole self assenting?"

Listening to the evangelist that night, I learned the meaning of existential doubt. I summoned to my mind the Sunday School room where my parents and I stood with Rev. Hosendorf. I could still hear the simple words of the prayer he uttered, his familiar tenor voice, the wild happiness I felt afterward. But what if that was a dream? Had I intended my choice powerfully enough? What if I had backslid? Lurid possibilities occurred to me. What if the devil had possessed Rev. Hosendorf that day? What if he had temporarily lost his faith or sinned? Had his prayer to save me worked?

Then with a jolt, I recalled that my best friend was standing beside me. I cracked my eyelids slightly to peer at her. Her blue eyes were open and round as a doll's, gazing around the auditorium with detached interest. She wasn't singing. She held the hymnal and respectfully watched the verses go by as I sang them from memory.

I felt Marjorie slip out of her place and start down the long aisle. My mother, who drove us to the revival, had picked up Marjorie too, one of my old friends from Christian school. She was a lone figure now, drifting down the aisle, wandering slightly from side to side. Marjorie had been saved six or eight times already. As I watched her narrow shoulders in her blue flowered cotton dress, I felt for her. She was smart, especially in math. Surely she knew that going forward would make us think of her as weak, unable to resist, perhaps loose-wired. I wondered whether she might feel that the evangelist needed her help. Possibly she had a crush on him. If so, I was with her. But I thought fiercely that I would be damned if I'd go forward. I gripped the seat in front of me so hard my hands grew numb. I swayed and felt lightheaded.

My best friend's face looked expressionless, but I knew how swift and razor-like her mind was. I was dying to know what she was thinking.

After the Evangelist prayed the final prayer, we put the hymn books back in the rack, climbed the long way down to our car, waited for Marjorie, and then drove home. On the way, we talked cheerfully about swimming. My mother promised to take us all to the pool at the end of the week. I kept waiting for my friend to comment on the revival. She appeared cheerfully unscathed, which seemed incredible to me. I believed she would offer her opinion to me later that week, since the two of us told each other everything.

Fifty years later, I live on the East Coast, and my friend, who still saves things, as I do, lives on the West Coast. We still talk by phone and email. She flew in to help us bury my mother last year. I have never asked her what she thought about that night. She has never offered to tell me.

That was one of the last revival meetings I attended.

Many years after our late summer revivals, I read the anthropologist Victor Turner, who wrote about Ndembu rituals in Africa. Of course, I thought, as I read his book. That describes what we were doing. It was religious ritual. Understanding African ritual clarified my own. I finally saw that revivals were among the most compelling ceremonies of my tribe. Of course, religious revivals were nothing new, even in the Fifties. Protestants have gone through periods of revival since the mid-1800s, and even before that, during Great Awakenings in America. There's a long tradition of traveling preachers, including Jonathan Edwards, John and Charles Wesley, Billy Sunday, and Billy Graham, who forged the fundamentalist tradition of revivals.

In revivals, fundamentalists re-enacted the crisis of getting saved over and over. The altar calls aroused sickening anxiety in me, on the one hand, and allayed it on the other. I believed that in those few moments of decision, all eternity was at stake. It was both thrilling and terrifying to live on a treadmill of repeated choice, as my people—and I—did. Of course, fundamentalists vary widely, and perhaps there is less emphasis on the moment of decision now than there was in the

Fifties. But I wonder whether there might be an inverse relationship between fundamentalists' language of certainty and their need to go back and check again, to attempt, over and over, to get right with God. It could be that the people who speak most frequently about "blessed assurance" do so because for them security poses a particular problem.

Getting saved and saving things. That's the language I remember from my fundamentalist childhood in the Fifties. *Getting saved* expressed our fixation on the future. It promised us heaven. It gave us a reason to live in the present. *Saving things* articulated our love of the past. It involved maintenance and caretaking. The two terms—getting saved and saving things—were like bookends. Between them resided everything current and now.

And what did we fundamentalists say about *now*, about the present? I think we were less sure about that. *Now* was a slender slice, a shy sliver of time, nascent and untrustworthy, and fleeting. The present, when I was a child, easily yielded the stage to the monumental past and the astonishing future.

I confess, it's hard for me in the third decade of the twenty-first century to remember how it felt to live in such a skinny, discredited present, partly because very soon afterward *now* became so glamorous, with its emphasis on feelings and on whatever an individual experiences in the current moment. *Now* has subsequently become the campground where we Americans have set up housekeeping—what we desire, the encounters we're having this minute, the causes and entertainments we're currently riveted on. History and the future seem to have disappeared down the rabbit hole of *now*.

For our old late summer revivals, I am grateful. I was a fairly heedless child, I suppose, and they jolted me into a violent and permanent awareness of a world surrounding and beyond the physical world I loved so instinctively and deeply. My later realization that revivals were a form of ritual doesn't mean that they weren't significant to me. As I learned much later, in graduate school, to classify something is not to dismiss it. Looking back on adolescent love, for instance, doesn't cancel either the pain or the validity of that love. It only helps to make sense of what happened.

Although I'm grateful for the old revivals, I don't attend services like that now. I don't think of getting saved as one catastrophic emotional choice anymore. I don't believe it's an event that cracks life into two parts, one that happened before and one that will happen afterward. I think of getting saved more the way I think about tending vegetables in the garden. It involves maintenance. Every week you water. You pull a few weeds every day.

I still iron clothes, and I try to pray the way I iron. When I was a kid, it was my job to do the family ironing on Saturday afternoons. While I listened to the latest hits on the radio, I pressed shirts—the shoulder piece, the collar, the cuffs—each part in order. I loved the scent of fabric under the hot iron. I loved the simple back-and-forth motion. I knew all of our shirts intimately. I could have identified them in the dark. I loved making them useful for the next wearing. As I ironed my family's clothes, I thought of my mother, my father, my sister, my brother—each of us, mornings during the coming week—taking the shirt off the hanger, finding pleasure in the crisp fabric.

Ironing never gave me the same emotional high as being fixed in the piercing gaze of an evangelist who offered me yet one more "absolute and eternal" choice, one more chance to change my life forever. But I've been through enough altar calls, those close calls, those breathtaking spiritual highs. I have decided it's more useful for me to think quietly about whether I'm as patient as I should be. I sometimes consider how to keep my mind from climbing around like a monkey while I try to pray. I wonder what Jesus meant when he told his followers to be willing to give everything away and whether that applies to me. Now I believe redemption involves maintenance. And I confess, I first saw that truth in the coded language of my fundamentalist people.

4

My Dead Brother Teaches Me to Travel

MY PARENTS NEVER SAW the point of traveling. They didn't particularly care to alter their perspective. Why change your point of view, especially if you're pretty sure it's right? They loved stability. Almost every Saturday night in Parkers Prairie they spent with their friends, Ruth and Dave Saunders, telling jokes and eating ice cream. They genuinely enjoyed visiting their parents. We taped pumpkins and black cats to our windows in October and set off firecrackers on Independence Day. In the fall, my mother and my sister and I shopped for one new dress each, and in the spring, we broke the black soil and planted vegetables. Sunday was church, Monday was wash day, and my mother baked bread every Saturday. We sang *Give me that old time religion. It's good enough for me!* My parents were fundamentalists. Repetition and certainty were what they wanted. Novelty and travel they didn't trust.

This created a problem for their children, for whom time passed more slowly than it did for them. I was an antsy, impetuous child who often felt trapped in our house in Lincoln, Nebraska. By midmorning, sometimes, I found myself wondering whether I'd eaten breakfast last year or the year before. At the age of eight, I began to hang out with Junior, the neighborhood juvenile delinquent, and I would sometimes steal into my brother's room, which was forbidden, to drive his

American Flyer train at derailing speeds. On long afternoons, I stared at the pictures in old *National Geographic*s until I could see a miniature figure of myself beside Old Faithful or inside the Grand Canyon. Now when I feel caught in that kind of futile repetition, I sometimes think of my older brother. He taught me that when the periphery of life closes in and I'm having trouble imagining anything but my own predicament, it's time to get out.

I would rush in from school, hot and sweaty, the screen door banging noisily behind me, my vision spangled from the afternoon sunshine. If the smell of Vicks VapoRub assailed me—then I knew. He had been laid low by asthma again. In the corner of Michael's darkened bedroom loomed a cylindrical green oxygen tank with a nozzle on the top and a tube running to his nose. Walt Schamber, our town doctor, would be sitting on the bed, perplexed and frowning. On the other side, my mother would sit, cradling her chin in one hand, her elbow propped on her knee. They murmured *heartrate adrenalin injection* over Michael, who lay there laboring to breathe. If it was really bad, no one even noticed I had entered the room because they didn't dare lift their eyes from him. No wonder Michael could be grouchy and exasperated. Even when he wasn't in bed, he lived in the center of my mother's full attention. He had a much harder time than I did getting away.

For our family getting away usually meant visiting my grandparents in Pipestone, Minnesota, and while we were there my grandfather would occasionally take us to tour the nearby Sioux reservation. It was by no means a vacation spot, but it provided what my mother called "a change." Centuries before, the Sioux had discovered how to quarry the soft red rock from the hills and carve peace pipes, essential for sacred Indian ceremonies all over the Midwest.

My grandfather is tilting his straw hat back. He scratches his head and drives us slowly down the unpaved roads of the reservation. We kids briefly stop fighting over who has to sit on the hump in the middle of the back seat. We blink at tumble-down houses made of raw gray wood siding where small scabs of paint still hang. When Grandfather pulls over to the side of the road, we scramble out of the car to inspect the items for sale. Liver-colored pipestone turtles and bookends and peace pipes lie on dark green tarps. A couple of Indian women with carved bronze faces sit at the edge of the displays. They don't chat or even raise their eyes to look at us but watch the ragged children who dig in the dirt and chase one another around the weed-filled lawns. Gas fumes from my grandfather's blue Buick dance across the yards in blurry waves. Even the soil smells hot. When one woman unfolds her limbs slowly, gets up, and walks over to help us, we tell her we're just looking, scramble back onto the broiling plastic seats, and drive off under the woman's stare. Our big car rocks into the red potholes and ridges of the dirt road.

I hate going to this dismal reservation, but I am also enthralled by its mystery. The children don't seem like children, like us, but like hens pecking in the dirt, and I don't understand why the young men sometimes stagger when they cross their lawns on Sunday afternoon. But the women seem noble, in an aggrieved way. Not that they're beautiful. Most of them look overweight and lumpy in their bright skirts and blouses, but I imagine it requires fortitude to sit in the hot sun on Sunday afternoon watching the occasional car crawl by. Recognizing how easily bored I am, I wonder whether I would stay under those conditions, even to take care of my children. In that way, these women are beyond my comprehension.

I was taught that the Sioux were poor because they didn't work or save, because they drank, and they didn't believe in Jesus. These were the facts I accepted. I knew that half a mile from the reservation, roads running by farms of white people were paved, but it took years before I understood the unpaved roads in the reservation were not the fault of the people who lived there, that their school was stocked with cast-off desks and textbooks from the white school in town, that their only curriculum consisted of auto mechanics and wood shop and Home Ec. In the end, our trips to the reservation did not release me from my narrow horizons but cemented me more rigidly into them.

The year we drove to the Badlands of South Dakota, I began to learn what it meant to travel, in part because Michael had become more discriminating. By then, he was seventeen, I was fifteen, and our sister, Julie, was twelve. We swam in a shallow, spit-warm lake and licked ice cream cones that dripped down our arms. In a roadside park, we climbed half-heartedly on jungle gym equipment that was too small for us. I nagged my mother to see the site advertised on a roadside billboard: STREAM FLOWING UPHILL!!

With hushed reverence, the guide led a half dozen of us through the cool woods to a hillside overgrown with ivy and scrub pines. Occasionally turning to caution us about our footing, he climbed ahead of us in his brown shorts and heavy boots to a place where a stream cut through the underbrush, squirting and pulsing over rocks. Uphill. Well, kind of uphill. Working to believe it, I could imagine that the bed tilted up slightly. Around the glade, several hills came together at different angles, so it was difficult to tell what was ascending and what was descending. The guide removed his hat reverently, as if introducing us to his own personal favorite Himalayan mountain and waited for our response.

Because this was my idea, I feel obligated to react. Amazing!

Michael took off his tortoiseshell glasses and squatted down to get a better look at the angle of the stream.

"It's a trick," he announced, standing up.

The guide's face turned flinty.

I could feel my own face flushing with shame. We had given the guide our fifty cents, which seemed to me like a promise that we would be a sympathetic audience. Moreover, I enjoyed the idea of a miracle far from church. The stream might not look exactly as the billboard pictured it, but it was better than anything we'd seen so far on this trip.

"That water isn't flowing uphill," Michael said.

"Take as long as you like," the guide said. "Just watch your step when you go." He turned, jingling our coins in his pocket, and walked down the path.

Not to be taken seriously must have hurt Michael's pride, which had already been battered from two years without a father, a period of steady attrition. No father to take him to baseball games, no father to help fly his model planes, or to teach him to fight. Two years of watching his friends take their fathers for granted. Michael was blond and slight, and he had a temper, which sent him into asthmatic fits.

He wheeled aggressively to follow the guide. He was beginning to wheeze. My mother trailed him and laid her hand on his shoulder. Michael whirled on her with a look of savage irritation.

"Don't," she pled.

He glared at her.

"Please."

He hesitated. The guide's brown shirt disappeared into the trees.

Michael must have known he couldn't win a fist fight, but maybe he didn't think it would come to that. He had a fast mouth. And he didn't like to be fooled. But more importantly, I think, even as a teenager, he grasped the difference between novelty and travel. Travel involves getting into someone else's point of view and it requires empathy. When you see water flowing uphill you don't feel empathy. Either you feel tricked, or you feel astonishment of the kind that doesn't do a thing for your soul.

By the next day, the whole water-uphill experience seemed tawdry to me.

Michael turned his lethal irony against whatever hemmed him in—our increasingly careful, frugal, Midwestern habits, our church's fundamentalist logic, the romantic notions of the women he lived with. He had to answer to the mother of three teenaged children, a young widow. She was often weepy, sometimes supine on the couch, hyperventilating, with fluttering eyelids. She feared for his life, quite literally. But she also feared for his soul. Michael would ridicule the arrogant, color-blind Mr. Sampson for wearing one red and one chartreuse sock to church. He would rail against Pastor Garland, who got the order of the planets wrong in his sermon. How could you believe a preacher about the Revelation of St. John, Michael demanded, if he didn't even know high school science? Michael mocked the notion that he had a Christian responsibility to carry his Bible to public school on top of his books. He chafed at my mother's curfew of 10:00 on weekends. Sporadically he exploded at her, but mainly he smoldered in a long, sarcastic burn.

Michael's physical activity was so restricted by his asthma that becoming a ham radio operator was his only way of getting out. Always geeky, he hit upon the idea at fifteen, soon after my father died, to send for the parts. He paid for them out of his allowance, stringing the wires, and rigging the thing himself. For once, Mother let him do what he wanted. In fact, I suspect she helped subsidize the project, though she never admitted that.

In the middle of one night, about six months after he got the radio working, I woke up in the bedroom I had painted a sweet, hideous lavender and heard static coming from Michael's bedroom. Outside, the night was utterly black because we lived on the outskirts of town, beyond streetlights, next to farmland, where my father built a house with his own two hands before he died. The scent of lilacs drifted in my window. I threw my sheet off and stood up to get my bearings, then crept past our chairs and the couch, which slept like young elephants in the dark next to the large, split-leaf philodendron in our living room.

I knocked at Michael's bedroom door. Knocking was a rule Michael invented; the rest of us barged in on one another. When he opened his door, I edged in the several inches I was permitted and slouched against his door jamb. He was a thin outline in striped pajamas sitting before the big, black contraption, his blond maverick curls illuminated by its faint light. On his head, he wore a huge black headset, which made him look like an aviator. Human voices, sparks and splinters of words, shot from the machine.

"Come in, come in!" Michael called into the mike. He moved the dial slowly, as if casting a net to see what he might pull in from the darkness. The machine squirted light. I knew he had found people all over the world who logged on to talk to him in English at prearranged times of the night. He craved hearing their voices. He once told me he was planning to travel to meet some of them.

I suspect that Michael needed his ham radio to get beyond the kind of fundamentalism he experienced at the Temple Baptist Church, which belonged to the Conservative Baptist Convention. No one in the church read widely or conducted any independent investigations, though, to be fair, most church members were overworked, underpaid, and struggling financially. We presumably belonged to the priesthood of believers and each of us had individual relationships with God, but we actually relied on the minister to tell us what we believed. I don't know how carefully the adults had even examined his credentials before they hired him. The leaders of the church—all of us—felt a profound need to believe in the fundamentals and we were all about continuity with touchstones, but the truth was, we didn't have either the time or education to examine what the touchstones were. In contrast, during Michael's long periods of convalescence, he read widely, eclectically. He was always intellectually restless.

That restlessness lay behind our family's dreadful *Lady Chatterley's Lover* episode. In 1959, D. H. Lawrence's novel was considered pornography by almost everyone in Lincoln, Nebraska. Ironically the novel became famous in part because ministers and moralists railed publicly against it.

Our minister preached against it one Sunday, arguing that reading it would contaminate us. In other words, I thought as I listened to his sermon, if we experiment, if we learn by experience, we will get infected with evil. That's what Adam and Eve did by biting into the apple in the Garden of Eden. I began to wonder how the minister knew the book was evil. Had he read it? Then why wasn't he contaminated? Maybe he had just *heard* it was evil.

In fact, I wanted fervently to stay pure. But by then, I was old enough to have found out that not everything I had been told by adults was true, and I understood the only way to be sure of anything was to investigate myself. The trouble was, I knew that investigating could get a person into a lot of trouble, so it was crucial to make some risk assessment. What, exactly, was the worst thing that could happen if I read *Lady Chatterley's Lover*? I didn't think reading a bad book was nearly as dangerous as *doing* something wrong. But I was tortured by the idea that if I read *Lady Chatterly's Lover,* my ideas might, indeed, change. I might no longer have a pure mind.

While I fretted about how to break out of this logical cul-de-sac, Michael bought and sneaked a 35-cent paperback copy of the novel into the house. I can't imagine where he found it, and I don't know how our mother discovered that he was reading it. Maybe he taunted her with it during one of their spats. But my mother talked my younger sister into rooting the book out of our house before it corroded Michael's soul. Enflamed with mission, my sister recruited me to help her.

While Michael was away one day, we ransacked his closet and drawers and desk. As I opened his closet and stared at his shirts and shoes, I realized for the first time that my brother might have a sex life. Because he didn't date much, I had thought very little about that. As I pushed back his trousers, I was punished by lurid, Dantesque visions of a deviant, monstrous, alternative brother feeding the furnace of his passions with smut. But what if it wasn't smut? Galvanized by my practical quandary, as I searched his room, I hit upon a way to decide without reading the book. I would simply look at the picture on the cover.

The picture turned out to be a raw-boned, good-looking male servant reaching toward a lovely, pale, formally dressed woman. He was in the act of stripping away her chemise, and so I concluded that Rev. Garland had been right about the novel. Clutching it in my hand as my sister and I spirited it outside to the trash, I could almost feel its electric sexual pulsing. It was not until years later I learned that cover artists rarely read what's inside the book they're illustrating, and if they do, they always exaggerate the sex.

In fact, I think now that reading *Lady Chatterley's Lover* was a way for my brother to participate in a wider cultural debate, to hack open some space beyond Baptist youth group meetings, beyond our clean and bookless split-level family. The year he bought the novel, which used the word *fuck*, the nation held its breath as the Supreme Court found that it was not pornography, but a work of literature with significant ideas. Of course, that didn't convince anyone in our church, and, in fact, the novel was not the sort of thing they'd have wanted to read anyway. It describes how an upper-class woman, whose husband is paralyzed and impotent, goes mad with frustration. She begins a long, slow affair with their gamekeeper. The two of them come to realize that sex is not debasing but a way two people can mingle their souls.

I don't imagine Michael ever got to this resolution. As far as I know, he never bought another copy. And he couldn't have found the book in the Southeast High School library. He never even mentioned that his book had disappeared. Maybe he didn't want to dignify our violation with a response. Or maybe he'd gotten what he needed from the book, a way of traveling, a method of finding himself in a larger world.

Although I felt guilty about rummaging through Michael's things, I suspected that he'd have been happy enough to rummage through mine. That, I sensed, might have been a lesser violation because I did not protect my privacy as fiercely as he protected his. What I knew was that we were rivals. He was my mother's first child, the chosen son, the fragile one, the one our house belonged to before I arrived. As soon as I could walk, my mother relied on me for help with her problematic, profoundly male oldest. *Honey, can you reach Michael's medicine? Could you get him a drink of water?* She would meet me at the door after school and warn me, *Mrs. Gifford sent him home from school and Dr. Schamber will be here in a minute. Can you play quietly?* I knew that Michael was smarter than me, but I could make friends better, and I was not prickly. I worked to become useful. I was learning to play the violin so well that I was featured in *The Lincoln Journal*. I sharpened my wit against Michael's repartee. Then with a precocity that utterly outflanked him, I began dating, fell in love, and learned by experience about sex.

My brother often loudly claimed to pity the men who were snagged by my female tricks. He referred to me as "the brawling woman" and quoted Proverbs 25:24: *It is better to dwell in the corner of the housetop, than with a brawling woman and in a wide house.*

"So go live on the roof!" I would yell at him.

"Kids!" My mother would shout from the kitchen. "Don't drag the Bible into it!"

That fall we piled our Chevy with Michael's hypoallergenic pillow, his physics books, his adrenalin and non-allergenic snacks, until the undercarriage hung low in our driveway. Then all of us climbed in and drove from Lincoln to a suburb west of Chicago. We carried his things into the dorm, and made his bed, and stocked his shelves, while he paced and scowled and grumped to get rid of us. Then we drove several blocks to a room my mother rented for $15 in the basement of a professor's house. That evening I gazed out the window at twilight on the lawn at the moon, which was so large and round and perfectly white that it might have been a sheet-music illustration. The night was flawless. My stomach fluttered. I had seen freshmen talking, laughing, swarming on the quad, and I wanted to go to college, too, immediately, and forever.

The next morning we left for home.

Michael, presumably, had gotten out.

The phone call came at 7:00 a.m. the next Friday. I could hear my mother clinking breakfast dishes in the kitchen. It was a sticky September morning, my windows flung wide open, and I could see a few reddening leaves in the crowns of the trees. I was just pulling on my Pep Club sweater, the heavy black knit with a big wooly gold letter S on the back. As my mother talked on the phone, something in her tone alerted me. I stepped out of my room, glanced toward the kitchen, and saw her sink to the floor. She didn't faint. In a real crisis, my mother was never anything but solid and practical. She crouched like an animal in the corner, looking stunned but asking questions. And I knew.

I knew.

It was her birthday.

We never learned the cause of Michael's death. My mother had been required to watch four autopsies in nurses' training, and she vowed then that none of her loved ones' bodies would ever be ravaged that way. Over the years, people who learn about my eighteen-year-old brother's death have wondered why my mother didn't need to know what killed him. But I've carried two children for nine months, kept them from running into the street, applied band-aids to their cuts, watched their bodies change in puberty. I understand why she didn't want to have to imagine for the rest of her life the knives plunging in, the sinews hacked, the heart torn out.

Still, without an autopsy, there has been no barricade of facts to keep misgivings from swirling around me like angry floodwater. About a decade ago, I began to wonder whether Michael, who was always pushing boundaries, committed suicide. By then, the records were long gone, of course. But Chaplain Evan Walsh, who called that morning to break the news of his death to my mother, reported that the night before Michael died, he was having trouble breathing. He checked himself into the infirmary. His asthma was profoundly worsened by anxiety. And he must have suffered the same nerves all freshmen feel. *Will anyone like me? Can I do the work?* For all his independence, he reacted to every nuance of the emotional weather around him. He must have felt both elated and threatened by the campus, which was so different from his uneventful life at home. He had been rescued from death many times by my mother's gifted, intuitive nursing. This time she wasn't around to save him.

But the irony of his dying on her birthday, was that coincidence? In the early morning, while it was still dark, he must have found himself in a strange bed in the infirmary, fighting to breathe. That kind of struggle would distort his face, turning his lips and fingernails blue. Like a woman in labor, he would get caught up in the battle, motionless, with a faraway look in his eyes, acknowledging no one in the room. He couldn't. I remember the hiss of the oxygen, the buzz of a fly, the mustard-colored afternoon light filtering through pulled shades. That morning in the infirmary, if he even remembered that it was our mother's birthday, I doubt that he cared. He was eighteen. He had been so bent for so long on separating from her. He was battling for every breath. And although I habitually attributed my own sentimentality to him, Michael was not sentimental.

As his body traveled on the train from Wheaton toward Lincoln, I drank my first cup of coffee. More than my first alcoholic drink, this was the marker I laid down to claim adulthood, the bitter, hot, aromatic taste of a new country. I was the oldest now; I was taking my brother's place. It seems odd that I felt so little guilt about it.

One of Michael's friends, the only other student from our town who had gone from Lincoln to Wheaton as a freshman that year, escorted Michael's body home on the train. By phone, he helped my mother make arrangements, an act so mature in an eighteen-year-old that it now boggles my mind. He had never paid any attention to me because I was only his friend's silly younger sister. That weekend, he spent hours in our living room, teaching me how to play cards.

Pulling a new pack from his pocket, he cut the deck in half, positioned the two halves at angles to one another, and began fanning them to intercut them. We fundamentalists were not allowed to play cards. Cards were the Devil's Bible, as my grandmother used to tell us, and, in fact, Wheaton students signed a pledge not to dance, drink, or play cards. But they had cleverly taken up a game called Rook, which is similar to Hearts, and that's what my brother's friend taught me: the subversive game of Rook.

"Watch," he said. "You need to know this." His bottom lip was tucked under his teeth in concentration as he shuffled the cards expertly several times.

I watched.

"Want to try it?" he encouraged.

The stiff cards fell to shambles in my hands.

He flicked me a look with his black eyes, took the cards from me, roughed them up a little, and showed me again. We practiced until I could do it. Then he taught me how to play. He turned the evening lively and casual, though stunned friends kept stopping by to bring food and pay their respects. Now I think my brother's friend was helping me to enter adulthood with a ceremony that, in retrospect, seems as formal as any Ndembu ritual. I would be expected to take my brother's place in our family, and at some level, I think we both understood that. We had been raised with religious ceremonies.

"You have to take the initiative, you have to control the game," he urged. "You should practice dealing. Pay attention. You'll need this."

I would be coming to Wheaton, too, he was telling me, and he was getting me ready. When he said goodbye several hours later, he left me his cards. I have never known how to thank him for an act of kindness that transformed the way I viewed myself.

Before we buried Michael, I felt him return briefly. Standing outside our church on the grass beside the hearse, I felt like I was losing my balance. The trees swam. I felt my brother moving beside me the way you feel the wind moving through a valley, and then I sensed him departing for good. I felt a great release, perhaps Michael's release as he left his body, which had always given him trouble. But I was sixteen and I thought mostly about myself. I experienced this as my own release.

Michael's funeral was, they said, a celebration of his homegoing. As was typical of Baptists at that time in the Midwest, the family, what was left of it, his mother and younger sisters, arrived at the church early. We spent a few minutes with his body which was lying in an open coffin. Michael's lips had been rouged and his blond curly hair was parted rather than swept straight back with Brylcreem, which was how he did it. As I looked at him in the close, sickly-perfumed air, my hands began to shake. I trembled all over with fury at the men from the mortuary on Michael's behalf. All his life, he had so easily felt violated. Even though he was plainly dead, I expected him to sit up and remark on the impudence of the morticians.

I know now, as I didn't know then, that these men are lightning rods for grief and anger. When my mother requested that they make an adjustment to Michael's hair, one of them gravely complied. In the last moment before we were ushered away from the casket, my mother spotted a fly, stepped over, and waved her hand above my brother's cheek, brushing it from his face. It was her last attempt to protect him. Shortly after that, they closed the lid.

It did not look to me like a way of getting out.

A year later, when I told my mother that I planned to go to Wheaton for college, she didn't reply. Wheaton was a wonderful and terrible magnet for me, an intellectual paradise, a holiday from our dull, repetitive life. I longed to join a flock of like-minded teenagers. Together we would soar into the sixties. But I knew that Wheaton was also a place where, if you weren't careful, you could die.

Several days after I announced my plan to go to Wheaton, my mother requested a talk with me. She was wearing her worn, blue-gray, pilly cotton nighty, and she was rubbing cream into her face, walking down the hall toward my bedroom. I was passing her on my way to the kitchen for peanut butter and a rusk.

"About Wheaton," she said.

I could tell she was about to say I couldn't go.

"I refuse to send another kid there alone," she said. She let that soak in.

"But I'll go with you."

It took me a moment to realize that she was bargaining rather than dictating. She had economic power over me, and she knew it. True, her power was complicated by the fact that she had already promised to pay my tuition. However, she didn't need to ask me; she could have simply informed me that she was moving with me. But she didn't.

And I could have told her not to come, but I didn't.

Later, I regretted our bargain. I had wanted to test my courage, to experience a new reality, to try my wings. As the buyers traipsed through our house, as we packed the Lenox in strips of newspaper, as I sweated and squinted and watched movers carry our furniture to the van, my heart felt like an empty shack. I believed I would never get out.

After the move, my astute mother loosened her grip on me. To save board and room in the fall, I lived at home, but I discovered that other freshmen women were required to be in the dorms by ten on weeknights. My mother announced that I was officially out of the house now, and, even though I was sleeping there, she would keep no curfew. After that, she never asked me where I had been, and she never met me in her nightgown at the door with heart palpitations. Occasionally I drove into Chicago with college guys who lived in town, who didn't have curfews either, and I sneaked back into my mother's house at 4:00 a.m. I suspect she never slept until she heard the door lock behind me, but she didn't raise a murmur.

I was mindful that this must have required monumental self-control on her part, yet I was restless. After damping down a lifetime of curiosity, after grieving my father's and brother's deaths, after working hard for academic glory to make my mother proud of what remained, I was crazy to get out. I didn't even know what that meant. If it had been the seventies, I might have tried drugs. Instead, I tried travel. I wanted to go somewhere radical. I had friends who flung their toothbrushes into rucksacks and traveled in Europe, but I wanted to go to a realm beyond any place I'd heard of. I wanted to tear the seams out of everything I had previously imagined. I think I wanted to go to a country my brother might have talked to on his ham radio. I knew nothing about Peru. Without realizing a revolution was in full swing there, I set off for Lima, and in Lima, I hopped a rickety second-hand bus to ride over the Andes into the jungle.

That summer, aware that I was already older than my brother had been when he died, I began to learn what—I now see—he already knew, namely that the novelty of travel wears off fast. For a girl who had spent her life in Lincoln, Nebraska, Peru offered plenty of novelty. As our orange bus labored over the Andes, I felt free of the flat, two-dimensional calendar-illustration world I had lived in. The steep, husky, endless, snowy mountains gave me vertigo, and I felt thrilled by the smallness of my own body and by the way the road ahead appeared to be a tiny gray thread. I stared thousands of feet down at three dozen iron crosses the size of plusses in my childhood addition problems. A woman whispered to me in rough, pidgin English that the crosses marked the spot where a bus had landed after meeting another bus and soared off the loopy, one-lane mountain road at sixty miles per hour.

Emerging from the bus in the middle of the Amazon jungle forty hours later, I encountered another astonishing scenario. Violently green, fecund jungle trees and vines soared above a small clearing, and the air above the rutted reddish dirt road swam in the sun. I stepped into a force-field of such muggy, aggressive heat that it seemed to come out of its corner and lunge for my body like a three-hundred-pound Sumo wrestler. All around me, the jungle was alive with a buzzy din. My eyes blurred and my head felt full and fuzzy as if it were stuffed with rags.

Within two hours, I was submerged up to my chin in a tepid oxbow lake with the children of missionaries. As I doggie-paddled, I noticed a shadow swarming around us and inquired what the shadow was. "Just piranhas," they explained, relaxing on their backs against their inner tubes, paddling luxuriously. The piranhas were sniffing to discover whether I had a wound, they told me. If they found one, they would strip me to the bone so fast it wouldn't even hurt. Otherwise, I would be fine. At this shocking news, which they offered quite seriously, and which I later found was true, I stayed in the water against my better judgment because I was convinced that this was a test of my courage and I needed practice at passing such tests. Later that afternoon, one of the girls, who took me in hand like a seasoned diplomat, introduced me to Max, her pet cheetah. She opened the cage and let Max out. The two-hundred-pound predator followed her around like a kitten while I struggled against my compulsion to climb into the cage and lock the door.

For the first week of my travels, I encountered one new and surprising thing after another.

But you can get used to anything, and then, to make you swoon again, you need another fix, yet another jolt of novelty. I became accustomed to the jungle after several months, to the blue, blue skies of morning, to the brief, violent thunder, and rain at 3:00 p.m. every afternoon, to the utter black of nights freckled with stars so large and vivid I felt I could touch them. Maybe I became accustomed to the jungle because I didn't know what it meant. It meant nothing, it *was* nothing but an exotic change from what I was used to. Or, to put it another way, I was an interloper in the land, a voyeur.

Then I flew with one of the missionaries named Bart to visit his tribe, and I began to understand the meaning of the jungle. After Bart landed the two-person plane on the river, we hiked through the dense foliage and stood veiled by trees, watching. The men wore loin cloths. The women were naked to the waist. Their flesh was the color of chestnuts. They appeared to be muscular and lithe with black hair cut in Dutch-boy style, like the hair of Bart and his wife. They had built airy wooden houses on stilts. They moved with the subtlety of ocelots, seeming never to do anything that was planned in advance, touching foliage, calling to their children, disappearing into their houses, wandering out again. They seemed to obey no clock. Eventually, Bart stepped out of the trees and motioned for me to follow. The Indians grinned at him in pleasure, and shouted greetings, and waved their arms, then hung back, nudging one another shyly, noticing me, giggling.

We interrupted their morning.

What was their morning?

And I considered: what was I to them? I had descended from the cloudless, azure sky in a two-seater that must have looked to them like an oversized vulture. I stepped into the 115-degree heat of their clearing, wearing jeans and a white shirt with tubes we call sleeves and a flap we call a collar. I carried papers with beetle-sized letters marching across them. My hair was short and blond. My face was pink and freckled. To them, I must have looked as though my skin had been bleached and I was a person who had been inexplicably shrouded in fabric.

I began to seem strange even to myself.

Bart had told me the members of his tribe didn't recognize themselves in pictures. They didn't believe more than one version of themselves could exist. A person can't be *beside himself*, they reasoned. How can a person hold himself in his own hands? Remembering that, as I stood there, I touched my face.

What stunned me, what I couldn't get my mind around, was the simple fact that it is possible to live with dignity and intelligence in a way so very different from the way I grew up. I began to understand my own culture as one of many. This was what Michael was beginning to see, I think. Not that he would have talked about it that way. He was only eighteen when he died.

You might say these missionaries were permanent travelers. Bart and his wife came from Cincinnati, and half the time they lived with missionaries from other tribes on the base, Yarinacocha. But they ate the food of their tribes, which they preserved and brought back to the base, and they cooked with pots their tribes had thrown. They spoke the tribe's language fluently. In fact, their job when they came a decade earlier was to listen to the people speaking, write an alphabet for the language, record its stories, teach the people to read, and then translate the Bible into their language. This, they expected, would take thirty years of their lives.

Now I can ask questions about this kind of missionary work that I couldn't have asked then. Was it right for them to enter the tribes? Was it fair to ask those people to convert to Christianity? I can only say what I saw, namely, friendship and love. I saw the tribespeople laughing and eating with the missionaries. I knew missionaries so changed by living with their people for thirty years that they now lie in graves, not in a Cincinnati cemetery, but out there in the jungle. I wonder whether the oil men who mapped the jungle in the 1960s chose to be buried out there.

One evening when the missionaries at Yarinacocha were harmonizing *Oh Suzanna* on somebody's porch, we spotted flames rising from one of the houses, yellow and red tongues hungrily licking the black sky, reaching for the high canopy of trees. The cry went up: a house had caught fire. The men ran to get water. The news spread. The house belonged to Bart and his wife. A bucket brigade formed as naturally as if it had been rehearsed. After hundreds of buckets of water, after the men dashed in, trying to save their pets and photographs, after the slow realization that no one could save the house, we all stood watching it burn. Inside remained nearly everything they owned.

When there was nothing left but embers against the dark sky, we all strolled back silently to somebody's porch, where Bart picked up his guitar and started playing again. Until 2:00 a.m., while the flames died down, we sang "Give Love a Chance" and "Take My Hand, Precious Lord" and "Bridge Over Troubled Water" and "Rock of Ages." On that night, I learned what it means to let go, to relinquish control. Bart and his wife allowed their boundaries to be reshaped, as travelers must.

To be reshaped was not the goal of my parents or my fundamentalist people. They aspired to being immutable as rocks.

I have been writing this as though I have known all along how smart my brother was about getting out, but until very recently, it didn't occur to me that he was the one who triggered my urge to travel. After all, except to go to college, he rarely left home. Ironically, it was by reading one of my own poems that I finally understood how fervently he longed to travel. Twenty years ago, when I wrote it, I was trying to explain to my son Jack who his uncle Michael was. Maybe it's not surprising that when Jack was little, when his blond curls flashed by, when I saw the quick glint in his eyes, I sometimes imagined my brother was back.

SHOWING MY SON A PICTURE OF MY BROTHER AT A HAM RADIO

Why are his lips so thin?
He was sick, that's why.
What is he doing?
Constructing the world
from noise and longing.

> Oh brother, adjusting the headset
> over blond curls the color
> of pencil shavings,
> sitting in front of that
> black box, twirling a dial.

Who does he look like?
Like the fisherman before him,
uncle or cousin who turned
sideways to the sea in Sweden
and slipped inside the wind.

> He is listening for
> some frequency, some flash,
> some language

beyond the periphery: Spanish,
maybe, or Japanese.

Who looks like him?
At night, deer, staring into headlights
and in the daytime, you,
looking at this picture in my lap,
kicking your sandals against my thigh.

    Oh brother, the genius
    in black and white
    who strung wires, heard voices
    in the headset only he
    could understand.

Did he die?
So young he never had a son.
He never met a person who
spoke Spanish, never
saw this picture.

    He watched his little sister
    run healthy rings around him,
    laughing so she couldn't hear
    any truth in all
    that static.

Who took this picture?
I did, his little sister,
standing in his doorway, wanting
to say I only speak plain English.
Come in. Come in,

    while he kept casting
    his voice into the night
    like a lonely net.
    Ask me what I've learned
    since then.

My Dead Brother Teaches Me to Travel

I have learned Death
is a tall interpreter and
you are another language
my brother speaks in,
your blond curls, so near,
I finally understand.

Sometimes, when Jack was little, I would be sitting on the floor, putting his toys away for the thousandth time. Sometimes he would stop running around his room and hurl himself onto my lap. *Thunk.* And I would hold him. He would rest his sweaty little hand on my arm. I would smell autumn in his hair. I would think about my brother, about how precocious Michael was, how difficult, how perceptive. It was only after I had a child that I understood what a great tragedy it was that Michael only lived to be eighteen. Most of us are still pathologically confused at the age of eighteen. If only he'd had time to sort things out. If only he'd been able to shake hands with the strangers he met on his radio. After our father died, how did he know he needed to practice traveling? Maybe he had some sixth sense. Maybe he realized that he would be taking a long journey. Maybe he was trying to imagine inconceivable distances, a little at a time. Maybe he was getting himself ready to go.

5

Shakespeare Asks to Meet My Mother

IT'S A HUNDRED AND THREE degrees in Lincoln, Nebraska, and my mother is sitting at the kitchen table, twisting the elastic steel armband of my father's big watch around her wrist. She is paging through a book as massive as the New York telephone directory. It contains all of Shakespeare's plays. The letters are the size of midges, written on paper so thin you see print from the other side as you read. She gets up for a drink of water. She washes out a few dishes. She combs her foamy black curls. She checks to see whether the mailman has delivered anything interesting. She stops by my chair to mention that I might want to go out and weed the garden. She sits down to study the big book. A dog barks outside, and she immediately jumps up to look out the window. She goes back to Shakespeare for a minute and turns two or three pages. "This is so dumb!" She twists a black curl around her index finger. "It's about a handkerchief!"

My mother is trying to support three children on the salary of a nurse, which is minuscule, and gnawed down every year by inflation. Before she can get a raise, the State Department of Education requires that she pass a Shakespeare course. Why Shakespeare, I don't know. She has no time to indulge in culture. But it is clear that, without a raise, she will no longer be able to support us.

I have just turned thirteen, and I can feel my mother's attention. It is like a big basket that holds my concerns easily, with plenty of space left over. She is a widow, but she is not a victim. She is so smart that the principal of the junior high where she is the school nurse phones our house after school to ask her advice. She's the one who decides whether we can keep one more stray dog, and she knows what to do about bullies. She laughs and gossips like a teenager on the phone with her girlfriends. She can cook a mean spaghetti sauce, and she's pretty. Everyone, as far as I know, admires her.

So I assume my mother is right about Shakespeare. That summer, the running jokes in our family go like this: Q. *How many Shakespeare characters does it take to change a light bulb?* A. *They used candles.* If Shakespeare's plays are that stupid, I think, why does he have such a big reputation? But, oh well, I am beginning to discover the adult world can be bizarre. We lock our ridicule of Shakespeare into the vault of family secrets.

Every morning my mother drives off to class at Nebraska Wesleyan in her ancient, chalky blue Chevy. She chugs back home in the stunning heat, sets up an electric fan, and tries to settle down to Shakespeare at the kitchen table. She is as kinesthetic as her own hair, coiled and springing. She prowls the house, waters plants, organizes drawers, washes a dirty window, throws vegetables into a pot for soup. She is in love with the life of the body. When the leaves darken into August, she has not accomplished that mysterious feat which no one can really explain. She has not changed the little black squiggles on the page into mental images of kings and clowns and lovers. The truth is, my mother cannot read Shakespeare.

If she realized that, she must have been alarmed. Much of her vitality and pleasure came from her confidence that she could support us. Maybe she felt like a passenger watching an in-flight TV news channel when the anchor reports an impending plane crash. The flight number is hers.

She grows tense and grouchy. The Shakespeare professor, she tells us one night at dinner, could never operate in the "real" world of broken legs, severed fingers, and stolen cars—the sorts of crises she manages weekly at Irving Junior High School. After all, the poor guy thinks the pretend handkerchief and the love juice in Shakespeare's comedies have the same status as an actual leg broken on an actual trampoline. Shakespeare, my mother points out, isn't going to pay our mortgage or keep our shelves stocked with spaghetti. My mother never understood how well Shakespeare sells. Or why. I realize that now. But under her influence, I firmly categorize her professor and all other intellectuals like him as ineffectual. I believe my mother, that intellectuals can function only because they have secretaries who keep track of their pencils and help them find their cars in the parking lot at night.

My mother's Shakespeare paper comes due. This paper involves not only writing, of course, but reading. And how can she write about plays she hasn't read? God knows she has plenty of imagination—more than enough to invent her own plots and characters. But she is aware that if she made up the plot, she would be found out. She absolutely must pass this course. So she sits down at the kitchen table with blue-lined notebook paper and a pencil, and she whips up a confection of ornate prose, picking up what she thinks of as the flowery style and diction of Shakespeare without divulging anything about what she has read. Her argument spirals around and around.

When my mother finishes the paper, she asks me to critique it for her. The year before, critiquing her paper would have been my father's job, but he died in December, and now we are alone, and she is trying to support us. The confidence she has placed in me is thrilling. I am just beginning to get a reputation in the family as The Child Who Reads. None of the drawbacks of that role have manifested themselves yet.

With the conviction of an unwashed subversive who feels she needs to defeat the councils of the washed, I read my mother's paper. I have begun to imagine Shakespeare as a football field where my mother's team is being mauled by the opposing team of her professor. I know who I am pulling for. I am gripped by the spirit of a cheerleader. *Hit 'em again, harder. Harder.* When I can't follow the argument in my mother's paper, I explain to myself that, after all, I am only thirteen. A person has to ease into the works of such a big-deal author. I point out a few piddling punctuation problems, but then I tell my mother that her paper is great, which is what she wants to hear.

I know there is something wrong with what I am doing. I know my mother's paper is impossible to read. I don't quite understand why. And I don't want to know. If I thought about it, I could probably figure it out. But I know that would take a lot of time, and I don't feel like working that hard. *Do whatever you can get away with*, as Flannery O'Connor once said in a different context.

My mother's professor awarded her a C on her paper. The threat of welfare passed. She received college credit and a salary increment. Rather than being grateful to him, though, she pointed to her passing grade as evidence of just how inept he was. And I agreed with her. The fact is, now I believe something very different. Maybe reading Shakespeare strengthened her professor's insight into character and enlarged his empathy. Shakespeare can do that to a person. Maybe the professor saw my mother as the protagonist of a tragedy. Maybe he gave her points because she was turning the script into a good play.

My inability to come to terms with my mother's Shakespeare paper marked a crossroads for me. My hubris then was not unlike my hubris on an afternoon ten years later when my dark-haired friend Nancy asked whether I could give her highlights with a Clairol kit. *Sure,* I said, *No problem.* How hard could it be, after all? I read the instructions. We laid out the blue tubes and the white tubes and the yellow tubes of goop. I tied a bib around her neck. We laughed and talked during the process and drank a little wine. I forgot to wrap her hair in foil. When she emerged with a big blond splotch on the top of her head—the sun rising through her scalp—I was prostrate with remorse. The next day she had to sit for hours while a beautician reversed her highlights.

Trying to please my mother about her Shakespeare paper initiated my descent into duplicity about reading. When I signed off on the paper, I knew I would be celebrated as the kid who had helped her defeat her teacher. My mother acted grateful and proud, and she wasn't faking. She took me to get a strawberry ice cream cone. I soaked up her gratitude without feeling responsible for the consequences of a judgment I vaguely realized was faulty. And then I forgot it. That fall, I became fiercely involved in defending a certain hedge fort on the playground against boys at recess, and I began to practice the violin seriously. I thought little more about my mother's Shakespeare paper for the next thirty years.

But the sides were drawn after that. I thought of life as offering two choices: my mother's active world or the corrupting, imaginary world of her Shakespeare professor. Ironically, that summer, I had begun to devour books. I had learned the trick, slipping off the collar of everyday life, following fiction anywhere it beckoned. I read books by Paul Hutchinson about the Sugar Creek Gang, which I imagined joining, failing to notice the gang was made up entirely of boys. But then, I failed to notice almost everything. I spun a cocoon of reading against the madness of a world where my father, disappear with no warning. The chair became my habitat. I camped there for whole days at a time, cradling one book after another—books that ignited breathtaking scenarios lit by magic neon lights. Occasionally, nagged by my mother, I would get up from the chair and step into the sweltering Nebraska afternoon to pick beans for dinner.

During those years my mother's creed was my creed, at least officially. She believed that if a person feels grief and horror while watching the fictional Macbeth murder MacDuff's children, that person has not stayed sufficiently alert to the demands of "real" life. That person is caught up in vain imaginings and may be lazy and bound for life's trash heap. I was failing my mother, I realized, because I secretly suffered and triumphed with characters in books. In public, I defended and sided with her. I didn't want the family to go under. And besides, she had a lot of power. On a hot afternoon, she could decide whether or not to take us to the swimming pool.

In the reading wars, I was a traitor to my own side. My mother's professor wasn't the main person I betrayed, of course. When Flannery O'Connor said to do whatever you can get away with, she went on to say that she usually couldn't get away with much. I violated a human principle so deep that it has roots in the beginning of time: I betrayed what I knew was true. It has affected my relationship with my mother ever since. Eventually, I had to reverse myself and openly honor books, or I could never have lived a free, happy life.

For me, reading is a sacrament. As I write that sentence, I imagine ghostly theologians pulling up in a ring around me, shaking their hoary white locks and muttering objections. But a sacrament is an outward and visible sign of an inward and invisible grace. And isn't that what language is? In the creation story, God tells Adam and Eve to name the animals and plants. Once they had words, they could make great leaps. They could explain crows and trees and radishes, and they could articulate what they felt, what they imagined about the animals and plants. Because of language, they could embark on the journey of their own lives, learning and remembering and passing on their experience. Without language, it would be hard to tell humans from beasts.

The Story Of My Life, Helen Keller's biography, describes reading as a sacrament. Helen Keller was blind, deaf, and dumb, and by the age of eight, she still hadn't learned to speak. She wrote that she felt imprisoned in a state of perpetual, savage despair.

> Have you ever been at sea in a dense fog, when it seemed as if a tangible white darkness shut you in, and the great ship, tense and anxious, groped her way toward the shore with plummet and sounding-line, and you waited with beating heart for something to happen? I was like that ship before my education began, only I was without compass or sounding-line, and had no way of knowing how near the harbor was. "Light! give me light!" was the wordless cry of my soul. . . .

Then one day Annie Sullivan traced the word *water* on one of her pupil's palms while she poured water over the other. Helen Keller's world cracked open—water/w*ater*—when the connection between words and things flooded over her. The world was no longer without form and void. Water was itself, air was itself, her hand was itself. "Everything had a name," she wrote,

> and each name gave birth to a new thought. As we returned to the house every object which I touched seemed to quiver with life. That was because I saw everything with the strange, new sight that had come to me. On entering the door I remembered the doll I had broken. I felt my way to the hearth and picked up the pieces. I tried vainly to put them together. Then my eyes filled with tears; for I realized what I had done, and for the first time I felt repentance and sorrow.

Learning to read ushered Helen Keller into the moral order. Her story is a conversion narrative.

As is mine. In 1950, I stood beside my mother in our kitchen, holding a worn Dick and Jane reader, sounding out the words, knowing I was faking as usual—that is, remembering the story rather than reading it. But then the story took off like a jet from a runway. I read pages and pages beyond anything I remembered. My mother stopped mashing the potatoes, frowned with pleasure, and told me that I had learned to read. I understood that somehow—I had no idea how—I was vacuuming the story off the page into myself. I did not merely feel a sense of accomplishment. I felt set apart. It was one of my earliest encounters with grace.

    I don't know why I didn't bookmark that day in my mind and honor it afterward. Well, I do know. Although I felt it deeply, I didn't understand how significant it was. There are no cultural markers for learning to read—no public celebration, no religious ritual. By the time I was thirteen, I had forgotten the essential holiness of that moment. I was a cracked cup. On the one hand, I couldn't stop reading. On the other, I couldn't stop believing that reading was a dangerous habit.

    This rift was not helped by the fact that I picked up two diametrically opposed signals about reading at school. The teachers hyped reading. In first grade, children who couldn't read were segregated into groups called *Blackbirds*, while those of us who flew through the primers were called *Bluebirds*. We avoided the eyes of the *Blackbirds* as we passed them on our way to the front of the class. And the division between readers and non-readers persisted. As teenagers, we were led to believe the non-readers among us were marked for lives of crime and addiction. Looking back, I wonder that we didn't stone those kids publicly at the end of the year.

Or they, us.

But in spite of public declamations of support for reading, high school was actually not designed for it, either. Students filled the building with restless activity. The teachers nattered on and on. We passed notes, carried on experiments, banged lockers, sprinted and screeched through the halls. We were always on display. There were no quiet nooks for hanging out with a book. No one admitted to liking books, even "smart kids." At times I thought they must have gotten A's without reading.

My mother sent mixed messages, too. She ridiculed readers like her Shakespeare professor, but she urged us to succeed at school. She was smart enough to know that in America, learning to read well was the way to thrive. However, she didn't expect any of us to *like* reading.

At home, I developed a reputation for being the reader of the family, which means being a dreamer, someone who can get lost in any fog that happens to roll in. As everyone knows, in a family, a person grows to resemble her reputation. A grandmother might say, *You drive just like your Great Uncle Elmer.* Or, *good grief, listen to her. She's getting funny, like her father.* When you're young, the aunts and uncles who haven't seen you for a while will stand around and make these comments in your presence—as if you were a piece of used furniture or an African violet they're thinking about purchasing. Whatever they say about you makes you think about yourself that way, which in turn pushes you further in that direction.

My mother often sent me downstairs to find a jar of canned plums or rhubarb for dessert. When I forgot what she wanted and came up with a jar of pickles she became eloquent in her annoyance. *Mankind could have evolved in the time it's taken you to find that. Go down and get it right!* I obediently climbed down and spent another ten minutes looking around, trying to remember what I was there for.

My mother blamed this lack of practicality on too much reading. She worried that I was so easily ensorcelled that I would not hear the sirens during one of our summer tornadoes, for example. She might find me wrapped around a street sign. Late at night, she sat on my bed, her face and hands stippled by the waving shadows of trees under the streetlight while she pled with me to change. But I couldn't figure out how to change. I had failed my driver's test because, the agent said, I was dreamy. I forgot my purse at school. I lost coats and boots. Reading carried me farther and farther downstream from her, standing on the dock, calling me toward responsible adulthood.

My mother might have been right—that there was something slightly sick about my secret, inarticulate reading. I suffered from a lack of critical distance. Whatever happened to the main character in a book happened to me, and I was helpless to extricate myself or make judgments about what it meant.

Ironically, part of what brought me out of my reading stupor was another Shakespeare teacher, a bull-necked former Marine who made us read *Romeo and Juliet* in tenth grade. When he blurted out in sweet, clumsy words why he loved the story, I thought I might die of joy. Someone else had dreamed exactly the same story I had read the night before! He made us read *Julius Caesar* out loud. Oh man. We were terrible, even I knew that. But the brilliance of the language lifted our clunky, illiterate little voices to heaven.

Later, in college, I discovered a second, better, more active kind of reading—hauling the glittering jewels from the cave into the sunlight and exclaiming to one another—*look at this! Isn't this amazing!* In high school, we talked mainly about plot. But simply to know that other human beings had the same story in their minds felt like the miracle of the loaves and fishes. This giant, awkward sergeant made the Shakespeare play into bread we passed around and ate in class. And I began reading in a different, more self-conscious way. I was gathering food for the table. I had a premonition that I might do something useful with my life, however crippled my mother thought I was by my addiction to reading.

Nevertheless, I was determined not to study any more Shakespeare than necessary. Even though I majored in an undergraduate English Department where Shakespeare was a requirement, I successfully petitioned to avoid my mother's old nemesis. It was the Jesuits in graduate school who finally forced me to read Shakespeare for my master's degree. And it was watching Professor Stan Clayes leap from the floor to the top of his desk in his virtuoso performance of *Henry V* that finally converted me to Shakespeare.

Since then, Shakespeare and I have been through every stage of love—astonishment, infatuation, disillusion, jealousy, worship. I've lived for periods of time in London and seen many of his plays at the Globe, where he may have acted. I've spent days in Stratford, where, as a boy, he ran the earth into his feet. I can picture him strolling around the town market after he dropped out of school, as it teemed with horses and herbs, vegetables and flowers. He must have studied people, bewitched by their charm and their evil. He probably helped in his father's tanning business, out behind his parents' half-timbered house. The day would dawn, bright and cool in the summer, the stink of lye floating on the air. Quick as a wink, he had a wife and three babies. He was probably desperate for money. Maybe he wrote couplets to sell for two pence with the gloves. At the age of twenty-one, standing outside his house in Stratford, listening to three babies wailing, he must have glanced down the road toward London. He was looking for a way to become Shakespeare.

Sometimes I think I understand Shakespeare better than I understand my mother.

I wonder now whether my mother realized that she was not reading Shakespeare that summer. I remember one night in college, climbing into bed early to read a translation of Kant's *Critique of Pure Reason*. I opened the cover of the book and fell into a deep hole. I climbed out, thinking I had made some bizarre mistake, like forgetting to put on my glasses. I started over. I kept feeling the ground shift under my feet. After a couple of pages, I couldn't remember what I had read. I calculated rapidly. If I'd spent an hour and couldn't remember what I'd read, I definitely wouldn't finish the assignment that night. In fact, I realized I might never finish reading *The Critique of Pure Reason*. It is astonishing, bewildering, humiliating to discover that you are holding in your hand pages of an English translation that you, as a native speaker, cannot read.

In fact, my mother never actually read anything but the Bible. Oh, sure, a cake mix box, maybe, and our report cards and Mother's Day cards. But she didn't read books. She had absolutely no interest in them. How could she read and understand the King James Bible every day, on the one hand, and yet never pick up any other book? In fact, no one in our church read. No one talked about reading. It occurs to me now that one young married couple read for pleasure, books about spirituality published by religious presses. My mother occasionally bought those but she didn't read them. She put them on our coffee table. Perhaps *not* reading is precisely what allowed my mother to remain in our church. It was over reading, after all, that I left my fundamentalist people.

Since my mother doesn't read, there's much we can't talk about because reading touches me in a way nothing else does. I would like to share the questions and humor of reading with her. Once I was trying so desperately to read a nineteenth century French novel that I invented things no one else in class recalled, because, of course, they weren't there. I have laughed about that with other readers, but never with my mother. She must feel the loss even more keenly than I do. She must have seen her teenaged child paddling away from her in the canoe of reading on a journey she either couldn't or didn't want to take.

It is a great irony that, nevertheless, she was the one who taught me to love stories—her own, and my father's, and those of her parents. With the verve and style of a fine soccer player dribbling and passing the ball down the field, she narrated the old tales. The past defines us, as my fundamentalist people argued. It is the story of God dealing with his people. Remember it. Write it in the tablets of our children's hearts: the story of Abraham's faith, the story of my mother's parents nearly losing their farm to hail, the story of how one winter midnight, just after my parents were married, they seized their playing cards, carried them down to the furnace in the basement, hurled them in, and watched them burn. They felt called to a life apart from the popular, drinking, dancing, card-playing in-group in Parkers Prairie, Minnesota.

My cagey mother aimed her stories directly at me. Maybe that's because I was the child who asked to hear them. I might read myself into ruin, yes, possibly, but my mother understood that if I didn't, I was the child most likely to hand down the legacy of the past. She fretted over my brother; she loaded her practical concerns on my sister. She handed me her stories more frequently and with more urgency as she recognized what I was becoming.

My mother is standing over a huge navy pot, lifting one dripping, steamy mason jar after another from the noisily boiling water. The kitchen thermostat registers a hundred and three, and a mist hangs above the stove, encircling her. I am leaning over the sink, sliding skins off peaches, my vision blurring as salty sweat drips from my forehead into my eyes. In the living room, George Beverly Shea is rumbling, *How Great Thou Art*. My sister, who stands at the kitchen table drying the hot jars, is, like me, stripped down to her underwear. Our faces are flushed, and our wet hair clings to our heads. Then we hear a chime.

One of us shouts, "Oh no! The doorbell!"

"It's Rev. Garland," my sister jokes.

We explode into laughter, three women who have been toiling since 6:00 a.m., loony from the August brain-numbing Nebraska heat. Julie scoots behind the living room drapes to spy on the caller. We wait, silent, jumpy as frogs on a griddle, hoping the caller doesn't walk around to the back of the house, where he might spot us through the big kitchen windows.

Julie hisses that it's a salesman. He's walking away. We relax.

"Girls," my mother begins. "I remember."

I remember. The powerful locomotive that pulled the boxcars of her stories behind it. At fourteen, she drove her brothers and sisters to school in a Model A. At sixteen, she was the lone teacher for thirty-two kids in a one-room country schoolhouse. By the age of twenty, she was staffing a hospital ER alone during the night shift. One night a couple of cops came in with a man's arm wrapped in a bloody army blanket. They thrust it at her and announced, *The body's coming later.* In surgery, she was the one who managed the eminent physicians, handing them instruments. They would swear and fling the instruments across the room, and she would have to calm them down. She was the recipient of half a dozen marriage proposals, most of them from doctors. She spent half a day stuck in an Otis elevator with a dead body. She watched as her parents' soybean crop got wiped out by hailstorms. She was chased and almost torn to shreds by a wild bull. When she worked as a nurse at St. Elizabeth's, she pulled the dead fetuses out of trash bins, wrapped them in diapers, brought them home, and buried them in our backyard under signs bearing their last names. As the school nurse at Irving Junior High, to hear her tell it, she regularly threw herself onto the bodies of students and teachers to stop geysers of blood from shooting out of wounds. It was her coaxing that persuaded an unhappy junior high math teacher to come down from the far edge of the school roof, where the woman was munching a piece of cheese and contemplating how far it would be to the ground.

I wonder now whether swapping stories could have healed the split between my fundamentalist mother and me. When my mother told her stories, what if I had reciprocated with stories from the books I read? Maybe there was a moment when, because I failed to act, we forever missed what we might have had in common. But I didn't know how to talk about the stories I knew. I couldn't even tell their plots. They felt locked away in a dark cave. And anyway, what my mother wanted was not reciprocity but an audience. Not just any audience, either. I was the child she wanted to hear the stories. And look, she knew what she was doing.

The subject of reading rose like Mount Everest between my mother and me. It was so big we couldn't even talk about it. I was Darth Vader, and she was Luke Skywalker, or maybe it was the other way around. I wanted her to read. I didn't much care what she read—cartoons, coffee table books, Our Daily Bread, romance novels—I bought them all for her. She politely thanked me and avoided opening them. I gave her copies of each of my books as I published them. She proudly displayed each of them on her coffee table, still packaged in their original cellophane.

At the age of eighty-nine, she told me that she'd had it up to here with assisted living. The eggs were watery, her home health care worker was not only lazy but possibly not refined enough. And the raffles and Hawaiian luaus arranged by Mary Francis weren't fun anymore.

"Okay," I said to her. "What would make you really happy?"

"My car," she snapped.

Before my mother gave up her Saturn, she got lost three times. She had to stop at a Rita's Water Ice stand and hitch a ride home with a male stranger, who unbelievably turned out to be not an axe murderer, but the angel Gabriel disguised as a middle-aged Dallas businessman. Before that, she hit a car while turning left in a no-left-turn lane.

"Oh, Mom, you don't want to drive," I replied in a light voice. "Think of the trouble—dealing with the insurance company, taking the car for service, comforting parents of the children you kill."

She cast me a lacerating look. *What do you know about it? When you get to be eighty-nine, you'll want your car back, too.* She knew what she was doing. It is terrifying to imagine being eighty-nine. But I couldn't make this decision out of terror over my own impending old age. My mother simply could not have her car back.

"Here's an idea," I said, "I'll order you some used books from Amazon dot com," thinking that by reading, she could take long, safe rides in her imagination to places she's never been.

"I want my car," she said.

I was responsible for withholding my mother's car—and happiness—from her. I was Goneril to her King Lear! Of course, this was a joke I couldn't tell her.

The last time I picked up my mother at the Philadelphia airport—that is, the last time she was capable of flying to visit us—is when I realized she was Lear, and I was about to become Goneril.

89

Her memory and her health had been shaky for years. On this trip, she misplaced several carry-on bags. We slogged around the airport trying to recover them, filling out forms, filing documents, speaking politely to clerks. And then she remembered that she hadn't carried those bags onto the plane in the first place. We laughed about it.

"Thank you, darling, for coming to pick me up," she said. "Driving all the way from Dallas!"

I said, "No, *you* came from Dallas, remember?" She—who once could locate herself within the space of a napkin ring—squinted, thought about it, and changed the subject.

With self-pity, I thought, *Now I'm the mother and she's the child.* It was summer. We drove by a roadside fruit stand, the kind of stand that is boarded up all winter. It was manned by sun-tanned kids. I gave myself orders: *Keep your heart open for business. Do not tack plywood over the window. Do not put up a sign saying CLOSED. You'll get better at this. You will have plenty of practice. Your mother is not going to recover. What she has is Old Age.* I knew this would be her last plane trip. The fact would devastate her because all her life she was so active.

I saw that she needed reading the way a sick person needs medicine. "How about stopping at Borders?" I asked her casually.

"Not on your life," she said. "I'm not ruining *my* eyes!"

That was the last time I tried to talk her into reading.

I will never quite recover from the irony that it was she who started me down the road that took me so far away from her.

Sometimes I imagine, once we're all in heaven, and after I've asked my father a lot of questions and he's given me the best answers he's got, I will go over to the booth where Shakespeare is sitting, signing his folios and answering questions. There will be a long line. I'll stand there gossiping a little in the warm breeze with other readers who adore the Bard. When I get to the front of the line, Shakespeare will look up at me and say, *I hear your mother's got some good stories. How about an introduction?* He'll get up, and we'll go find her. The three of us will swap stories. My mother will stick around—not because she needs a bigger paycheck to support her children—but because she finds out that she really likes the man.

6

Writing as a Subversive Activity

I BEGAN WRITING IN high school because it was the only way I could think of to subvert the classroom rules without being sent to the principal's office. I suspect that high school was a place of great agony for me, as it is for many people. To relieve the monotony, I signed up for a Latin course taught by a tiny, fiery, red-haired spinster who believed in Latin as a Force for Good. She was legendary for making her students act out snippets of Latin plays. She trounced us regularly in her spicy Latinate diction for our anemic attitude toward Life, which she suggested might have been so bloodless because we had been brought up in the excessively polite Midwest. When I rose in the morning to the tedium of Civics and Algebra and Hygiene, I knew she would be lying in wait for us in her Latin classroom—Spitfire, Grammarian, Storyteller—who marched the intrigue and bloodletting and glamour of the Roman tyrants up the front steps of the building and right into our high school classroom.

Shortly after the semester began, this blazing old crone got sick, and the mother of one of my unfortunate classmates became our permanent substitute. Or rather, babysitter. She spent most of the class period going over the vocabulary lists at the back of the chapters. And the rest of what she said was so predictable it might have been pre-recorded. As her voice droned and time slowed, I felt frantic. Every minute in that class felt like an hour sitting at a railroad

Writing as a Subversive Activity

crossing waiting while hundreds of boxcars rolled by. Seconds were elongated. They ticked grotesquely into the future. There were sixty such seconds in each minute and fifty minutes in each class. Time became unspeakably cruel.

To avoid going nuts, I scanned the horizon for exits. Our teacher would call roll. *Three minutes.* Then there were PA announcements. *Nine minutes.* In these interstices, under the teacher's radar, in the back of my Latin notebook, I started writing a cowboy novel. I told no one, but it changed my life. Instead of dreading Latin all day, I looked forward to surprising events unfolding at the corral. I was still in Latin, of course. Seeing a body in the chair, the teacher counted me present.

I had learned how to subvert authority at the small fundamentalist school my father helped to start the year I was in second grade. There I more-or-less invented my own education. The lack of proper books and supplies meant we pursued whatever aroused our curiosity. School was a circus of different grades and subjects, and each day we debuted new acts in the big tent. Oh, there were rules and a rough kind of order. But each of the two classrooms included four grades; our teacher juggled activities like a ringmaster. To survive, she had to be part trickster, part queen, part mother, part psychologist.

Because our books at Lincoln Christian School were donated, they were all different from one another, and so we didn't have to slog week by week through the chapters of a common text. We dodged from topic to random topic. One of the kids brought a book about Eskimos, so we spent two weeks studying where Eskimos live, what they eat, how they talk, what they wear. We passed books from one to another. I became infatuated with the idea of building an igloo village. My father entered into the spirit, buying chicken wire, plaster of Paris, and a plywood board on which to mount the village. While Miss Meierhenry worked on addition and reading with second graders, a bunch of us fourth graders stirred a batch of plaster of Paris. We discovered that when you add too much water and stir, it spatters all over the table and your clothes. When you don't add enough, it gets lumpy like cottage cheese. And as it hardens, it heats up. We made igloos every day for a week, daubing the stuff all over our hands and faces and legs. For one entire math period, while we were supposed to be practicing subtraction, we cracked the plaster of Paris off one another, fascinated by the way it showered across the floor. Miss Meierhenry, who could be strict, who occasionally spanked one of us, cut her losses, grinned, and sent us to the broom closet in the basement to clean up. While we swept up slivers of plaster, she moved on to fifth-grade geography. We were thrilled that, by charming her, we had subverted our math class. It was possible, in fact, to amuse and beguile our teachers who knew our families and, I believe, cared deeply for us. That's partly how I learned the power of subversion.

In fact, from its very beginning, the Lincoln Christian School subverted the larger culture by virtue of its very existence. The city and state had set up, accredited, and supervised primary and secondary schools, of course, and the rule was everyone must attend them. In this way, we would achieve a kind of mass culture. But my fundamentalist parents and those of the other kids in the Christian school didn't want any part of mass culture. Not that they knew how to set up a school. How could they have? Neither of my parents had a college degree. There were a few other Christian schools around the country at the time, and maybe they served as inspiration and models. But our family couldn't afford to make long-distance phone calls, and we didn't travel. If my mother and father were part of a national independent school movement, they didn't think much about it. They were on their own in the middle of a large country with a handful of other parents. What they didn't have in information or institutional backing, they made up for with confidence.

Looking back, I wonder at the courage of my parents, who had no natural inclination to take risks, who never traveled except to visit their parents, who lived such otherwise conservative lives. They and their friends invented that school and brought it into being out of nothing: a building, two teachers, some used desks and books, coat hooks and brooms, plumbing and chalkboards. At the beginning, they had no idea what a curriculum was, and they didn't know where to find teachers. The first year, they calculated what the tuition should be, guessing at expenses. They networked to find students who might enroll. Every year afterward, they tried to set the tuition low enough to attract students but high enough to cover expenses, and when they failed either way, they went into debt.

Eventually, they visited the State Board of Education, filled out paperwork for accreditation, and fervently prayed that it would be granted. If it wasn't, the school would be out of business. I watched as year after year they willed the school into being, made mistakes, nearly lost it, recovered, and survived to open the next fall. For them, it must have felt like building a bridge across the Grand Canyon. To look down made them feel dizzy, so they didn't look down. They just nailed one plank in place at a time. They trusted their weight to that plank while they nailed down the next.

Watching, I came to have faith in the odd process of creating. I learned to live that way long before I knew how to write. Writing involves trial and error, not so different from the daily adventure of thinking up a school and voyaging into the unknown to build it. When you start a book, there's nothing but a vision, a tickle in your throat that you feel you may never be able to articulate. But you sit down. You write every day, and eventually, you hold a book in your hands. Before the ceremony that marked the first graduation from eighth grade, my parents and the other founders looked back and remarked with astonishment that they had created, yes, a school.

So I'm eight. My father has been diagnosed with a heart condition and can no longer run his general store in Parkers Prairie; therefore, my parents devise a new adventure. They take a road trip through the Midwest to find a city they like, and then they move us to Lincoln, Nebraska. That fall, instead of taking us to the public school, my father drives us to the fledgling school he has set up with a group of friends during the summer. As we float through traffic, my parents go over the facts again. We will feel weird at first, but we'll find new friends. My lucky sister, who is too young to go to first grade, sits over the hump in the back seat, swinging her legs, which don't reach the floor. My brother sits on the other side of her, quietly looking out the window. I push one shoulder through the two front seats and touch my mother's sleeve to make sure she's still there, and still my mother.

We park and descend concrete steps into the basement of a church. The ceiling is so low that if you glance up you see aluminum heating ducts. Dirty sunlight shines in the small, high, rectangular windows. All I can see through them is a piece of blue sky with raggedy clouds scurrying by. Kids stand askew all over the basement. I don't know any of them. My chest feels hollow, and I hold my breath. I don't like the musty smell down here.

I grasp my mother's hand while she talks to another adult. I look up. "This is Mrs. Friezen," my mother tells me, squeezing my hand. Mrs. Friezen is a vertical woman with pointy features who wears a nice, flowing wool plaid skirt and a rust-colored hand-knit button-up sweater. I would like to touch its braided pattern, but I know enough not to. She smiles and says hi. I am surprised at how deep and commanding her voice is. Scrunching down to my height, she shows me a book with colored pictures, letting me turn the pages at my own speed. Her skin is the beautiful color of a walnut shell.

When Mrs. Friezen walks to the front of the class and welcomes everyone, the room quiets, as if she had twirled a dimmer switch. One of the fathers prays, asking the Lord's blessing on the first day of school. He requests that the Board of Education might give our new school accreditation this fall so we don't have to close. Then the parents begin moving toward the door.

I see tears swim in the eyes of the shorter blond girl beside me. I'm thinking, *I'm not crying! Not me. But oh boy, oh boy, is my mother leaving me here alone?*

"We'll have fun," Mrs. Friezen announces. She invites us to sit at the tables, then sits down, opens a book, and begins reading a story about a girl called Heidi.

> On a clear sunny morning in June two figures might be seen climbing the narrow mountain path; one, a tall strong-looking girl, the other a child whom she was leading by the hand, and whose little cheeks were so aglow with heat that the crimson color could be seen even through the dark, sunburnt skin.

I forget that my mother is gone until it's almost time to go home.

On cold fall days, Mrs. Friezen makes her daughter Mary Ann, who is also in second grade, wear exactly the same kind of garter belt and long brown stockings that my mother requires me to wear. When we sit at our desks, the garters press red indentations in our thighs. In the girls' bathroom, Mary Ann and I compare our angry red marks. We hate the way the stockings slow us down when we run. We are the only girls whose mothers require that we wear them. We think our mothers are unfair, that they are possibly mistreating us. When Mary Ann suggests that the next day we should refuse to wear our stockings, I am awestruck by her defiance. I agree, and we make a pact. The next day the temperature is below thirty, the sky is spitting snow, and we both show up at school wearing stockings. Now we have something else in common: our mothers are both tyrants, we tell one another.

We are learning to subvert our mothers by watching our parents resist the mass education system in Lincoln. It may not have dawned on our parents when they started the school that reading and math are not all we'll learn at their school. We're also absorbing the attitude that subverting authority is a good way to live.

To get to our new school, my brother and I take a city bus into the heart of town, walk a couple of blocks, and hop on a second bus. My parents warn us not to talk to strangers, to stick to our business. After a couple of weeks, I could do the route with my eyes closed. One morning, my brother and I duck into a corner store to buy sunflower seeds and Mary Janes, candy cigarettes and bubble gum. We begin to stop in every day. Mrs. Friezen doesn't allow us to eat candy in school, so we devour the sweets before we get off the bus, but I hide sunflower seeds in my desk. All day I sneak them into my mouth, cracking the shells open one by one with my teeth, and eating the savory nuts. I am learning new facts. That the teacher doesn't know everything. That I can go anywhere I want if I have a dime for the bus. That people my parents don't know can be interesting.

I decide to take control of my own education. One of the parents contributes enough used spelling books so all four children in our grade have one. That week Mrs. Friezen assigns the first chapter. The following week, she assigns the second. All of a sudden, we have to sit at our desks and copy a lot of words and invent sentences that use them; handwriting counts towards the grade. I can see where this is going, so the following weekend, I slave away for hours and finish all twenty-three lessons. On Monday, I hand them to Mrs. Friezen. With blood rising to her face, she opens a drawer in her desk, puts them in, and sternly explains that I need to write out one lesson per week, just like everyone else. She only blushes when she's angry, or scared, or something else is up, so I conclude this is not about educating me. It is a plot to keep me quiet and sitting at my desk. When I tell Mary Ann, she commiserates, and my estimate of her goes up a notch.

Although Mrs. Friezen never relents on spelling lessons, shortly afterward, she asks me to help her teach Annabell Lee Stein to read. I jubilantly check a health book out of our library, which is half a shelf of donated books, and slide in beside Annabell at her desk. We have just come in from recess, where we were playing Run Sheep Run. Annabell's hair forms a dark brown nimbus about her round face. Her cheeks are ruddy, and I can feel warmth radiating from her shirt and jeans. She bends to stare at the drawings in the math book of children washing hands. Stabbing my finger at each word on the line, I read to her about how colds spread, while she listens as if I were the announcing angel. *Washing hands prevents colds!*

My eyes brim, and I flick my head. A drop lands on my hand. In my last school, only teachers got to teach. This is more like it! I stop reading, turn to Annabell, lay my urgent hand on her arm, and assure her that even if I have to climb mountains or cross a desert, I will, I *will* teach her to read.

"Okay," she says agreeably.

In the tiny fellowship of our school, every day is turbulent. We smart from the vendettas and jealousies of our fort skirmishes, of Fox and Goose, and Red Rover, and countless best friend arguments. In fifth grade, we girls create a miniature chapel in a basement broom closet, draping a scarf over an orange crate to suggest an altar, laying down a braided rag rug someone has brought from home. One of us brings a Bible and together we fashion a cross from two pussy willow branches.

In class, if one of us is angry or swallowing back tears, we raise our hands and ask to go down to the tiny chapel. The 3x5 foot space becomes a respite from the shifting, shocking soap opera that is our lives. Sitting around the altar, we quarrel loudly and read Bible verses until we reach some kind of agreement or until we're worn out. Because the school's cleaning equipment is stored in the closet, the chapel reeks of the rust-colored granular compound our janitor scatters before he sweeps. To this day, when I smell a sweeping compound, I'm transported to that broom closet.

On some days the teacher sentences us to go down to the chapel to straighten things out. Some days, we visit it more than once—on very bad days. We learn we can avoid schoolwork by pretending to be pious, so we begin to subvert the devout instincts that moved us to set up the chapel in the first place, gossiping and giggling down there until the teacher sends a student to summon us back to class.

After school on Wednesdays, a bunch of us take the city bus from the Lincoln Christian School to Roberta Sheets' house, where her grandmother runs a Bible study. Roberta lives with her grandmother and her mother in a rundown part of town. She doesn't have a father because her mother had her out of wedlock—a sad story, our parents tell us, but Roberta's mother has repented and is now redeemed. Nevertheless, she wears low-cut dresses and she paints her long fingernails crimson. She looks younger than the other mothers, and she laughs a lot. When she comes to school to pick up Roberta, you can hear her giddy laugh in the entry hall, and it makes you want to rush out there to get in on the fun.

So even if she is a grade below me, Roberta belongs to our group. She helps build our forts and fiercely defends them, throwing herself into our fights against the boys. And when it rains, the lucky duck gets to tromp in puddles because she is wearing the tall yellow boots her grandmother gave her for Christmas. At the afternoon Bible study, Roberta's grandmother, with a whiskery chin like a troll, plays games with us and serves milk and cookies. Their house seems perpetually filled with the scent of baking. Years pass before I realize that Roberta's grandmother is taking care of me on Wednesday afternoons because my mother is working and my father has heart trouble.

Any differences that might flare up between the wildly diverse, oddly sorted parents of the school are put to rest quickly when they meet to solve our accreditation problem. We pull together against the public school authorities. Some days my father sits at our dining room table and fills out stacks of papers. Before Christmas, the Nebraska State Board of Education plans to send out a man to decide whether we pass the test. I don't even know exactly what the test is, but my parents tell us kids that the outcome will depend on us. The man will want to find out what we've learned by talking to us. "Volunteer to show the man your papers," they tell my brother and me. "Be friendly." In morning circle at school and evening devotions at home, we pray that God will make the State Department of Education give us a passing grade.

Then alarmingly one night our parents call a family meeting to discuss an even greater danger. Some students are withdrawing from school because it's too far for their parents to drive them twice a day. Without their tuition, the school will fold in a month. Outside snow is falling, and white pads of snow cover the bushes like hats. I have been looking forward to a snowball fight against the boys the next day. Now I imagine walking up the sidewalk to the school and finding the red door shut, a chain and padlock around it. Words jam together in my head. My parents tell us not to give up, that we'll hit on a solution together. My mother quips that my father should start a bus service.

She means this as a joke, but the next Saturday, when she's at work, my father takes us to an auction where a crowd of people mills around an icy parking lot. I see a leathery-faced man in a cowboy hat stub out his cigarette, climb the steps to a small stage, and start babbling. Keeping his shoulders perfectly still, he makes his mouth spin out of control, "Who'll give me thirty, I have thirty here, now thirty-five, who'll give me thirty-five?" He rattles away, and then he suddenly jerks to a stop. To me he appears to be having a seizure, about which I know because my nurse mother has described seizures and acted them out so we will know what to do if we witness someone in the middle of a seizure. Or maybe the man is speaking in tongues. I've never seen anyone speak in tongues, though JoAnn, one of my friends, who goes to the holiness church, has described it.

"Forty, forty, I have forty, who'll give me forty-five?"

My father tugs at his earlobe.

The panel truck is charcoal gray, and one fender is slightly dented, but when my father gets in, he turns the ignition key, and it starts. He whoops with pleasure, and when we ask, he informs us that the lolla-ka-trigger-of-the-come-and-go-rod is just fine, and that's all that matters. We should pick a name for her. Throwing all kinds of names into the air, we engage in a skirmish, and then settle on Betsy. The next week my father paints Betsy red, bolts wooden seats along her inside panels, and starts a free pick-up and drop-off service to the school.

It isn't long before my father is cutting out big letters on his band saw in our garage. The whine starts low, *gmmmmmmmmmph*, and as he pushes the wood through the blade, it rises to a high *eeee*, then eases back down to *gmmmmmph*. The saw's melody is the exact shape of the wood's pressure against the blade. Since our garage doors are open, I'm thinking of how the saw's tune rings through the neighborhood. Sawdust falls under the table saw onto the cement floor and accumulates in blond cones. It stings my nose with the perfume of pine, what I think of as the scent of my father. Now and then, a few red and brown maple leaves hop into our garage on a gust of wind. We are fortified in sweatshirts against the chill autumn air, listening to the play-by-play of a Cornhuskers football game. My father, who is wearing goggles, holds up a gigantic letter C and wiggles it in the air. That afternoon he cuts out all the letters, LINCOLN CHRISTIAN SCHOOL.

Later we help him paint the letters red. He climbs a ladder. Standing on the ground, I yell advice to him about whether the letters are straight or crooked as he bolts them to the school building.

As parents around the city discover that our graduates score grade levels beyond their age on tests, they enroll their children, and our subversive school flourishes. The school board has purchased a small, centrally located plot of land and built a gray cinder block building. It's a neighborhood of nice, middle-class houses, not a precinct for red letters, but we want everyone to notice the school and realize it's thriving.

Then after lunch one day, Ms. Meierhenry welcomes the corpulent, mild-mannered man from the Board of Education who is clad in a gray suit and who keeps a pleasant look fixed on his face. He lowers himself to an adult-sized chair which the sixth-grade boys have politely lugged to the back of the room. As the third graders file up for their reading group, he looks on amiably.

I turn around in my desk and peer back at him surreptitiously over my shoulder. His eyes are closing and, as I realize that the poor man must be bored, I am tempted to feel offended. I know how awful boredom feels, but hasn't he seen our miniature African twig huts? Moreover, taped to the wall are tracings of our own hands—which we have brilliantly converted into pictures of zebras and fish. I raise my hand and ask for permission to show him these things. When he smiles good-naturedly, looking like my father's oldest brother, and asks me good-natured questions, I know, I just *know* we have him on ice. Several weeks later, our School Board gets a letter saying that the Board of Education has tentatively accredited the Lincoln Christian School.

When I switched from the wild and woolly world of Christian to public school, my practice with subversion came in handy. That fall, my teachers repeated tediously what I knew cold. Other students took that repetition for granted, but it infuriated me, because with so few of us in each grade, our teachers at the Lincoln Christian School became familiar with exactly what we knew. We didn't get by with faking, but we were never forced to review information we could prove we knew. We were allowed to sew costumes for plays, or read science fiction, or write music, or practice baseball, or do whatever we wanted, as long as we kept relatively quiet. So I was shocked to be taught by adults who knew nothing about me and who, for about a third of every year, required that I sit through lessons I could have taught. I did not have the guts to get up and walk out, so I moved away on paper, by means of my imagination. Another kid might have begun sketching cartoons; my escape was to write stories.

Since those days of my cowboy novel, my writing has been subversive. I rarely ever write in order to explain what I already know. Instead, for me writing is a fumbling toward awareness. Over the years, I've gotten a little better at technique. But when I write, I'm nearly always uncertain of what's coming next. Writing, at least for me, is most often a groping towards what I want to say. It is a learning process through which I have discovered most of what I know. If I roll up my sleeves and work wholeheartedly at meter and metaphor, which is my job as a poet, some kind of truth occasionally shows up. I suspect this is typical of what happens to most writers and painters and musicians. Through our work, we discover what we know.

As I write, I'm hardly aware of where I'm sitting, or what the weather is, or exactly who the reader will be. It's more like sauntering down a street, glancing between two houses, and spotting something fleeting and insubstantial. I wander back to see what's there and find a cave, maybe, and spend the morning exploring. It often feels familiar. And when I return from that place, no time seems to have elapsed. Except, of course, now it's noon, and I have to pick up my child from school for his violin lesson.

To go somewhere else in the imagination this way requires a bizarre combination of hard work and relaxation. Writing involves pursuit, of course, and forward motion and a sense of form and rules, but, at least for me, at the heart of it lies diversion and play. After all, it's about going after new words, trying out syntax, devising metaphors, wrestling with the language to get closer than you've ever come to the truth. It involves courting the improbable, picking up stones that might *not* fit the wall you're building, turning over rocks that might *not* be hiding a salamander. The relaxation part involves letting ideas lead to one another, lowering your suspicion about whether a notion is practical, not forcing closure because the image has somewhere it still might need to go.

Going through all the failure and wasted writing requires patience of the sort required for sitting quietly in the backyard during most of a workday and watching the leaves wave in the wind. And enjoying it. A person doesn't get credit for checking her watch, wondering how much longer she will be forced to stay there. You have to savor it, or it doesn't count. You don't tally up the hours it takes to write a piece. You pour into it whatever time it takes.

All of this may sound more bizarre than it actually is. I suspect it's not much different from what happens to anyone who is riveted on an internal landscape. Get caught up in a game of golf or spend a morning gardening. Try planning a vacation in Venice or the Peruvian jungle. Or turn off the television and just sit still. Pick up the end of some thread and follow it, daydream, see whether it doesn't take you to a place of memory or imagination, where time seems to stop. If it's going well, you might feel an unearthly sense of peace.

This subversion of practical everyday life often feels hazardous to me. It's easy to zone out, to float away, to get your skirt caught in the gears of the imagination. After hours of writing, I have trouble remembering what else needs to be done. I wander around the house for a while, looking at furniture without really seeing it. Sometimes I find myself holding my phone, unable to remember the standard greeting. Once I "came to" and found myself holding the phone. I said, "Hello, who's this?"

The voice on the other end said crossly, "You're the one who called *me*!"

Oh, I thought, that's true. I did.

But I couldn't remember why.

This reminds me of my friend, a highly trained actor, who claims that while she's on stage performing, she has trouble remembering she's in a play. She doesn't recall eating her breakfast or leaving her house, and she becomes a little manic. In the end, she couldn't go on with her acting career. A story or a poem can also act like a Siren, making you want to abandon everything else. Then it's good to have a mast to tie yourself to, or you might jump into the sea and swim after a mirage. Being a mother is a pretty good way of tying yourself to the mast. After making over thirteen thousand dinners, I have come to believe that there might be no mast more solid to tie oneself to than the vegetable market and the kitchen.

I learned the improbable combination of holding still and voyaging required by writing from my fundamentalist people. I sat quietly for hours every week listening to sermons. I bowed my head and kept my eyes closed through thousands of prayer meetings. Because music was so crucial in our Baptist services, I learned to play the piano, practicing scales an hour a day. Then I took up the violin, sometimes slogging through six hours of etudes a day in the summer. I memorized hundreds of Bible passages perfectly, because reciting half-correct verses showed a lack of respect for the Book. And yet, despite all this enforced stillness, at Lincoln Christian Day School we made things up as we went along. To anyone from the outside, the place must have looked like chaos.

Once I went to public high school, Lincoln Christian Day School faded from my memory, and I rarely thought of it until five years ago when I was asked to read my work at the seventy-fifth anniversary celebration of the literary journal *Prairie Schooner*. I hadn't set foot in Lincoln since the day we drove out of town, just after I turned eighteen. Doubting that the school was still in business, I checked the web and indeed found the phone number. Startled and curious, I phoned. The baby sister of my best friend answered. She had become the mother of a high school student and was volunteering in the office. She invited me to visit.

In Lincoln, I sat for almost an hour in front of the school, gawking at the low-slung, contemporary, rambling brick building that sprawls on acres of lawn. Inside, I introduced myself to the principal, the librarian, and a young drama teacher. The school has dozens of teachers now, they explained, and thousands of pupils. An hour later, sitting cross-legged on the gym floor with a class of theater students, I told the story of how the school got started. I just opened my mouth and it spilled out. My father had been dead for over forty years, and I had never told anyone this story. I had never understood it as a story, much less as a triumph. I assumed that the school had long since perished. I am ashamed of predicting failure. What kind of daughter am I? Later, at least, I sent a picture and biography of my father to the librarian. She took me into one of the long turquoise-tiled halls and showed me where she would pin them in the Founders' display cabinet. Now my father is officially recognized as a Founder.

I didn't send my own children to a Christian school. There are things about the contemporary Christian school movement that worry me—the way it has participated in censoring textbooks, for example. And I didn't want my children separated from the world, as my parents called it. Wonderful as my father's school was, it was not wonderful because it sheltered me. What sheltered me also separated me from many of the people I now love, including my husband, and created in me a vast sense of loneliness and alienation. Until years later, I didn't find anyone who even comprehended the questions I was desperate to have answered when I was a student there. But my fundamentalist people taught me the skill of subversion, for which I will be forever grateful.

Behind the scenes, outside the conventions, in a place that challenges the agreements by which human beings are routinely bound—that's where writing seems to take place. It's subversive first. Then comes the hard, sometimes tedious work of revision. And then the work goes public. That is how, as the poet, Stephen Dunn, has said, we can make available to others "the strangeness that is our lives."

7

Saving Images

WHEN I WAS A CHILD, I believed Jesus might return any minute. I had a clear picture of what that would look like. I thought of this picture as the thing itself. I'd be outside, building a fort with my friends at recess, or riding in my father's red panel truck. At the reveille of trumpets, I would look up to see Jesus's actual tanned feet slicing through the clouds like the prow of a ship through water. The light of the entire universe would rivet on his dazzling white robe. I don't know where I got this image. Probably from some Bible story book, or maybe our minister, Rev. Garland, described it in one of his sermons. But as I later found out, it *was* an image; it was not the thing itself.

One fall night when I was sixteen, sitting in bed, doing math, listening to the rollicking lyrics, *It's a one-eyed, one-horned, flying Purple People Eater* on the radio, it dawned on me that Jesus might not be coming back in exactly those terms. I was astonished, first, then horrified. I lunged out of bed, flung the door open, ran into the Nebraska night, and padded around our dark neighborhood, watching lightning play just beyond the horizon. Thunder growled. The locust trees along the boulevard tossed ominously in a rising wind.

If lightning had reached out to strike me, I would not have been surprised. I had been taught that we are responsible for what we think and feel, that we believe what we choose to believe. So I assumed I must have decided to not to believe in the second coming. I couldn't recall making any such choice. But one moment I knew exactly what Jesus's return would look like and the next I couldn't imagine it happening. The second coming had given my life tension and significance. When I couldn't imagine it, suddenly my whole understanding of human history crumbled to dust around me. I thought I had lost my faith.

What I had lost, though I didn't realize it at the time, was a very specific image of the second coming. When that image was wrenched from the reality it had previously stood for, I began to notice images, to think about them. And after that the nature of all images changed for me. Of course, I couldn't have explained it that way at the time. Then, I was just terrified. To me it meant there would be no second coming. If it wasn't going to happen exactly the way I had conceived it, it wouldn't happen at all because I certainly couldn't imagine it happening any other way. Subsequently, I worked hard to get the image back, and it did return, but there was something around and under it that hadn't been there before—namely, the catastrophe of losing it.

Until a couple of years ago, I had forgotten the events of that night, probably because, at the time, I didn't have any language for what had happened to me. Just six months before, my older brother had died in his first week at college. And three years earlier, when I was thirteen, we'd lost our father. I had discovered that if you need to talk about death, at least there's a conventional language. While I hated that language and couldn't bring myself to use it, just hearing other people talk rationally about death made me feel saner and less alone. But how can you talk about the problem of losing your faith if you don't have any language for it?

In some ways, losing my faith felt more catastrophic than losing my father because I had been taught that faith is more important than life. How does the old hymn go? *Faith of our fathers living still in spite of dungeon, fire, and sword.* Perhaps because faith was so important in our church, we didn't consider doubt an option. We downplayed anything that didn't lead to triumph and joyful Christian living. To know God, we were told, is to be happy. Our parents taught their children to sing, "I'm inright, outright, upright, downright Happy all the time!" Of course, this was a bold-faced lie. We sang it before therapy was widespread. It was before sharing, before Catholics and Protestants visited one another's churches, before sensitivity training, before encounter groups, and before everyone was reading memoirs.

My parents warned us against trying alternatives to the religious forms and beliefs we learned from them. They cautioned that we would encounter what they called temptations to leave the faith. If we left the faith, they predicted, by which they meant their exact version of the Protestant faith, we would not lead happy lives and eventually, we would go to hell for all eternity. So, unable to articulate my questions and afraid of pursuing any language to express them, I could barely imagine them. My failure was so private and so complicated by fear and guilt that it has lain buried for forty years under the debris of my teenage years.

The dusty summer streets of Lincoln, Nebraska spelled themselves plainly, from 1st to 54th running north to south, and from A to Z east to west. The town is reliably perpendicular and parallel. I still associate the nurture and simplicity of my early belief with that small Midwestern city, its square houses, Saturday afternoon Cornhusker football game play-by-plays blaring from open windows, and the sweet-smelling smoke of burning leaves in October.

Early in May, my mother and father would pound stakes in the ground at either end of the garden and run strings between them to mark off rows of carrots, sweet peas, corn, tomatoes, all the familiar crops. Every year my father insisted on planting something exotic like kohlrabi to expand our palates, but we kids wouldn't eat much of it. The straightforward, blunt seasons brought us hard drenching rains, heavy snows, and punishing heat. Most mornings when we didn't have to go to school, we set out on our two-wheelers to explore without anyone worrying that we would form street gangs or be kidnapped.

In memory, I climb the steps to Temple Baptist Church on a quiet corner in Lincoln, and walk past the planter of English ivy through the modern glass doors. I stand at the back, where I sat for my father's funeral when I was thirteen, and look toward the altar. But there is no altar. Not of the kind I expect after decades of worshiping in an Episcopal church. There is a plain rectangular, oak communion table. Above the table, on the platform, stands an unadorned pulpit with a practical-looking pulpit light. The doors to the baptistery, behind the pulpit, are closed.

There is nowhere in this church to fix my eyes. I have been told why. Our eyes are supposed to stay fixed on Jesus. And Jesus is God, who cannot be trapped in an image. This truism seems obvious, but on reflection, what does it mean? If He can't be mentioned or pictured, how can we know anything about Him? This becomes a knot I can't pick apart. I am sixteen and I want to ask questions, but every question I formulate sounds either dumb or smart-alecky. *How can my eyes be fixed on something that isn't there?* My Sunday School teacher tells me that our inner eyes are supposed to be fixed on the *idea* of Jesus. *Why not a picture or a statue?* I ask. *Easy,* he answers so effortlessly that I imagine him whipping his Superman Cape around himself. We're commanded not to worship images. I know that. I've memorized the ten commandments, including the one against graven images.

It's noon on Sunday, just after communion, and water rushes into the baptistery. My mother has been elected a deaconess, which means that after communion she helps wash two hundred miniature glasses. She is gossiping in the church kitchen with other deaconesses while we kids climb the steps of the front platform with its choir benches and oversized wooden chairs where the pastor and music director sit. Stealthily we unlatch tiny doors on the preacher's side of the podium and discover breath mints. We hear running water and check out the baptistery behind the choir benches. It's a large, square metal bin that reaches approximately to the middle of my chest. Upon investigation, we discover that the water in the baptistery is . . . well, *real*. Not that I haven't known it was water all along. But the tub is being filled from a metal tap that looks exactly like an outdoor faucet. The janitor, who stops by to check on it, tells us the water has to stand all afternoon so it isn't too cold for the evening baptism. Such practical news about what goes on behind the scenes in church strips mystery from our familiar rituals and sets me wondering.

I face the baptistery and stare at it analytically. The metal tub is hidden by the blond wood paneling on the wall behind the choir. The baptistery doors have been swung open on their hinges to reveal, framed by the paneling, a painting of an outdoor scene: a river, the sky with scalloped clouds and flying birds, and some trees. The picture creates the impression whenever Rev. Garland baptizes a candidate—that's what they were called, candidates for baptism—that the water is not plain water and the event is not happening in a church, but outside. For the first time, this strikes me as odd.

I've seen dozens of baptisms. The candidate steps down into the water where Rev. Garland is waiting for her (in a preaching suit, which, I suddenly realize, must be waterproof. Who sells such suits? And do you need to show a badge proving that you are a preacher in order to buy one?) Then as we watch, he places his right hand across her back for support. With his left hand he slips a men's white hanky over her nose. Then he lays her down backwards in the water and quickly swings her up, using the hanky to mop her dripping hair and face. Immediately the preacher closes the baptistry doors, gets dressed while we sing a hymn, and comes out to say the final prayer. But why has everything been arranged—the wood paneling that frames the cutout, the picture of the river, the doors which keep the river hidden most of the time—so that from the pews, it appears the candidate has been baptized, not in a tub of tap water here in church, but in the flow of some river?

I turn from the baptistery frowning. Slowly, as I gather communion cups from the pews, which is my job, I drift toward one of the deaconesses, who is also collecting cups. "What's that picture in the baptistery?" I ask her.

The woman is tall and big-boned and she's wearing a flowery dress with a wide, red, patent leather belt and a big bow under her chin. She pauses, her big arms hugging three racks of glasses to her ample chest, and stares at the baptistery as if to locate the answer.

"Well, honey," she says with kindness, "that picture is important. That is the Jordan River, where Jesus was baptized."

"Oh," I say stupidly.

I am thinking, but wait, surely that isn't the Jordan River. It's a *picture* of the Jordan River. I don't say that, though, because I know it sounds sarcastic. And anyway, I'm pretty sure I know what she means: the picture in the baptistery is a likeness of the Jordan River. But this is the first time I've ever thought about the fact that a picture is an image that means something other than itself. Such a simple idea. Such a complicated idea. As I stand there thinking about it, she walks off to wash the miniature cups. Her husband and kids are waiting for her outside, and she needs to get home to make their dinner.

I remain standing there. To me the picture looks just like the Platte River in western Nebraska, and furthermore its chunky trees and naive perspective make it look like it was painted by a child. If that's supposed to be the Jordan River, I think, it must be a bad painting. My head tumbles with questions I can't sort out. They gather into a bulge in my throat. If I could think of the words, I would ask who painted the picture and whether the person had ever seen the Jordan River. What if it's not accurate? And what happens if you get baptized *without* a picture of the Jordan River? If the Jordan River is so crucial to baptism, as the deaconess told me, why don't we go stand in the actual river the way I hear on the news that some people in India make pilgrimages to the Ganges? After all, baptism is so important to us that we call ourselves *Baptists*.

For some reason, no one else in our church seems concerned about any of these problems. That Sunday night, during the evening service, feeling my boyfriend's arm around me, I sat in the back of the church, relieved not to be thinking.

However, I have started down this path, and before long I spot images everywhere. For example, our individual communion cups perch in a round stainless-steel tray encircled by a rim and begin to look like individuals contained within the walls of the church. Our unadorned pews are hard and upright, maybe illustrating how we should live our lives. Or am I making these meanings up? I don't know how to tell an image—which is not only itself but a representation of something else, exuding charisma and danger—from a mere object, which is itself, and harmless, and literal.

The next day in English class it dawns on me that poems, which we are studying, also contain images, that is, things like beds and rooms and people. Or not those things, but rather, representations of things. To me, this seems like a remarkable, earth-shaking insight. I pose a clumsy question to my English teacher about a poem she assigned last week, Richard Wilbur's "Love Calls Us to the Things of This World." I'm not sure I get what's going on in the poem, though she's told us the words describe the poet waking up in a big city. There's a wash line in the poem, for example, and some nuns and shirts. My teacher acts thrilled that I've stopped by her desk, but she doesn't seem to comprehend what I'm asking. She turns the pages of our American Literature textbook and shows me a photograph of Richard Wilbur, sitting under an apple tree, reading a book. He is hardly any older than I am, looking extraordinarily real, and as handsome as a young god.

Sitting on our living room floor that night, I read his poem over and over. Slowly, as if the images were parts of a photograph developing in a liquid bath, their connections grow clear. I am stunned by how I begin to inhabit its words, which describe waking up in New York City, hearing a wash line outside the window reeled on a pulley. I can see white laundry pinned by hands to the line, flying in the wind, the way the poem describes it. I begin to love this poet, not only because he is so splendid looking, but because he is so eloquent. That night, I let my math go. I read the six or eight poems of Wilbur's in our English book over and over, longing to become articulate. I grope to comprehend how he does it.

I have no idea what to do about my private awareness that images seem to be appearing everywhere, that such ordinary items as vegetable soup or a shirt can be made to represent something. This awareness is not unlike my growing, fumbling awareness of my own body's sexuality. What I know about images feels portentous and exciting, but it must be kept separate from the world of my church. I have been taught by my church that religious images such as golden crosses and miters and clergy's robes and elaborate altars smack not only of fakery, but of idol worship. I wonder whether there could be a secret world that my fundamentalist people don't understand.

Then in church, favorite old hymns begin to reveal complications I haven't comprehended in all the years I've sung them. During the sermon, I page through the hymnal, reading words as if for the first time. I wrestle with "There Is a Fountain."

> There is a fountain filled with blood
> Drawn from Immanuel's veins
> And sinners, plunged beneath that flood,
> Lose all their guilty stains.

But how could blood bleach out stains? It made no sense. And then there was "Onward Christian Soldiers." No one we knew was a soldier, except for a middle-aged friend of ours, a major at the Lincoln Air Force Base. The words, perhaps, meant Christians were *like* soldiers? I became uncomfortably hyper-aware of language. I desperately wished I could rewind back to the Good Old Days a month before, when I wasn't obsessed by images, but simply enjoyed singing.

It was shortly after this that I lost faith in my image of Jesus's second coming.

Now, many years later, I am trying to recall how I thought about images before that day I lost the likeness of Jesus's second coming. I suppose I thought what seemed natural and obvious. Sitting in my high school chemistry class, I could close my eyes and remember my bedroom. I knew absolutely it was my bedroom. I knew that when I went home from school, I would lie on the bed and do my homework. It never occurred to me, for example, that my parents might move away during the day, that when I walked home from school some other girl would be listening to the radio in my bedroom, or I would find some other bedroom waiting for me. I believed with such utter childlike certainty that the picture of my bedroom I had in my mind was really my bedroom, that it never occurred to me to doubt it. In the same way, I knew we drove a blue Chevy. I knew what the maple tree beside my friend's house looked like. There was a whole inventory of images I could resort to in my memory which portrayed my life accurately. If you had asked me, I'd have said the images *were* my life and that's all there was to it because I didn't think of them as representations. Not yet.

Looking back, in fact, I see that our emphasis on literal reading concealed from us that we used images. Although we thought Catholics were wicked because they worshipped images (or so we said), the fact is, we clung to images, too—in our hymns, for instance. And we carried actual black King James editions of the Bible to church, to work, to school, in our cars, everywhere, in order to symbolize the status of the Bible as the foundation of our faith. We quoted Biblical passages rich with images. We lowered believers into baptismal water of death and raised them up with Christ. We made up prayers, which we claimed were "from the heart," but they sounded almost identical to one another, and they were, in fact, profoundly ritualized. We ate bread and drank grape juice to commemorate Jesus' death. Most of us hung copies of the Warner Sallman *Head of Christ* in our homes. No wonder, no wonder. Images are necessary for thought. The more sternly you outlaw them, the more likely they are to sneak up the back staircase.

What my people *actually* outlawed was not images themselves but the discussion and consideration of images. Before I asked the deaconess on that Sunday afternoon, she probably never thought about what the picture in the baptistery meant, because we were into absolute equations between an image and its meaning, with no discussion about aesthetics and no interpretation. God created heaven and earth, for instance, in one actual week. And Jesus would appear in the sky in the end time as concretely as the prow of a ship sails through the water. No one ever opined about the Warner Sallman *Head of Christ*, "Don't you think it's a little schmaltzy?" No one asked whether such a passive, delicate Jesus could have whipped the money changers out of the temple, maybe because we didn't view the picture as a representation, but as the thing itself. The Sallman picture of Jesus *was* Jesus.

But oddly enough, the people in my church weren't consistent about that kind of literal reading. For example, they guarded against any absolute identification between God's blood and the communion wine. One of the great, central debates within the Christian faith, as I began to realize later, is whether the bread and wine actually *become* the body and the blood. Or are they a *metaphor* for the body and blood? Or maybe they merely *remind us*? Many thousands of people have been killed defending one of these positions. At every communion service, our Baptist church made a big point of the fact that the bread we ate and the grape juice we drank were merely a memorial, certainly not the thing itself, as, for example, is taught by Roman Catholic doctrine. I don't remember anyone explaining to me *why* they believed the elements of the Lord's Supper did not become the actual body and blood.

My confusion about this was further complicated by the fact that Welch's grape juice was our stand-in for wine. The deaconesses stored great glass jugs of it on the shelves in the church kitchen. One Sunday, when I was hanging out with the deaconesses as they washed the communion cups, I edged one of the jugs off the shelf.

"What are you doing?" my mother asked.

"Having some grape juice," I said, reaching for an ordinary plastic glass.

"You can't drink that!" my mother announced, lifting her hands out of the dishwater, shivering them in the air. Her hands were covered with long gloves of bright soap bubbles. She started moving towards me.

"Why not?"

"You just *can't*," she said.

Before she reached me, I pushed the jug back onto the shelf. If we had been at home, I'd have asked whether it was too expensive. Or was it wrong to drink what belonged to the church? But I knew better than to challenge my mother in public. The other deaconesses

Saving Images

laughed, then turned back to the communion cups and picked up their chitchat where they left off.

Now I suspect that my mother felt the grape juice I was about to guzzle down was blessed with some special power. Maybe she didn't quite believe it was nothing but a *reminder* of Jesus's blood. I don't know. But it's interesting to note that we occasionally drank Welch's at home, though only as a special treat, because it was pricey. What was the difference between the Welch's in the church kitchen and what we drank at home?

Even if I had been able to ask these questions, the people in my church could not have helped me. Our minister, himself, possessed little interest and less language for discussing this kind of issue. He warned against too much "head knowledge." A hundred years before, German academics had argued that the Bible was riddled with historical error, and after that, many mainline denominations in the early twentieth century began to read the miracles in the Bible as allegory. My fundamentalist people fought back, arguing that the Bible was the literal and inerrant word of God. They really had no patience with anyone who doubted that or who made a fuss over the niceties of linguistics or theology. Of course, the commentators did not believe these issues were "niceties."

And our family knew no one who wrote poetry, or painted, or composed music. In fact, much of the poetry I'd ever read seemed remote and tied to the tedium of high school. So when I lost my ability to sustain one fundamentalist image of Jesus's second coming, there was no one to explain that it didn't signal the end of my Christian faith but might have signaled the beginning of my life as a poet. I was beginning to think about metaphor, beginning to consider why some images resonate so powerfully in readers.

Recently, I told the editor of an eminent literary journal about the night in Nebraska when I thought I'd lost my faith; he confessed that he'd had a similar experience. He claimed many artists he knows have told him similar stories. Could this crisis over images be common? Maybe it's as typical as going back to your old neighborhood to discover that the jungle where you hunted for panthers is only an average-sized backyard with a tiger cat. Except what hangs in the balance here is not accuracy about your childhood, but the eternal salvation of your immortal soul. I am reminded of a story my friend told me of her thrilling run-up to her first communion—buying the ceremonial white dress, rising early on Sunday, taking the ritual bath, walking to the rail, being handed the body of Christ, only to shrink with horror because up close the wafer looked and tasted like a scab. The demystification of an image, the fall into irreverence, and then irony. I don't remember a single one of my fundamentalist people ever talking about similar experiences of demystification.

When I was sixteen, the demystification I experienced felt like what happens to a child who believes wholeheartedly in a literal Santa Claus and then discovers that Santa is only the Spirit of Christmas. To say *there is no Santa Claus* doesn't mean pictures of Santa Claus have vanished or that Christmas presents stop coming. Of course, you might worry they'll stop, but the main point is that you know you've been tricked, or at least you've misunderstood important things. Granted, I could turn in my mind to the image I'd lost, as if it were a page in a book. I just couldn't have it anymore without being aware that it wasn't the truth, that it was merely an image. I thought petulantly, *Sure there'll be a second coming! Like snow on the Fourth of July!* I never said this out loud because I feared it might kill my mother.

That extra level of knowledge—that an image might or might not be accurate—created in me a vast, world-weary, adolescent irony. If I could see the strings behind the puppet image, I wondered, how could I be sure it wasn't fake? I wanted to reserve my love for what was *real*. Lying on our couch when I was seventeen, reading about Holden Caulfield in *Catcher in the Rye*, I began to view adult society as fraudulent. I began to abhor all forms of fraud. When I got to college, I found friends, mostly men, who had perfected the tossed-off mock. I never learned to do that myself. These issues of truth and the representation of the truth were life-defining for me. About them I remained halting and inarticulate for years.

Although I lost my fundamentalist faith—that is, my belief in reading images literally—I didn't give up my faith. Or it would be more accurate to say that faith was all I had left, paradoxically, since very little literal proof or fact remained for me to believe in. I switched churches at the age of nineteen and dutifully trudged forward in the Christian life, hanging onto the disciplines I had learned as a child: reading the Bible, attending church, taking communion, and praying—though at times, it all seemed tedious. For months, for years at a time, I felt very little personal connection to God. I knew, because my fundamentalist people had taught me, that feelings aren't everything.

I began to delve into the provocative problem of how to read. I loved poetry with what amounted to religious zeal. I sensed that there might be some connection between poetry and my loss of fundamentalism. But what? I had read very little poetry and had no idea how to find more. In those days, there was even less poetry in bookstores than there is now, which means there was almost nothing, and there was no Amazon.com. Once I discovered that Richard Wilbur lived in Connecticut, and Leslie Stahl broadcast the news from Washington, I very simply associated culture with the East Coast. I had never seen the East Coast, but I felt its magnetism. I began to believe I needed to go there.

Naive as that was, I suspect that what drew me from the Midwest to the East Coast was no more insubstantial than what draws many people to settle in new places. In the cheerful, straightforward Midwest where my family lived, where strangers made eye contact and greeted one another on the sidewalk, I began to feel out of place, though, in truth, I didn't know anyone on the East Coast. I was unusual in Midwestern circles because I protested the Vietnam War and marched for Civil Rights. Like many students in the mid-sixties, I adopted a mode of irony. I knew people who did drugs and joined communes. I suppose everyone our age did. I tried pot and an encounter group. My friends wrote their own marriage vows and repeated them barefoot in gardens. I discovered exotic new foods like pizza and began drinking wine. In the middle of the upheaval, I packed a few belongings into a U-Haul trailer and moved to the East Coast.

Every morning I took an Amtrak train from Wilmington, Delaware, where I settled, to study at the ivy-covered University of Pennsylvania campus. I read fourteen hours a day, and eventually it dawned on me that all those Salinger characters who hate fraudulent images concocted by deceptive adults are nothing but images themselves. Furthermore, Salinger's diatribe against deceit is just one more diatribe in a long American literary tradition blasting images. Wasn't Hawthorne railing against hypocrisy in *The Scarlet Letter*? Wasn't Thoreau urging us to strip old images away to discover a fresh authenticity? He recommends that we should go back to nature. But isn't "nature" itself an image that represents a complicated construct of ideas? Think of the novelist James Fenimore Cooper, the photographer Ansel Adams, the once popular Nature Company and its many knock-offs. Isn't it quintessentially American to glorify nature and lambaste images? Maybe the wish to disrobe in order to find "the honest truth" is a noble impulse. But, of course, every *honest truth* in literature is another image. In the end, undress as we might, we can't think without images. They are the building blocks of consciousness.

When I started working on my PhD dissertation—which, not surprisingly, turned out to be about images—my advisor asked me to look at the rabbit/duck sketch in Ernst Gombrich's book *Art and Illusion*. If you look at it one way, it's a rabbit. If you blink and look at it another way, it's a duck. By showing it to friends, I discovered there are people who can't see the rabbit, who only see the duck. And vice versa. But the triumph of that sketch is that most people can see both. It really is two things in one. The rabbit both is and is not. The duck both is and is not. Just try showing the sketch to twenty or thirty friends. Their comments will seem weird, strange, hard to predict.

During some of those mornings at home when I was supposed to be scribbling my dissertation on a legal pad, I stared at Gombrich's rabbit/duck until I got pretty good at making myself see whichever I chose, but I have never seen both at the same time. The sketch always forces me to shuttle back and forth. And that process—not the rabbit or the duck themselves—is what is important. By practicing the transformation, I gained some control over it. Having lost its power to

Saving Images

surprise me, and when there was nothing at stake, it began to amuse me. It functioned as a puzzle. Who really cares whether the thing is a rabbit or a duck? What's important is an observer's flexibility of vision.

I would like to say that the rabbit/duck picture helps me remember that images are never true or false, that they can only represent a thing more-or-less adequately. But, in fact, I often forget that. I am a sucker for words and music and dance and painting. I keep falling in love with them and mistaking them for the truth, and then, like Snoopy, I experience a rude awakening. I re-learn painfully that there is this built-in ambiguity to images, that no image is ever the thing itself. Meaning does not adhere to images. To be understood as the Jordan River, or as an image of Christ, a painting needs to be interpreted. That's what I think my fundamentalist people didn't understand. And so they never realized that there is a difference between losing an image and losing faith in the thing behind it. Or at least they could never explain that to me.

Ultimately, around the time I had my first child, the year I finished my dissertation, I said to myself: *Well, this ambiguity, at least, is not lack of meaning. If I can move between two meanings, I'm not without either. The rabbit-duck sketch doesn't mean Nothing, it means Both. Surely there is no reason to get so bitter over the instability of an image. Ambiguity is not the same as meaninglessness.*

What followed was a new stage of belief. Or perhaps I should say a second kind of belief. Shortly after I stopped seeing images as literal, I began to understand metaphor in a new way.

Metaphor is one of many ways poets use language to fuse two images. It's written like an equation. X=Y. But unlike mathematical equations, the equation of a metaphor is a radical absurdity. X is not only *equal* to Y, it is also utterly *different* from Y. Say the moon is a woman hunting in the sky. At the risk of belaboring the obvious, the moon is not like a woman in most senses. It's not shaped like a woman, and it's not alive. But when you read the metaphor, for one fleeting moment, you see the two terms as married. And you understand the truth, which is a third thing, a surplus, the point of the comparison, which transcends either of the two terms.

Metaphor cannot be taken literally because at its heart lies paradox. I believe now that metaphor is a way we humans can talk about what we know of the transcendent.

I'm grateful for metaphor. I don't believe for a second that a writer, while thinking in metaphor, can be truly hopeless or without vision. Metaphor begins as the itch to live and to create. The new image often seems wacky or childlike or unorthodox. It is sometimes misshapen. It is frequently astonishing and uncooperative. But above all, metaphor is born of hope. It's new and palpable. All right, yes, it's provisional. It might not work. But it is the child of possibility.

My life since that fateful evening in Lincoln, Nebraska, has been, to a large extent, about learning how to read and write metaphor. Twenty-six years after my terrified bolt into the dark streets in Lincoln, Nebraska, I found myself sitting in our family room on the second floor of a nineteenth-century townhouse in Philadelphia, trying to write. It was summer. I was the mother of two children. To be a mother was to be taken up with physical tasks. It was morning. I was in my early forties. I was teaching in a university but spending most of my non-teaching days with our youngest child. By this time, we had a computer. Our second child, Jack, was two. For an hour a day, I could count on his watching Sesame Street. I snapped on the program and snuggled beside him on the blue couch. We had no air conditioning, so he and I were hot and sweaty. Once Jack's brown eyes locked onto the screen, I quietly slipped away and sat down several feet behind him in front of my computer. There I wooed language. I never turned the TV volume down because the smallest flutter could shatter his two-year-old attention. So Big Bird and Maria and Oscar the Grouch carried on behind me, getting all mixed up in my head with the lofty, abstract, serious ideals of poetry.

The amount of time I had to write was determined by how long Jack watched. I could never predict this. I glanced over at his tousled blond curls frequently to make sure he wasn't choking, or dumping cereal on the cat, or cutting up the couch with scissors. But that's about all I knew. I knew I had to take care of my child, and I knew I had to write. And I knew the two were frequently at odds. I often hurled words at the page the way a potter throws clay onto a wheel, quickly, messily, urgently. In that unsatisfactory, provisional way, triangulating between my child, Sesame Street, and the great works of poetry, I learned how to use images in poetry.

It would have been helpful if someone had explained to me when I was a child in Lincoln, Nebraska that I was not losing my faith; I was just losing faith in a particular image. But who might have done that? Should I blame my distracted mother, who had been shunted out into the world to support the family after my father died? Could frail old Mrs. Duacheck, bundled in her black seal coat, have turned to me as we were waiting to shake hands with the minister and explained the nature of imagery? Or, for that matter, was it the minister's job? How could they even know that's what I needed? It's not like I had made my strange, difficult questions clear.

It would be one thing if the people in my church had been punitive or cruel, but they were good-natured and warm. They swapped recipes for green bean hot dishes and lemon meringue pie. They complimented one another's cooking. If there was a need, they would clean one another's houses and take care of one another's children. One of the ancient church ladies spent weeks cross-stitching a cover for one of my mother's antique chairs. True, the people at Temple Baptist wrangled over the size of the new parking lot. And at prayer meeting, you could hear some rip-roaring gossip in the prayer requests. But we were devoted to one another. We were a besieged town that had closed its gates, rationed its water, and shared out its candles. I was held in the arms of that church. I wanted to belong, and I understood their warnings. If I fell out of the nest, I would return to them smelling unfamiliar, and the mother robin would no longer touch me.

When I became so fascinated by images, I deviated from their doctrine. They condemned the use of images in religious ritual. But I couldn't get away from images. And so I no longer felt welcome.

The fact is, fundamentalists have always made the lives of artists difficult. The Puritans, the spiritual ancestors of my Baptist kin, argued that statues in church—as well as images on canvas or in the theater—are idols. With this in mind, the Puritans in 1640 smashed Catholic statues and shattered stained glass windows in churches all over England. About the long fundamentalist war on art, I can't help but feel grief and anger. And yet I can't stop loving my fundamentalist people.

Many of my artist and intellectual friends believe fundamentalists are stupid. They're not stupid: they're my mother and my sister and many of the street-smart, loving grownups of my childhood. I think of their hymns, altar calls, adult baptisms, the Lord's Supper. I think of the way they dressed, of the way they talked about being saved, and I realize they have a canny instinct for images. Though the last thing they wanted to do was to discuss images, when I was a child the fundamentalists I knew might have felt more keenly than anyone, except for artists, the power of images to transform. They had plenty of images, and they believed fervently in the possibility of transformation.

I don't think fundamentalists—either those I knew in the fifties or those of today—realize there's a difference between losing an image and losing faith in the thing behind it. I wonder how many of their children besides me have blundered into this abyss of questions, how long they have been lost, how badly they have been hurt. To my people, I would say, *don't blame the arts. You need the arts. Images are not, of themselves, bad. You think with images, too, because no one can think without them. And there is a difference between losing a representation of the truth and losing the truth itself.*

And I want to add, *lighten up. You're not the arbiters of truth or how it is expressed. The truth is strong. The truth can take care of itself.*

Out the window of my study, in the purple of sunset, I watch a rabbit emerge from an azalea bush, stitch our backyard, and disappear into the English ivy by the back fence. He's small, just shedding his baby fluff for the speckled camouflage of adult fur. He must have been born last spring. Frost on the grass, tender young lettuce, a juicy carrot--the images he sees and remembers must be brief, instinctual.

Saving Images

I have a very different kind of memory than he does. It includes a poem, dashed in haste two decades ago when my child was still so young I could lift him off the couch onto my lap. It includes the recollection of myself as an earnest, believing child and the story of myself as a teenager, damned and trudging the streets of Lincoln, Nebraska after dark. These are stages in a journey—the child, the disillusioned teenager, the mother, the poet, the grandmother—stations on the way toward learning what it means to be human. I believe they are markers in the process of redemption.

8

Like Postcards from a Friend

IT WAS ONE OF THOSE clear, cool mornings early in September when the sunlight falling through trees turns everything translucent green. It might have been the morning of the world. I was just thirty, still exultant over passing my PhD exams in literature. Days before, I had convinced my husband that we should buy and lay down a shaggy grass-green carpet in the fourth bedroom of our brick townhouse. Here I planned to hole up for ten months and write a four-hundred-page dissertation on the English poet Edmund Spenser; and, if things went my way, by summer, I would be called *Doctor.* That title would qualify me to find the job of my heart's desire, teaching Spenser's *Faerie Queene* and the great Shakespearean plays to students in a university.

    My husband left for work at 8:30 a.m., his black wingtips turning the corner, his feet patting the steps, the front door closing. A momentous quiet settled in the house. I sat down at my worktable and picked up a pencil and a legal pad (because this was eleven years before we had a computer), and then, in the nursery next door, the baby turned over. It was not the sound of her turning over in her sleep. She was awake. I knew that. I knew things about her even when I didn't want to. Like the proverbial Eskimo with dozens of words for *snow,* I could distinguish, even from another room, a dozen different ways she turned over. There was her startled-bird motion of fear at finding herself out of the womb and alone, for example. Then there was her leisurely, ruminative way of turning as if she were about to discover a profound idea. And her swimming motion, her way of shifting for the sheer pleasure of exercise.

Not that I chose to be this excruciatingly sensitive to my new baby's every move. It came over me, the way a wave in the ocean can wash over a person. I tumbled and floundered, tossed willy-nilly by its force slamming me in a new direction. Academic books and abstract ideas were no longer as compelling as they had seemed. To get any reading done, I had to clench my will, shut out my child, and rivet my mind on the project that earlier had given me pleasure.

And then, as I was puzzling over how my child had rearranged my life, suddenly, I heard her whimper. I could see her brilliant blue eyes. They would be turned toward the door where she expected me to appear. I could feel her loneliness in my hands and arms.

It was not as if I didn't realize that I had a choice. I knew I could either go to her or stay put and write the first sentence on the blank yellow legal pad. I stared at my hand holding the pencil. It looked like the claw of some creature I didn't recognize. I couldn't remember what I wanted to say about *The Faerie Queene*. The poem had been written four hundred years earlier. As if the historical difference weren't enough, Spenser invented a quaint language called Antique English, which sometimes made me feel millions of miles away from the poem, as if I were staring at it through a telescope. Furthermore, I couldn't, honestly, think of anyone who would want to read what I was about to write, even my advisers at the university. I knew that getting down four hundred pages of serviceable prose was all that stood between me and a PhD. Given that there were no tenured women faculty in my department at the University of Pennsylvania, I didn't entirely buy that I, a woman, could earn a PhD. Academia might as well have been a neighborhood where, I was coming to realize, we couldn't afford to live. I was starting to wonder if a university job might be beyond me.

I went to pick up my child. I took her to the park.

Back then, I was desperate for community, friends, a network, people to talk to. I had lost the fellowship of my fundamentalist people, their picnics and hymn sings and prayer chains. I didn't fit anywhere. Around that time, the woman across the street told me to read Alice Munro. I had never heard of Alice Munro or of many other contemporary authors, either. I had been madly spinning through Chaucer and Shakespeare and Donne and Browning and other male writers for the last seven years and hanging out in the graduate seminar room with other graduate students. Nothing I read was contemporary because I decided that I wasn't about to have university professors tell me what to think about my own century. I had an attitude, I suppose, and the price I paid for it was isolation and loneliness. But we had just moved, and the woman who came over to welcome us to the neighborhood with cookies turned out to be an endless source of good books and gentle, healing advice of every kind. When I opened Alice Munro's short stories, I felt as if I were reading postcards from a friend.

In those days, I was mad with the need to Do Something Important. Not that I was sure of what to do. It was the early seventies. The seams of the world had already split open. Many of us had protested about civil rights. Then came the assassinations. Between them, we strode with banners down the wide avenues of Chicago, protesting the Vietnam War. We stopped traffic and made obscene gestures at the police, who were billy-clubbing our doctor friends who were wearing white coats with red crosses above the pocket. We shouted at rallies and gave press conferences announcing that we were going to dump Lyndon Johnson. And we won at least part of what we wanted. But beneath all the action, I felt skeptical. A lot of our behavior felt shallow to me. Our attacks on the older generation sometimes rang in my ears as self-righteous cant. Calamity threw its shadows all around us, and it was not easy to figure out what to do.

My confusion made me feel that it was all the more urgent to do something fast. Time, I had learned, is the great enemy. The Baptist church, where a decade before I spent all day Sunday and Wednesday night in prayer meeting—as well as other days for special services—had seeded deep within me an awareness of the fleeting nature of time. *Work for the night is coming,* thrummed in my brain, like a heavy beat under a melody. *Work for the night is coming, when no man can work!*

Oddly enough, Time was the theme also of my mother's jewelry box. On its glass cover was etched a handsome woman with a parasol, and beside her floated the words: *Do not waste time, for time is what life is made of.* This box occupied a sacred space in my mother's inner sanctum, at the heart of her combing and dressing rituals. Both the box and its philosophy had been handed down from my mother's mother to my mother, and I inherited both when I was less than thirty.

The horrifying brevity of life was underlined by the death of my father when I was thirteen. Specialists had given him two options. He might live for as long as five years with his heart problem. Or he could elect to have immediate surgery. He had a fifty percent chance of dying on the operating table. The pressure of choice, the high stakes, the bad odds, and above all, my inability to do anything to change it, made me wild. He decided not to have surgery. He preferred the certainty of more time with his kids. As he grew sicker, both my mother and father acted with great courage. They set about equipping my mother to support the family, and as I watched, I concluded that women had better find some way of supporting themselves and their children.

My desperation to Do Something Important also arose from hearing all my life that since much had been given me, much would be required. What gift could be more vital, my parents asked, than a warm, loving family and education in a Christian school? In return, they contended that we'd better arrange our lives to give something back. *But what,* I wondered. I'd had a few things published. When I was nineteen, I had been honored with The Atlantic Monthly Prize for both poetry and fiction and awarded tuition at Bread Loaf School of English, where, for the summer, I was the Atlantic Monthly Scholar. Moreover, I was crazy about reading. I really believed words and books could change the world. So although neither of my parents had finished their undergraduate degrees, I made a break for it, skewing off to graduate school to earn a PhD in English.

There I found myself betwixt and between. Instead of looking for the Second Coming and deferring to one another in love, my fellow students smarted off and pestered one another with practical jokes. When one of my friends, Joe, had to miss a Victorian class, he phoned Nathaniel for the assignment, and Nat instructed him to read *Sartor Resartus*. So Joe stayed in all weekend, slogging through Thomas Carlyle's long, impenetrable prose book. On Monday, our professor, who had assigned a mere two chapters, praised Joe for exceeding the assignment. My friends teased Joe about this for months.

Only I didn't get the joke. Why on earth do that to someone?

My new friends guzzled punch spiked with 120-proof alcohol, and they had a knack for just the right slovenliness. They told slightly off-color (never quite offensive) jokes. Listening to them clown around in the English seminar room was, for me, educational. They unsheathed lethal irony against almost everyone, though I have to say they were unfailingly nice to me, even though I must have seemed very different from them. For one thing, I had learned to dress tidily, and I couldn't get the knack of their studied negligence. Furthermore, I had no tricks up my sleeve, nothing to amuse them, zilch. And when I thought about it, I wondered whether there might be something a little saccharine about the way I talked, or possibly just naive, or maybe just Midwestern bland. Of course, I never made the mistake of bowing my head and reaching to hold hands with them before praying at mealtime, but occasionally I let slip a phrase like *Oh boy!* or *Good grief!* or *Lord only knows!*

I drew the line at emulating their brio, but inevitably I picked up their language and, I suppose, some of their gestures. When I went back at Christmas to visit my fundamentalist people, they seemed puzzled and somewhat distant. One of my old friends let me know I had changed. And truth to tell, their language and dress and customs seemed slightly out of joint to me. I flew home and caught a cab back to our apartment, trying to piece out what had happened. The bottom line: I didn't fit into either group. Then in a month or so I got pregnant, which you weren't supposed to do in graduate school, and I designed and sewed a vast cape to cover my growing belly. I wore it everywhere, in winter and in summer. After that, I really was hopelessly out of place in graduate school.

Around the time I began writing my dissertation, I was just beginning to realize that I would be peeling a lot of potatoes for the rest of my days. The reason I didn't understand this until so late was because I was not the girl who peeled potatoes at home. That was my sister. I was the child who read. And since emerging into adulthood, I had been living the cushy life of a student. Undergraduates don't cook. Ideas reign supreme in universities, and the cafeteria makes the meals.

By contrast, I now found myself drowning in details. Everything we owned, every single spoon and paper clip, had just passed through my hands twice. I had packed and unpacked it to move. And then there was the daily-ness of taking care of another human being, the diapers, the stroller, the playpen, the bottles, the special implements for washing the bottles, the lamby she couldn't do without, and on and on. I was beginning to realize that, by marrying and becoming a mother, I had emerged as The Keeper of Things. I was overwhelmed by all the stuff.

More puzzling, I was bereft of words to explain my loneliness. After all, I seemed to be living a normal, even privileged American life. Uneventful as my life must have appeared to others, every day I awoke to a crisis. Not that I complained. I felt it would have been small-minded to grouse about details. Or maybe that isn't quite it. More likely, I couldn't put my finger on what was wrong. Someone has to wash the dishes, doesn't she? Yet it certainly seemed odd that I was washing dishes every time I turned around. I felt grimly determined to become efficient, to learn to get quickly through what I had once thought of as the small details and then move on to Something Important.

The first time I opened a book of Munro's stories, the difference between her and the writers I had been studying in graduate school sheered my breath off. Munro's fiction is a bounty of familiar smells and sights and sounds for women who work and have children. The stories are set in places like skating rinks and school bookrooms. I could smell the disinfectant, taste the root beer, feel a fish sliding out of the water and splashing into the boat. Stories so robust with particulars must have been called into place by the writer's meticulous attention and care, I thought. They made me recall the first writer I loved, Richard Wilbur, and his poem, "Love calls us to the things of this world."

Only with this difference: Alice Munro's worlds felt exactly like my own: changing diapers, and sewing skirts, and draining the boiling potatoes. Within the borders of her fiction, a tea strainer meant something. I soon understood that she saw significance, not only in symbols like a rose, which we're supposed to know is a symbol for love or something like that, but in everyday objects. Not that she heaps symbolic meaning on objects. It's more that her characters find significance in their things, the smallest stuff of everyday life. It is a question of Munro having her eye upon the sparrow.

Here she is in the story "Miles City, Montana," describing a woman after a long car trip:

> I was thirsty, and got out of the car to look for a concession stand, or perhaps a soft-drink machine, somewhere in the park. I was wearing shorts, and the backs of my legs were slick with sweat. I saw a drinking fountain at the other side of the park and was walking toward it in a roundabout way, keeping to the shade of the trees. No place became real until you got out of the car. Dazed with the heat, with the sun on the blistered houses, the pavement, the burned grass, I walked slowly. I paid attention to a squashed leaf, ground a Popsicle stick under the heel of my sandal, squinted at a trash can strapped to a tree. This is the way you look at the poorest details of the world resurfaced, after you've been driving for a long time—you feel their singleness and precise location and the forlorn coincidence of your being there to see them.

Sitting here as I write this now, thirty-five years later, it is impossible to express the joy I felt when I first read this passage and others like it in Munro's stories. Someone had already hacked a path through the perilous landscape ahead of me. Much of the literature I had read in graduate school had performed the service of showing me profound truths about human experience. But no writer had cataloged my own terrain, which was the bewildering landscape of a woman with a kitchen and a child. To put it in terms my fundamentalist people might use, when I read Alice Munro's stories, I heard a "still, small voice." Without her stories, I believe I would have endured my twenties silently, rather like an animal, and then I'd have forgotten them, since I had no words to tell or remember them by. In short, Alice Munro showed me my own strange, solitary life. She gave that life meaning and connections.

I began to think of Munro's stories as a means of grace.

Every day I dragged myself like a mule to the legal pad in the room with the green rug. Frankly, I got very little pleasure out of it. I was becoming less sure that I could finish a PhD. No one from my class had yet. In fact, an alarming number of my peers had been flunked out, and some had quit. But I gritted my teeth and hunkered down to work because I couldn't think of any other way into a world of power and ideas outside my own study.

My even-tempered child grew and developed with the miraculous speed of all normal children. Soon she was crawling beside me on the floor and playing with her toys. Because she watched me every day and mimicked what she saw, she could hold a pencil properly by the age of nine months. By then, she was talking, too.

My husband and I began to take her with us wherever we went. In restaurants, after she was done eating, we let her climb down from her highchair and toddle from table to table, enchanting people. We had her pegged as a diplomat. We were scandalously proud of her. From time to time, I would look at her and think with astonishment that, if I ever got done writing my dissertation, this child would have a doctor for a mother. What a strange household for her to grow up in! That's how I found it easiest to imagine my own improbable future, through the prism of my child, who seemed contented to be used in that way. She was already a little character. Already we could predict what she would be like: talkative, straightforward, sensible—in short, ready to do anything to accommodate our plans.

At night, after I tucked my child in bed, I read Alice Munro's stories compulsively. All of them turned out to be about people I felt I knew. Munro passes over those already in the club. She doesn't seem interested in big money, though she's fascinated by what money does to those who don't have it, and she doesn't give a hoot about people with political power. They appear as giant lifeless figures on the backdrop of a stage where the focus is on what the little people in the story will do next: the old man who is in despair because he will never see his brother again, a high school music teacher pinned in place by gossip, neighbors in a housing tract who are dissecting one another with knives of jealousy. They are people of straitened means from small Midwestern Canadian towns, people who are in some kind of minor trouble.

In the story, "Jesse and Maribeth," for example, I found myself reading about the love relationship between two preadolescent girls. It wasn't anything sexual, which is the meaning we Americans tend to give *love*. I'm talking about that sweet, intense, life-changing attraction between girls very early in life that makes them say they're *best friends*. I'd had a best friend. But I had never read about best friends in fiction.

And I've read very little about the subject since, though I know more contemporary fiction now than I did then. I suppose the idea of best friends has been dismissed by most writers as too small. It's just not in the running when the subjects are picked. But reading the story, I was back there—whispering confidences in the dark until two in the morning, when the two of you are giddy from lack of sleep, swearing one another to secrecy, until a bleary-eyed parent appears at the door with a final, ominous warning that he will separate you.

Stories like this one cast light backward through years of my life and make clearer events I had never understood. And there was another thing. Reading them assuaged my impatience at not being out in the world, doing something. It also made me consider and sometimes appreciate the jewel-like value of the life I was leading. I realized my life was not anonymous. Someone had taken note, someone brilliant.

Because of her fiction, the kind of life I was living suddenly felt valid, felt real, felt interesting.

Then I stumbled upon other people who had read Munro. In fact, for a while, I began to look for her readers. In the absence of our close fundamentalist community, I started to feel another kind of kinship, the fellowship a reader feels with the writer who has created a home, who has offered spiritual nourishment. It included Munro and her readers.

Later I felt that kind of bond with my own readers. A story or a poem, I began to realize, is part of a conversation. In the stories that I was reading like postcards, Munro not only addressed her readers but replied to writers she'd read herself; so through her, I connected to them. What I am describing, the kinship between texts, has been called *intertextuality* by literary critics, but I'm not talking about a static network of connections between books. I mean the remarkable way reading creates a living neighborhood. That neighborhood is not a geographically defined place but a spiritually connected community, vast and potentially endless, like the kingdom of heaven.

I was misled by that early, euphoric feeling of belonging. Several years later, when I had a teaching job, I arranged with colleagues from other institutions to invite Alice Munro to do a reading at each of our campuses. I wrote the letter: we would pay her well, I said, and we would be so very honored to host her. It never entered my head that she might say no. Her handwritten picture postcard back to me came promptly, and her reply was polite. She never left home to do readings, she said, adding a few jaunty sentences, and then, thank you very much.

I was shocked. I had felt such a personal connection while reading her stories that I thought of her almost as a friend.

And then I laughed. *Hello!* Of course! I didn't know Alice Munro. The reader doesn't know the *writer*. I only knew Munro's *narrator*. But the puzzling fact remained that I felt I knew her better than I knew many of my friends. Her characters might as well have been chums I'd grown up with: lower middle class, many of them, not particularly well educated, struggling with finances, tossed by the economy and work, slangy, vulnerable.

I came to believe that the way Munro frames the neglected and forgotten is not an accident of where she was born or a matter of her casual preference. Like all good writers, she moves to where the energy is. In the crosshairs of a story, Munro locates a person who can change because she has suffered, and as a result, opened her heart. That's why Munro prefers troubled and anonymous people as subjects because they don't have the finances or the power to keep themselves safe. They live under dreadful pressures.

The irony of that began to dawn on me—the advantages of being poor and exposed. It is the irony Erasmus pointed out in his brilliant *In Praise of Folly,* which I had read in graduate school. I began to see the significance of making thousands of dinners, mixing pablum, singing the alphabet song, all while keeping myself as steady as the backboard behind a basketball net. Not that I shouldn't Do Something Important. But if I could, I would need to do it gradually, painstakingly. In a major sense, I understood that one has to be a fool. One must peel potatoes and diaper children and get *joy* out of those things. One must enter this kind of detailed life of service in a spirit of love and forgiveness. This felt like a great paradox. I saw it as a terrifying threat to my future plans. It seemed to threaten everything I had been working for.

My child sat on the same green carpet every day, getting sick of watching me draw tiny squiggles on a yellow pad. But until I got a job, I knew we'd have no money for daycare. And I couldn't find a job until I had a PhD. We were trapped in one of Joseph Heller's catch-22s. With a frenzy that made me shut out almost everything else, I plowed forward to bring the dissertation to an end before I buckled under the financial pressure and went out to find some other work, clerking in a grocery store, maybe, or applying to be a secretary.

During those days, I would sit on the floor alternating between writing about Spenser and showing my daughter how to stack her fat, bright-blue and red and yellow plastic doughnuts or singing the alphabet song or conversing about characters in her books or on

Sesame Street. I could actually talk to her while taking notes on the *Faerie Queene*. Sometimes I was frantic to work, frantic to do something important, but I tried not to show it.

One Monday morning in March, when I opened the door to her room, my daughter, who was by now a toddler, hung back. I told her I would take her out for a walk soon. We went into my study and sat down on the floor. All night I had been feverishly working out an idea for the last chapter. She waited courteously for a few minutes, then tugged on my jeans to go. I turned to her with what must have been a vacant stare. She tugged again. "Okay, I'm coming," I said, but I didn't get up. A thought was forming, and I was wooing it, hoping it would distill into an English sentence. She must have recognized the look in my eyes. I had done this before. In fact, I was capable of wooing an English sentence for hours.

With volcanic force she erupted, an eruption that seemed more terrible because she had always been so even-tempered. She deliberately turned her back to me and braced her chubby hands against the wall. She looked over her shoulder, twitched up her face, and screamed.

I leapt up. It seemed like a natural catastrophe. She wouldn't stop crying. I felt her for fever. I changed her clothes, which I thought might be itchy or too tight. She screamed with outraged fury. I think it was the first time it really dawned on me—as I have had to realize over and over again—that she wasn't an extension of me.

I understood. I had made impossible demands on her, and I felt prostrate with terror, lest by these demands I had already destroyed her. God had trusted me with a child, and after only a year, look what I had done! I had locked her in a dungeon with a cellmate, me, who was, most of the time, abstracted and silent. I was aware, even then, that this vision was slightly hysterical. But there you are. It's a thought I've had more than once since, that one of my children might not survive some ghastly circumstance, often caused by some adult, frequently by one of us, the parents.

There is something funny about this scene and my guilt, now that I know from experience how children bounce back, how most of them take whatever is given to them and tend to make the best of it. I think now that the persistent health of young things is a kind of mercy. But it shouldn't be presumed upon. And that day, I felt childlike, gauche, awful remorse.

I apologized to her and took her out. The sky was one foaming broth of clouds when we started walking toward the park. Before we arrived back home, the sun had come out, and I felt a sense of quiet grace. The walk had given me some perspective. Miraculously, it was what I needed. My child was happy, and I was able to write. In less than a month, I finished the dissertation.

When my child was a year old, I hadn't yet read Munro's story, "Miles City, Montana"; it hadn't even been published. But later, I felt a pang of familiarity when I read these words:

> So we went on, with the [children] in the back seat trusting us, because of no choice, and we ourselves trusting to be forgiven, in time, for everything that had first to be seen and condemned by those children: whatever was flippant, arbitrary, careless, callous—all our natural, and particular, mistakes.

Carrying on any kind of long, close human relationship is like housework. It requires a lot of finely calibrated small moves. The ones between a child and her mother are, perhaps, the best example. To get one child to the age of eighteen requires six-thousand, five hundred and seventy-some days. The days are filled with diapers and carpooling, hurts, and repercussions, grudges, strategizing on both sides, frustration, scolding, rebellion, and forgiveness. And also joy and grace.

9

How to Read a Poem

THE PINES GLITTER WITH frozen sleet as my Honda slides down I-95 to the university. It's the first day of the semester. I hang my coat on my office door hook, beat my mittens against my desk to crack the ice off them, glance in my mirror, and tame my hair. Then I slog out the beautiful Memorial Hall doors and down the mall to meet my 11:00 a.m. poetry class.

The students have wadded up their coats and stuffed them under their chairs. Their cheeks are scarlet, their hair moist from the freezing sleet. An aroma of wet wool permeates the air. They are striking, young, alert, some tanned from an after-Christmas getaway to sun country. I don't recognize any of them, and they don't know one another. Our project for the coming semester is to read together.

"Let's go around the circle," I say. "Tell us your name, year in school, major, the name of the last book you read, and . . ." I pause. "Your favorite food."

A young woman with black retro glasses begins. "Erin Mc-Closky, junior, English major, *The Shack* by William Young. Um. . . . ." It's nearly lunchtime. She rolls her eyes, imagining a universe of gorgeous chow and settles on "Pizza."

The young man sitting next to her is wearing a Hawaiian shirt and flip-flops. "Rasheed Collins, freshman, undeclared, *The Audacity of Hope*, pineapple."

Next a red windbreaker. "Laurel Spiletti, senior, English, *One Hundred Years of Solitude*, ice cream cones." Laurel's nose is red. She sneezes.

"Gesundheit," several of us call out. A titter of nervous laughter.

Eventually I call on one of the students to read a poem aloud. When she's finished, I ask another student to read it. We sit for a moment in silence, letting the poem soak in.

"This poem is a story," I say. "What's the story?" The students duck their heads. Their lips move. They frown. They bite their pens and write in their books, gestures they believe will give me the message that they are thinking hard. They look anywhere except at me. If they make eye contact, I might call on them.

I re-read the first line aloud. "Come on," I coax them, "Just tell me what literally happens."

Alec raises her hand. "I think the tree in the first line is really a woman."

An intake of breath. This is a daring beginning. Several students' faces leap with interest. Then a hand waves in the air.

"It says right here it's a *tree*," Matthew objects.

"Can it be both a tree and a woman?" I ask.

"No. The poem means what it says."

"Wait!" It's Jess. "There's a bough. Like bow wow. It could be, you know, a dog?"

"What do you think about that, Matt?" I ask.

"I think it's lame. Look, it says B-O-U-G-H. THAT'S A TREE."

"It might be a pun. You know?" Jess defends herself. "Bow. Bough."

Some students appear increasingly excited at the prospect of a teacher letting the discussion go on like a run-away sled. They appear to love the notion that whatever anyone says will be a possibility. The truth is, to me, the line in the poem feels more and more attenuated, as though all their meanings might stretch it till it breaks apart, but I don't say that.

However, some students begin to frown. I have taught long enough to know what this portends. Either they believe they know what the poem means—and it's not any of these outlandish things the other students have said—or they believe I know, and I should tell them. This proliferation of meanings is barely tolerable to them. It's a waste of class time—time they have paid for, time they don't want to spend listening to any more silly guesses. They don't look at their classmates, who are talking, but glare intensely at me, and I understand that they're impatient for me to step in and tell everyone the gist of the poem.

After about fifteen minutes, the talkers are all talked out, at least about this poem. Like beagles, they want to move on to the next one. Jackson raises his hand and demands from me a meaning he can write in his notebook before we move on. I glance down at the page where the poem swims gracefully in its white space.

"I don't think a poem *has* one clear, easily stated meaning," I tell him.

I don't want to translate poems into pithy adages these kids can recite back on the exam. I don't want them to take dictation from me all semester. The point of this class is for them to learn how to read any poem they pick up. That's why I have urged the students to articulate their ideas, why we spent time arguing over the meaning of lines, because I know of no way to start a class in poetry without a good long siege of student talk. They have to feel safe to try out meanings. If I just tell them what the poem means, if I don't ask them, or if they think someone will make fun of what they say, they'll keep their guesses to themselves. Eventually they won't bother to conjecture about what a poem means at all. And those conjectures are the early stages of reading.

Nevertheless, at Jackson's request, I step in and ask more directive questions. We move toward something that resembles a group reading of the poem, based on a close reading of its language. But Jackson, in his black ski jacket, is now scrunching down in his seat, scowling. He drums his pencil on his notebook. Outside, the landscape is darkening. Purple and black clouds are rolling in.

Leaping From the Burning Train

I think Jackson wants the same kind of certainty I wanted when I was a fundamentalist, and that if he doesn't get it, he might make life difficult for all of us.

There is a myth that all is well in poetry class, that reading poetry is a gentle pastime, and teaching it is a pleasant, low-risk job. After all, what could possibly go wrong in a class whose sole task is to read Shakespeare and Elizabeth Bishop and T.S. Eliot? The truth is, poetry class is unpredictable and sometimes volatile. Teaching poetry has led to some of the most hair-raising, passionate events of my life.

There is a great deal at stake in a poetry classroom. I suppose you could say that reading is the true subject of the class, how to read a poem. Reading goes to the very heart of my students' identity. When they arrive in my class, since they've been reading for twelve or fourteen years, they're already driven by closely-held beliefs and intense emotions about reading. As children they were placed in the Blackbird or Goldfinch reading group, maybe, and those innocuous labels branded them. Some of them were taken out of regular class by a reading tutor. Some stuttered or couldn't get the hang of reading aloud. Others flew through the simple books their classmates found difficult and they felt bored to nausea, having to repeat, repeat, repeat what they already knew. Reading has been the source of suffering or triumph for my students their whole lives—and for better or for worse they carry that history with them.

Add to that the fact that poetry tends to focus on love and death, speaking with great intimacy about our most personal and deeply-felt emotions. Poetry speaks through concrete images. To put it another way, poetry embodies passion. It renders thought physical. Students sit alone in their dorm rooms or on the quad reading, experiencing the passion of the poem along with its speaker. Many of them bring this passion to class with them. On the one hand, they want to talk about this experience; and on the other, they *don't* want to because, after all, how much can they afford to disclose about themselves? What if their reading of a poem isn't validated by the other students and the teacher? What does that say about them? Blurting out an erroneous reading can feel like telling their fantasy lives to a room full of strangers. What if they make fools of themselves in public, not about a chemical formula or a geological formation, but about a love poem?

And they are not discussing these love poems in intimate groups with other students exactly like them. A classroom at my university is a miniature society, a tiny America where very different kinds of people gather. I have taught high-fashion runway models and cadets in military uniform and kids from chicken farms who commute from their downstate homes. I see white boys with dreadlocks and fundamentalist Christians who carry black Morocco-bound Bibles and young women with shaved heads. I taught a student who baked cookies several times a week and brought them to class to sell. One semester I taught a student who was driven to the door of Memorial Hall in a limousine every day. I taught a beautiful, middle-aged black woman who, although she lives on welfare, has spent her entire life attending one university or another. Admittedly, most of my students' stories, when I hear them, do not sound this extraordinary, but that may be because at the age of twenty most kids want to at least appear to fit in. Gathering students from different economic, religious, and social backgrounds and urging them to reveal, not only their own ability to read, but also whether they have understood the issues of love and death, sometimes turns explosive.

And then there are the other pressures of school. Many of my students are polite, or at least detached, but increasingly they seem disgruntled by exorbitant tuition. Some of them feel fury at being required to take courses they believe they won't use. Many of them are outraged by any grade lower than a B. Last year when I gave one junior a B+, she glared at me with patronizing contempt and explained savagely, *I do not get Bs.* Another wore a headset to class on the first day, his shoulders keeping time to music. After class I explained that headsets are not allowed during our class discussions. He stared at me with uncomprehending astonishment, as if in all his vast experience he had never heard of such a dumb rule. He muttered something I couldn't hear. *Excuse me?* I asked as graciously as possible, keen on working this out before his attitude infected the class. He wheeled around and sprinted off.

What flashes before me, sometimes, is the scowl of the student in the poetry class at Virginia Tech. I remember hearing about the way he slumped in his chair, pulled his wool hat over his eyes, and smoldered; the way his teacher, the poet Nikki Giovanni, recognized danger two years before her student shot thirty-two students and faculty. I hardly ever worry about this possibility, that is, until a slight, nervous student who never talks in class and who always wears a string tie knocks on my office door at 5:30, long after my office hours have ended, when the building is deserted. It turns out he wants me to help him learn to scan meter.

Several years ago, I pulled into my garage an hour's drive from the university and was disturbed to see one of my students hurrying up the sidewalk to our house. Then I realized it was he who must have left cryptic, unsigned notes for me around campus. He began popping up at the coffee shop, appearing outside faculty meetings, and once he emerged out of the shadows beside my car in the parking lot, late after a poetry reading. Eventually, I had to call the police.

Toward the end of the semester, Jackson shows up in my office.

It's spring. Because we start the semester in February at our university, our classes run through May. The year has hurried around a corner into spring, and the dandelions are just lifting their tufted yellow heads. Already it's hot, ninety-five by the thermometer outside our kitchen. I feel ready to throw down my pencil, and so do my students. Our nerves are frayed, but we still have final classes and projects and exams to go.

I have taken to praying sometimes in my morning shower for Jackson, who is wearing shorts and a t-shirt these days and has reached such a high pitch of frustration that the young woman who sat beside him at the beginning of the semester has moved to a different chair. As I lather my hair in the morning, I am brainstorming about how I can help him, feeling both motherly and irritated because I haven't been able to convince him to learn to read. Remembering his omnipresent scowl, I can guess at how he filled out his Rate-the-Teacher form.

During our last class session, he seemed to take up half the oxygen in the room.

That afternoon I am doing email in my office when I hear him skateboarding down the hall towards me. He arrives at my door, twists into the air neatly, catches the long board in one hand, and leans it against the wall. Then he plunks his backpack down and plops into my blue Ikea chair. I step away from the shelter of my desk and sit in a chair across from him.

"You're sure good at that," I say.

He squints at me from beneath the shock of straight dark hair falling across his forehead. He wants me to cut the bullshit.

"What can I do for you?" I ask.

"I came to see if I've got the right answers for the test." He dives into his backpack and pulls out some folded notebook paper.

"Okay," I say.

He begins reading the titles of poems, followed by the interpretation he has gleaned from our class.

I say, "But Jackson, you can't just write an equation like that."

"You're grading us based on, like, what?"

"How well you can read metaphor. Whether you can talk about meter and sound. Whether you see how they all work together to make meaning."

"You're giving us an essay question?"

"Right. Didn't I tell you that this morning?"

"Like we have to explain what some poems mean, in an essay."

"Yes."

"So I came to find out whether I've got the right meanings."

"We can talk about that. But remember, I'm giving you some poems you've never seen, too."

"That's totally not fair!"

"Look, we've been learning how to read. What I'm testing is the process."

"I know how to read!" He glares at me.

"I want you to be able to read any poem you pick up. Not just the ones we looked at in class."

His eyes say that I am making this subject much harder than it needs to be, that I am a poor excuse of a teacher, that I am making his life wretched.

"You know something?" he explodes.

"What?"

He is too frustrated to answer. He half-rises from his chair. We're moving onto dangerous territory. I ransack my mind to think of something to say that might connect with him.

"Reading is like skateboarding," I say. "Or singing. It's a skill."

He is not beguiled by my reference to skateboarding. He drills me with a cold look.

"I'd be happy to practice reading a new poem by looking at it with you," I offer.

"I want you to tell me whether I've got the right meanings so I can study for the test!"

"A poem doesn't equal one phrase or sentence. I can't tell you it does because it doesn't."

He stares up at my poster of Kew Gardens.

"Look," I say, "if I could attach meaning to a poem the way a mother attaches a child's mittens with Velcro, I would. But I can't. A good poem can be read a number of different ways. Even legal opinions—for heaven's sake—even *they* are subject to interpretation."

I realize I've lost him.

"I know it can be maddening," I say.

He leaves my office soon afterward, skateboarding away.

Sundays, after the choir sang, Rev. Garland stepped to the pulpit and warmed us up by reading a few gorgeous verses from Revelation. He was taking half a year of Sundays to work his way through the last book of the Bible, which was a favorite with Baptist ministers. Revelation, with its spectacular images of rivers springing from thrones and angels eating books, is not easy to read, and because he believed it was very important, he wanted to translate it for us. Rev. Garland was a copper-haired, hot-tempered young minister with beautiful hands and manicured nails, the pastor our parents had wrangled over and then finally hired to lead Temple Baptist Church out of the 1950s and into the next decade.

On this Sunday, Rev. Garland launched into the spellbinding story of two prophets who would become famous in the "latter days" and appear to everyone in the world and then be brutally killed and dragged through the streets. After that, he told us, the battle of Armageddon would create a conflagration so blistering it would melt the dirt.

He encouraged us to marvel at how the Bible was able to predict the invention of TV, because that, he told us, is exactly what it did by forecasting that the prophets would be seen by everyone in the world. Before TV, he reasoned, no one could figure out how *everyone* could see the prophets, and so it was tempting not to take this passage literally. But he argued that this proved that every word of the Bible was written by God, who from the beginning knew the future, as we do not, including the invention of television. If there were other things about the Bible that we didn't comprehend with our tiny minds, we should simply trust and not question. All will become clear in God's time. I scribbled notes in the white space on my bulletin, took the notes home, and laid them carefully in one of my drawers with my other notes on Revelation.

I collected his explanations of Bible passages. When I read a Bible passage, the words worked like tracks on which I ran the engine of familiar meanings from Rev. Garland's past sermons. The meaning chugged along with satisfying predictability until I reached a section of verses I hadn't heard him explain. Then meaning broke down because I had no general principles to apply to reading the Bible. To me, reading meant translating the words on the page to a prefabricated meaning that I had in my memory, remembering the code Rev. Garland had given us. I hung onto his interpretations for dear life because I had been taught that the salvation of my eternal soul was bound up in the words of the Bible, and I wanted to be damn certain I knew what they meant.

Last semester a slender, pretty, brown-haired young woman in the first row of my poetry class sat looking up at me with her green, green eyes during a student discussion. I don't know whether she was listening or whether she had gone away to some vacation spot in her mind. She never talked. I had no idea what she was thinking.

But on the second exam, she wrote, "I signed up for this class having no idea what I was in for. I realized I was out of place and literally lost as soon as it began. Why does one line have to have a thousand different meanings when it's only five words long?" She concluded by admitting that during the semester, her ideas had changed. She had learned the thousand meanings depend on "where you're coming from." She added with irony, "It must be hard to write something that has no meaning, so it can have a thousand meanings."

Reading this felt to me like watching my house burn. I'd thought the class was fairly successful. Many students talked. Some of them began writing their own poetry. And a number of them started buying poetry on Amazon. Moreover, it's not as if I hadn't given them direction. Although I rarely rejected their ideas outright, we followed the logic of each of their readings carefully, assessing whether the text could support the interpretation. At the end of class, I never supplied paraphrases of the poems, but I did make clear the contradictions in their readings, and I suggested alternatives. So I was surprised to read my green-eyed student's bitter cry of anguish. After I gave back the exams, I asked her to stop by my office. I wanted her to talk to me about reading and also about her many absences.

When I offered to take her coat, she declined to give it, instead perching nervously on the edge of my blue chair, her gloves drooping from one hand. In her black trench coat, she reminded me of a blackbird, poised, ready to fly off.

"You're right," I said. "A poem can't mean just anything. It isn't a Rorschach test."

Her eyes darted around the room.

I forged on. "You know how we've talked about backing up our readings by citing words and lines."

She glanced from the snapshots of my children to my wicker basket filled with theater programs to a tea set one of my former students had sent from Korea. She was merely enduring this interview, waiting for me to finish. She felt she didn't have time to waste in my office, or maybe she was too anxious to focus.

Soon she stopped coming to class altogether. She was a senior. She may not get another chance to learn to read poetry, which is a luxury only the lucky can afford. I learned a little about her later, and on the basis of that, I can tell you she is already living a life that would surely be better with poetry in it.

I know there are professors on our campus who might have made her happy because, like Rev. Garland, they dictate paraphrases of poems and ask students to reproduce the paraphrases on tests.

One winter day, after my colleagues turn off our hall light and go home, a young woman edges through my door. I can tell who she is by her book bag, which she pushes in first. Amanda is writing a poetry honors thesis with me, and my office is like her second home, so she drops onto my kindly blue chair and doesn't bother to disguise her feelings. She glares, which is what she does when she is angry. I ask her how her marathon went last weekend, and we chat about the cold, until she gets herself under control.

In one of her lit classes that morning, she reveals, her professor decoded an Emily Dickinson poem as if it were a physics equation. He expected the students to slavishly copy what he told them. It took him about four minutes. Then he moved on to translate the next poem.

My student raised her hand. "I have a slightly different way of reading the last poem," she offered. My colleague stared at her blankly.

"Here's where I differ."

He let her talk, then, without comment, pushed on to translate the next poem.

Amanda rages about the fact that a literature professor, of all people, would treat a poem so shabbily. She had proved inadequate to defend the brilliant ambiguity of Emily Dickinson. She slumps in the blue chair, depressed, and one of her books falls to the floor. Well-traveled, bright, mountain climber that she is, she is not used to being defeated.

She lost her father a year before to cancer, and I think she's a little angry at him for leaving her. Maybe she's just beginning to realize how fallible human authority can be. She might have been a fundamentalist at one time, but she's learned how ambiguous the world is, and she is bound and determined that ambiguity will be acknowledged by her professors.

"Can you get him censured?" she demands. "Or shall I report him?"

She clearly means this.

I tell her—gently, I hope—that my colleague can't be censured because of reading differently than we do or because he doesn't allow his class to discuss the meaning of a poem.

"That's not reading," she retorts. "He's a literature professor, and he *doesn't read*!"

In a drama class I taught a decade ago, a young woman named Barbara offered an interpretation of *The Glass Menagerie,* which differed wildly from the reading toward which the class was inching through lively discussion. Barbara's idea was new to me and fascinating and potentially important, so we abandoned the track our discussion had been on to pursue it. When I asked Barbara to explain how her interpretation fit the details of the play, she retorted that she had no idea, but her high school teacher had told her that's what the play meant, and her high school teacher was very smart, smarter than any professor at this university.

I felt surprisingly hurt, and I probably sounded recriminatory when I explained that an interpretation of a play doesn't fly unless you can show how it relates to the characters and plot. The other students froze, undoubtedly feeling self-conscious and awkward, and I wasn't able to get the discussion started again.

In retrospect, I sympathize with Barbara's frustration. If you don't work out that literal one-to-one equation between a text and its meaning yourself, you tend to forget the details.

But what happened to the other students in that drama class, I think, is what often happens when students are just beginning to jump on their interpretation bicycles and ride by themselves. If someone comes along and pushes them down, they are too discouraged to get up and try it again. Every poetry class offers the chance for real discussion about reading and about what great poems say about love and death. The space can provide students an oasis for peaceful human exchange in their hectic days. It can foster civil discussion among students who are so different they might never meet under any other circumstances. But all this is unbelievably difficult to achieve.

It's not just the fundamentalist readers. The students who love to proliferate meanings can also torpedo the chance for real discussion. I have observed over the years that they tend to be students who enjoy the buzz ambiguity can give, the ones who chafe under structure and authority. On the first warm day of spring, they clamor to move the class outside. They're crazy about the notion that everything they guess about a metaphor seems right. At least at the beginning, they think that when they selected the poetry course, they stumbled onto one long holiday.

At our university, they are often the same students who easily question their own cultural assumptions and decide that every culture is equal, none is superior. Logical contradiction, weird context—whatever, they're easy. Sitting in a class, everything seems abstract, and anything can seem permissible, at least theoretically. Ask one of these students whether she thinks it's a good idea to roast and eat her dead grandmother in order to ingest the woman's courage and wisdom. She'll laugh and shrug. "Sure, it's just another vibe. We respect it. Whatever." This kind of sloppy flexibility is just as likely to prevent real discussion as a fundamentalist reading.

I'm pretty sure my green-eyed student who complained that five words can generate a thousand meanings missed so many poetry classes because she was pregnant. She told me as much. At least that's what I believe she was saying. I suspect that while the class was talking about poetry, she was feeling nauseated and picturing a little cradle. She was probably scared, and she might have been worried about money. By the time she took the exam, she wasn't pregnant anymore. She must have had plenty to think about besides poetry.

Maybe as she contemplated a thousand equally right meanings for one line, she felt overwhelmed by uncertainty: the baby, whether to stay in school, whether to marry the father, whether she even wanted to be a mother, all the poems' meanings, the choices, the way meanings clash, like the jarring facts of her life. If the uncertainty got to her, I'm with her. I remember what it felt like. Too much uncertainty and your whole life can come unraveled.

Even in this country of freedom and endless cereal choices, even in this century of relativity, what a person can say about a poem is limited by what the poet has written.

I once taught poetry to a class where most of the students never talked at all because three or four students spoke so early and so persuasively that they became the seers. They wrote the best papers, too, and since I ask for three or four of the best papers to be read in class, that further established their celebrity status. I agonized about what to do because I didn't want to dampen the enthusiasm of the Big Four. Yet by the middle of the semester, even though the students sat in a circle, all their eyes were turned deferentially toward me. When they talked, they repeated the stars' interpretations, as if reciting the pledge of allegiance. Class discussion was all about polite detachment—from one another and from the poems they were reading.

After I assigned the second paper, which required a close reading of a poem, I asked the Big Four to stay after class. I proposed that in their papers they should invent and argue preposterous meanings for the poem I had given the class to interpret.

They stared at me.

Not to worry, I told them. I would give them good grades for being outrageous. They could use their imaginations, base their wrong interpretations on metaphors and lines in the poem. They should argue carefully and persuasively. Being both consistent and wrong would be a lot more challenging than it sounded. I was asking them to do this because I hoped they could initiate some controversy in the class. I wanted to have at least one good fight over the meaning of a poem.

It worked, sort of. On the day the four students were asked to read their papers in class, the other students leaned back, predicting the same old same old. But after hearing two papers, some students began to squirm. Some of them frowned in puzzlement; some stared down at their notebooks in embarrassment. One finally raised his hand and said, "Are you telling me that was a good paper?"

"Well, what's wrong with it?" I asked him.

There was long silence and a little fidgeting. Then he spoke briefly, nailing the paper's faults. A few others chimed in. We fell into a real discussion for the first time. I don't suppose more than a third of the students talked, but I counted that as a breakthrough.

Then I admitted that the four papers were a put-up job.

No kidding, the students said. They laughed.

I had worried that they would feel tricked, but they didn't. Maybe they were impressed that I cared enough to set something like that up. Eventually, we went on to talk about how you can know whether what you're saying about a poem is right or wrong.

Does the class vote?

Do you search the web?

Do you just write down what the teacher says?

It was a fledgling discussion, but a discussion.

After a couple of months some of them felt more comfortable venturing opinions about poems. Talking about poetry didn't scare them as much as it had before. Self-confidence, like a good, stiff breeze moved through the sails of their dinghies. Some of them found they could sail alone. Teach students the meaning of a few poems, and those are all they'll have. Teach them how to read poems, and they'll be able to read poetry all their lives.

It's the last class of the semester, and Jackson is scowling from the back row. Maria, who has turned up with blue fingernails today, defends a particular reading of a poem. Z (a student who changed his name from Josh to Z in the middle of the semester) says no. He argues for a different reading. They're both flamboyant personalities, and each has established a turf with followers. Now they disagree. The air feels heavy with tension. A nervous quiet descends on the students. Which of them is right?

I tell them, look. Both readings are interesting. Why not let them stand side by side? The metaphor in the poem is multivalent, so we don't have to choose. Let them both live, and we will learn to hold the two meanings in tension. This is what I am learning on my faith journey, to be happy with a little less certainty, to be comfortable with more dissonance.

Jackson gets a C on his final exam, not as bad as I expected. But he doesn't get the point of reading poetry. The truth is, I grieve over such students. Maybe, I tell myself, when he's forty-five, sitting in a high-rise somewhere reading a poem in *The New Yorker* it will dawn on him that the words bring news about his own inner journey. Maybe someday he'll feel lost, and wanting to map his own internal space, maybe he'll see that poetry offers a language for doing that. Then he won't care so much about someone else's right answer.

Jackson's desperation to be sure of the answers reminds me of my own fundamentalist childhood. He faces my exam as if it were the final judgment. How will he be able to make a good account of himself before the Grader if he doesn't have the answers? Without a key, he doesn't trust himself to interpret the text.

Jackson is a literalist, or rather, a fundamentalist, who refused to give up the possibility that some authority will tell him what the poems mean. Oh, God, I think, if only certainty were possible, I would give it to him! Jackson has mistaken my authority over his grade and over what happens in our classroom for a much more powerful authority. He wants to think of me the way I thought of Rev. Garland, and so do some of the other students. But I can't let them—not because I want to deprive them of something they need—but because human language is metaphorical and inevitably requires interpretation.

Frankly, now that I've given up Rev. Garland's key, I'm not sure how to read the book of Revelation, but I'm not as troubled about that as I used to be. How many ways have we found to read *Hamlet*? How many nuances have readers found in *Tintern Abbey?* Every time I've thought I was sure I'd found the best reading for a great text, I've learned there's another facet I haven't considered. Eventually, basking in the joy of new readings, I realized I no longer needed the certainty that there is one true eternal meaning for every text.

I know that teaching the process of reading, rather than the meanings of specific poems, frustrates some of my students. But to say it that way, in the language of education texts, makes their struggle seem less fiery and dangerous than it really is. Each student bears a long and unique history of defeats and triumphs over reading; each of them faces the intimate text of a poem and experiences it alone; each of them must find a language to talk about her experience in the company of radically different readers. To suggest that my fundamentalist students are merely going through a stage in the learning process is to pretend that I know their irritation and worry will be resolved. But I don't know that it will.

All I know is that we gather in this classroom Tuesday and Thursday at eleven in the morning and with every class a morning of our lives passes. It is momentous. It is, in this flash of time we call our lives, all we have. I honor the seriousness of it. My students will never be twenty again, and I am spending my own real, fleeting life with them. Some students, like the young woman with the green eyes, sit in class fighting tears. Others are fighting mad. Reading poetry is not a detached or simply intellectual process. It is deeply emotional, and it is hooked to everything we are and believe.

This is my benediction for my students. When the semester is over, I hope they can pick up a poem and read it without me. I hope they'll look for other readers to talk with about it. I hope they'll have enough courage to work through the text of poems to grasp their complexity. May the fundamentalists among them come to relish, first, the adventure of not knowing, then the pleasure of looking carefully at the words, and then, the slow dawning of meaning. May they learn to hold that meaning in suspension, because any interpretation of a poem is gloriously subject to revision.

For eons, human beings have used poetry to talk about the most profound issues of their lives. My students need poetry because, as they struggle for money and power, it can keep them in touch with what is deep inside them. It can remind them to look beyond surfaces. It can tell them again, when they forget, what it was like to be a child. It can connect them to some essential questions about why we are alive and what it means to be human. In this hyped-up, speedy, illusory culture, they need to reflect on that kind of inner truth. That is why I believe it is important to teach them to read. I won't always be with them, but the poems will be.

10

Diary of a Rehearsal

THE DIRECTOR HANDS OUT coupons for dinner at a nearby restaurant, warns us to be back for rehearsal in an hour, and heads for his office, muttering darkly that he needs to return phone calls. We are in rehearsal for *The Tillie Project*, a play the director of this theater has commissioned me to write. I'd like to make some revisions to the script during this break, but to do that I need quiet, and the theater doesn't keep an office for me. Playwrights don't hang around theaters these days the way they used to. Most of them are safely dead or, if they're alive, they're busy reinventing their lives in some other city. But this is the first production of my new play, *The Tillie Project*, and I have been summoned by the director who commissioned it to work with the cast.

I am in an awkward spot. I don't belong with actors, but I have a coupon for the restaurant where they'll be eating. They're gossiping and laughing, heading in a group for the door. Several of them turn and call to me, *Come with us*. They look back, open-faced and beguiling in the light which floods through the door that one of them has already wedged open. The November wind blasts in. I can't believe they actually want to share dinner with someone who has multiplied their headaches by changing their dialogue, not once, but several times and who, for the sake of a better script, will change it again.

Hours before, sitting around a wobbly table on the stage under the director's scrutiny, the actors read straight through the script for the first time, discovering what gallant or corrupt or tormented character they will be playing. They have two weeks to commit their parts to memory and learn blocking. In spite of the notorious perils involved in a new script, they radiate enthusiasm, even the one who's been cast in the three smallest parts. He is an experienced character actor who could probably transform himself into a radish if he wanted. But at the moment, he appears as his own reassuring self, mid-stride toward dinner.

"Come on," he calls, opening his arm and holding the door for me. I'm regretting that I didn't give him a bigger part, but as soon as I think that, I know it's silly. Writing for the theater, more than any other writing I've ever done, demands austere choices, demands exclusion and paring down.

After a quick, functional dinner, we use the bathrooms, fill our bottles with water, and head back to the theater. The director is prowling around in the wings, stepping over a pile of two-by-fours and sections of a roof, looking for the sound guy. Lila, the young ballerina-like actress who plays the heroine, runs her fingers through her hair to disarrange it, then pulls on a long skirt. She gets a faraway look in her gray eyes and disappears into the murky backstage area. I whiff burned sugar and feel slightly drunk on the scent.

Padding down the dark aisle toward the luminous stage, I think what I often think in rehearsal, how strange the business of theater is. While other people are exiting the expressway to their daylight jobs in law firms and corporations and fast-food stores, we are gearing up for a day of make-believe. I'm not used to spending all day around people, particularly such electrifying ones, and to tell the truth, I get sick of the repetition in rehearsal. The big velvet curtains and pink-red lighting on the stage make me feel drifty and unmoored. I wonder, as I often have, what on earth would make a person want to spend all her days, a whole precious life, in the theater, pretending?

On Tuesday, the last week before the opening, rain is bucketing down, pulling fall leaves to the ground, creating a slick brown film on

Diary of a Rehearsal

the streets. Not finding a parking place, I abandon my Toyota in a No Parking Zone and barely make it into the theater by ten. Once inside, I close my umbrella and toss it carelessly on the floor. After I confer with the director and watch part of the rehearsal, I'm itching to move my car, which will soon be ticketed. I feel around for my umbrella. It must be somewhere here, under one of the hundreds of seats. Not finding it, I get up and search in earnest, but I stop short of crawling around the whole theater on my hands and knees. I decide I'll dash out in the rain and re-park my Toyota without my umbrella.

Pushing the door open, I notice a slender young guy in jeans and a cheap t-shirt who plays one of the smaller parts and therefore, while others rehearse, frequently helps build sets. He is standing under the overhang, smoking. "What do you think you're doing?" he asks. "It's pouring!"

"I'm just moving my car." I grin and shrug, trying to convey my wholehearted thanks for his concern. What I would like to tell him is that, unlike actors who are so physical, I live in my head. Why should I care if I get a little wet? I'll dry. He motions me to wait, snuffs out his cigarette, sprints into the theater for his umbrella, flicks it open, and accompanies me to my car. Then he insists that I take the thing, so I won't get soaked when I walk back. As he dashes back to the theater, I wonder at his care, his respect for the weather, his concern for our bodies.

When I return from re-parking my car, he's pacing the stage, working out blocking with another actor. At the side entrance, two actresses are snacking on pretzels and crying out with glee as they try on one another's shoes. In one of the aisles, an actor is stretched out in meditation, breathing serenely, his eyes closed, a faint smile of delight on his face. The set designer has put up a WET PAINT sign on the proscenium and is paddling around the stage, in and out of the funereal burgundy curtains, dodging the rehearsing actors. In the wing, stage right, an actor stands observing lighting changes that turn the performance area into a pool of lavender, then blue, then white, then red. An actress approaches him from behind, snakes her arms around him, and imprisons his torso. He stands quietly, amiable as a horse being saddled. They settle into an extended embrace until the director calls them for a scene. Their affection is as innocent and unthinking as that between a mother and child. The sheer physicality of it all boggles my mind.

I am another species from these actors. Yet I feel profound affection for them, not least because they are indispensable to me. Actors do for scripts the kind of favor that builders do for architects. Only after the builder incarnates the plans in wood and windows and a roof can the architect know whether his idea succeeded or failed. Until I hear an actor saying one of my walk-on lines as he enters the set, I can't be sure whether the line is too long or too short. If the rhythm of the dialogue is off, or the pacing of a scene seems wrong, I often discover that by listening to the actors.

Besides, most actors I have known are brave and gifted people. They climb around on a cluttered stage, making entrances and exits on time, elegantly weaving patterns as complicated as the steps in a ballet. Their flexibility and grace confound me. Their balance and technical mastery amaze me. And I am touched that three dozen actors—more—wanted to audition for each part in this script, even though it's untested and it will be performed for only eight weeks. I am awed by their resilience, moving like vagabonds from one job to another, setting up miniature communities over and over, and then bidding their fellows goodbye.

During my years in the theater, actors have taught me a vast amount about the body. I, the fundamentalist, who never danced or wore makeup, who was taught modesty in dress and bearing, when I am in the theater, I become acutely physical. I find it hard to account for this strange way of being in the world. It has nothing to do with sexual promiscuity. It is unlike anything I know.

Call it style or demeanor, I have learned how much it counts. Rehearsals for my first play were held in a large garage in Brixton, an area in South London where the theater could rent space for a few pounds a day. At the time, Brixton was haunted by addicts and thieves, but our actors walked there at noon with the majesty of street barons, and no one troubled us.

Diary of a Rehearsal

A different, American production of that same play was rehearsed for two weeks at the World Bank in Washington DC. I never got used to the grandeur of the immense marble lobby, through which the powerful and the rich streamed at all hours of the day. But in the exhausting Washington heat, the sub-sub floors of the World Bank were blessedly cool.

The third week of rehearsal, the director asked several actors to bring props from the theater to the Bank. As the actors emerged from their battered Volkswagen Beetle with mops, a lantern, dishes, and a hunting rifle, the DC police surrounded them, yelling. "Put up your hands!"

One of the actresses, skilled from many years of beautifully controlled hysteria on stage, began sobbing, "I'm an actress! I'm an *actress!*"

Traffic stopped. Horns bleated. A throng gathered. Several people in the crowd, no doubt fearing violence, threw up their hands. The actors froze. The cops conferred with one another. After a long discussion, the bizarre truth dawned on the police. They put down their guns and talked to the actors.

The fact is that actors can seem very different in their street clothes than they do on stage. When I first taught script writing, I invited an actress to visit my workshop. I had just seen her play Lyubov in *The Cherry Orchard*, so I knew she was a statuesque and dominating personality, though I had never spoken with her face to face. We agreed on the phone to meet outside the door to the classroom where my workshop was held. For ten minutes before the bell rang, I stood scanning the foot traffic for her. When she didn't come, I was worried because I had nothing else prepared for the day. I couldn't believe she'd be late; theater people learn to arrive on time, or they don't get work. As students and professors disappeared into their classrooms, I noticed a short, pleasant-looking, blond woman standing across the hall. I stepped over and asked her whether she had seen Kathleen Pirkl. Kathleen Pirkl smiled and shook my hand. Off stage, in real life, she had resumed her own proper height and bearing.

When I was growing up as a fundamentalist, theater was forbidden. I never saw a play, except for dismal school performances, until I was eighteen. The first good play I ever saw was performed on the shallow stage of Edman Chapel at Wheaton College in 1962, performed by students, one of whom was Wes Craven, who had written it (and who went on to become a famous horror film director). It was only in the mid-sixties that children of fundamentalists in America began writing and acting in religious colleges, where they were meeting one another and then, against all odds, valiantly opening theaters around the country. A few of these are now arguably among the best regional houses in America. But until the late sixties, one of the strongest taboos of fundamentalism was the taboo against theater.

Back in 1642, before theaters in America, the Puritans, the religious forebears of fundamentalism, succeeded in closing London theaters. They brought two charges against actors. Actors are promiscuous. And they lie. As a preacher named John Rainolds put it in the mid-seventeenth century: "The vanity and unlawfulness of plays and interludes hath often been spoken against by the holy men of God." Indeed, for half a century preacher had railed against playhouses, which were located on the south bank of the Thames River, among the revelry of taverns, bear-baiting, and whore houses. The actors, all men, many of whom spent their time in the red-light district, seemed hardly better than the whores they were accused of visiting. Puritans were supposed to work hard and lead sober lives, which did not include trips to the theater.

To the Puritan attacks against his theater, Shakespeare replies through the speeches of some of his most loveable characters. In *Twelfth Night*, for example, Sir Toby Belch gets sick of being ordered around by his niece's dorky Puritan steward Malvolio. When Toby suggests that Malvolio lighten up, the servant stiffens and haughtily instructs the old knight to stop drinking. Fed up with the servant's arrogance, Toby quips, "Dost thou think because thou art virtuous there shall be no more cakes and ale?"

When I go to dinner with the actors on Tuesday night, they thoughtfully refrain from pumping me for information about their characters or arguing that their parts should have more lines. By now, they have inhabited their characters for several days. They believe in the integrity of their characters, and they long for the opportunity to advance their loves and motives. One actor tells me that at night she dreams the dreams of her character. She has gone places I have never been in the skin of the character I invented. The cast has even worked out a pecking order that is, in part, based on the social status of the people in the script. This strange slippage between the script and reality reminds me of the rehearsals of one of my other plays, during which one actress frequently reminded her friends in the cast that she was the queen and they were not.

The truth is, I feel uneasy about the way some actors blur the boundaries between themselves and the characters I have invented. Toward the end of rehearsal when my first play was being produced in Washington DC, one of the actresses, a pretty, large-boned young woman with an extravagant mop of black hair, showed me a secret spiral notebook crammed with writing on both sides of the page. She explained that she had written this journal documenting her character's life before the character entered the play. I didn't know much about the theater yet, and after reading several pages of the journal, I was puzzled. How in heaven's name had the actress divined what the character had lived through before the action of the play opened? I certainly had no idea of it myself. I thought of most of the characters in my plays as having very limited existences, limited to their function in the plot. For me they were not substantive, but conditional upon the actions I needed them to perform in a particular script. In that way, I could even say they were accidental.

Now I know that what that actress was doing is common. In fact, The Method, as it is called, is promoted by some schools of acting. Many actors imagine their characters' lives before the action of the play opens in order to explore what motives drive their characters, to discover more fully what the characters feel. They need to sense in their bones the coherence of the characters they play. This is still mind-boggling to me, the one who creates and tends the whole script. It is part of what makes a week in the theater seem so odd, what makes these courteous, gifted actors appear so alien.

Before evening rehearsal, the director is standing in the orchestra pit, bending over a big chart. I greet him. He turns to watch me shake off water like a spaniel.

"It's rained every day this week."

"Yeah."

"Nice to be inside." I say, snapping my umbrella shut.

"You might want to keep that open," he laughs. "We sprang a leak last night." He'd been in the theater until midnight with the costume designers.

I wonder what made this talented man, who could have done almost anything he wanted, decide to spend his life making believe.

While he takes Act II from the top, I go back to sit down. In the orchestra pit, beneath the actors, prowling back and forth like a cheetah, he is alert to their every twitch and turn. Suddenly he springs onto the stage, and the action stops. He huddles with an actress. He murmurs to her in a kind, confidential voice. From my seat about halfway back in the dimly lit house, I cannot make out what they're saying, but she has a worried expression on her face. She looks like a baseball pitcher who's in trouble. He bends to her like a coach who has taken a trip to the mound. Maybe they need a rewrite. I consider going up to the stage to confer or at least calling to them.

But no. My rule is, we must try to make the script work. It's madness to revise every time an actor hits a snag. The script would be perpetually changing. What would happen to the narrative line? What would happen to the other characters' parts? The director withdraws, the actress sticks her chin out bravely, and they take the scene from the top again.

I look around for someone to explain, to translate, someone to klatch with, but the director is conferring with the lighting designer and the actors are on stage, earnestly working on a scene, trying various ways to make it work. Good actors have a talent for buying into a script, before they know whether or not it will make a good play.

Diary of a Rehearsal

Until a play opens for the first time, *no one* knows whether the script will work—not the director, not even the playwright.

That's why, as a playwright, I have often been grateful for a cast's resolute and prior commitment to the characters and the story of my scripts. In the end, whether it involves skill or talent, actors must posit that a story is true, in some important sense, before they enter rehearsal or see any proof that it is. Against the literal logic of the everyday world, they exert the constant pressure of their belief, in spite of the low pay, the long hours, and the often cold and ugly rehearsal rooms. This kind of belief, where does it come from?

Because a good actor can summon an audience to astounding belief. Some of them possess the *je ne sais quoi* that makes them appear to be inventing their lines on the spot. I watched such an actor in the Olivier Theater in London, merely by strolling across a stage, bewitch thousands of people into believing that he was navigating an ocean. I have seen actors, driven by faith, and princely in their skill, convince audiences, including me, of scripts that I had previously read and found implausible.

When I was in fourth grade, we wrote and rehearsed plays. Though I attended a fundamentalist school from which theater was banned, a group of us kids threatened and beseeched our novice teacher to let us write and put on scripts for the younger kids on Friday afternoons. By Friday, we were all bedraggled and sick of books. The big hand of the clock moved so slowly through the large black minutes that our teacher couldn't find enough for us to do. So she allowed us to write and act, but only in the damp, gloomy basement.

One Friday afternoon during our play, the little kids broke into giggles during a sad, intense scene, and their giggles burgeoned to guffaws which spread like a winter cold. The performance dwindled to a full stop. First one of the actors and then another just gave up. We stood around on the stage, awkward and without lines. It was deeply embarrassing, but we tried to appear nonchalant.

I think all of us wished we could start over, but we were too infected with the miserable reality of the concrete block basement, where we were using a wash line as a curtain rod and a sheet for a curtain. We were too aware that we were pretending—only *pretending* to be criminals and princesses—characters that weren't even in a book, characters we ourselves had cooked up. Our sense of enchantment had evaporated and all the delight we previously felt had leaked out. We couldn't cross the line and incarnate our characters again, because we couldn't believe in them enough. For a little while, in fact, we couldn't even strike up a convincing conversation among ourselves. Our faith, even in our own personal stories, had flagged.

It's Thursday morning and I am thinking all this while sitting in the theater, watching the cast of *The Tillie Project* rehearse. I still can't explain why actors commit themselves to the theater life, why they want to make believe.

And then I look up. The actress who plays Tillie has walked on and is rehearsing the scene where she makes a life-changing decision. She is laying out the argument with ferocity, pig-headed, bent on changing the course of her destiny. She is riveting. I can't stop looking at her.

At that moment I see.

We're not *pretending* here in this dark, empty theater.

It's real. We're doing something real.

I'm not sure what to call it. I call it transformation.

I'm remembering the day before, back at home, I had taken a phone call from a friend who told me that her long-hated father had e-mailed to say that he had cancer, that he had been given two months to live. He beseeched her, his daughter, to stay with him for a while. Suddenly she had to make a choice. There was no escape.

She phoned me to talk because she knew she had to answer him, had to decide either to go or not to go. She knew that what she chose would change her. She would live with the consequences of that choice for the rest of her life.

It's at that moment, sitting in the theater with the red velvet curtain and the smell of burnt sugar, that I realize my whole life has been about that kind of choice and the way it can transform everything. Conversion was the whole point of our revival meetings and church services when I was a child. Before I was eighteen, in my fundamentalist church I had heard thousands of altar calls. Maybe that's why I've always loved theater, because every good play dramatizes either a character's transformation, or his refusal to change.

Moreover, transformation in the theater doesn't occur only when a character in the script changes; it happens every time an actor steps into a role. When we were kids, rehearsing, we went back and forth between our own everyday selves and the characters. Everyone knew that Linda C.'s father was a bus driver and that she lived on Oak Street, but in one of our plays she acted the part of a princess. Whenever we stopped rehearsing, she became Linda again. Linda, princess, Linda, princess. *Wait. Slow down. Try it again.* And then in the glorious last hour of Friday afternoon, as the lower grades watched, we fourth graders—people those kids saw every day—converted ourselves into circus bears, exotic foreign dignitaries, and witches.

So I'm thinking all this as I sit in one of the red, plush chairs in the audience, now examining a xerox of the stage set. And I'm aware that the actors are flying, or to put it another way, the rehearsal is going really well. And then the director yells for us to take a break. Everything stops. The actors stretch. They launch themselves toward the bathroom or into the wings to check their cell phones. The actress who plays Tillie wanders down from the stage, beams at me, and holds out her Tupperware box of celery. I thank her and lift out a cool pale green stick.

Even though I know Equity rules dictate that actors get twenty minutes break every two hours, it's disconcerting when they abruptly stop arguing and begin giving one another backrubs. Watching, I lose my bearings again. Should I walk up and tell the actress with her Tupperware box how much I like her blouse? Or should I mention that I'm grateful for her insight into Tillie's character?

If I do, she'll squirm. She'll tell me, after all, she's only doing what she does every day. But I know this is what she *tries* to do every day and what she succeeds at only on some days. Part of what makes the play work, when it does, is her skill. But there is also power flowing through these actors which the actors don't control. They don't control it any more than I do. And most of them know that.

The truth is, the force of the Tillie story has gripped us all—me first, as I was writing the script, and now these actors. It is making itself visible through us. I have stumbled upon the answer to the question: what are we doing here on a Thursday morning in November? We are tapping into some kind of power which is extraordinary, spellbinding, amazing. Maybe it's worth rehearsing for weeks to feel that power even once. Maybe it's worth doing almost *anything*, because when it does come, it feels like transcendence pouring through us.

This is a mystery. I have not seen it happen often, and when it happens, it is inexplicable. It does not happen only with exceptionally talented actors or ones who are famous. Many of these cast members live fairly pedestrian lives in New York and commute half an hour to this theater, mostly by train. Moreover, the power of the production doesn't arise from the fact that I wrote the play for this cast. I didn't have the faintest idea who these people were, and they still don't have a clue about my long and sometimes frustrating struggle to hammer out the script. I haven't told any of them what I think the story means. Yet they have managed to find the characters I invented while I was sitting alone at the wooden desk in my study.

How did they do that?

It is said that the stage is a sacred space. Twenty-five hundred years ago, the Greeks used the high altar in their temples, the altar where Bacchus revealed himself, as a stage. An altar is a place of incarnation, the place where, in some Christian churches, the bread and wine become the body and the blood of Christ. God comes down, as we believe, and appears to us in the Eucharist. It is where we who are gathered become a kinship of believers, a communion of saints.

What happens in the theater may be less consequential than what happens at the altar, because it does not involve the incarnation of God, but I am beginning to understand it does sometimes incarnate transcendent power. A human body, the instrument. A script, the meaning. Time and space, the medium. At these moments, theater isn't "pretending." In fact, it is not far from holy. Maybe that's why even the actors' shenanigans, their impersonations and mimicry and acrobatics fascinate me, because actors are the most palpable instruments of an art which is shrouded in mystery.

In fact, this peculiar power, which I feel when I'm on stage, prevents me from walking around up there, unless I'm invited by the director or needed for a talk-back after a show. I don't go backstage either, where the actors dress and become their characters. I don't know how to transform myself the way they do. Insofar as I can transform anything or anyone, I do it by writing. I don't belong on the stage.

Meanwhile, as I'm sitting twenty rows back, chomping on a piece of celery and reflecting on the sweet mysteries of the stage, the actress who plays Tillie throws herself down on the boards up there and does sit-ups.

"Your places," the director calls. And then, soon after, "Scene One." Tillie bursts through the front door, holding a bird cage aloft, sporting a broad-brimmed hat, caterwauling that she's sorry she's late for her new job. She's a raw young kitchen maid. The man she was flirting with at dinner several weeks ago is now her boss, and she nervously awaits his pleasure. It's not the actors' costumes that convey their characters, or their props, either, or their gestures, exactly. I can't put my finger on why this makes me so happy. It's working. The script is flying.

And I'm remembering a Minnesota Saturday night several weeks before Christmas. Snow has been shawling down all day. We kids and my mother have eaten our dinner. She's upstairs putting my little sister to bed, and my father is working late at his store. I am sitting quietly in a tapestry-covered, overstuffed chair in our living room with my legs jutting straight out, I'm so small. The living room is dark with only the blue tree lights shining and the spruce gives off a warm, evergreen fragrance. Under the tree rest a few wrapped presents, but the main attraction is the crèche my parents put up every Christmas season. In the stable, a tiny baby Jesus lies on a miniature blond pillow of hay, his head encircled with a halo.

I begin saying the same word over and over, lazily, until it doesn't sound like itself any more. *Crèche, crèche, crèche, crèche.* The lights from the tree cast spectral radiance around the room so the couch and the tables and magazine rack and plants appear luminous and unfamiliar. This is my living room, I know that, but I have never seen it look this way before. Outside the wind picks up, hurling bits of sleet against the windows.

Then I think I see the baby move.

I climb down from the chair and sit on the floor beside the crèche, right in front of the baby. I perch there, cross-legged, focusing on the baby Jesus, staring, hearing the wind clawing for my attention at the windows, but I don't look at it. I focus on the baby Jesus and try not to blink, squinting to make sure that if he moves again, I won't miss it. A steady draft blows across my legs as I sit webbed in the bluish shadows of the room. I feel something, a spirit, maybe, shift inside me.

The baby never moves again. But I understand something after this that I didn't know before, though I can scarcely believe it, and I certainly can't say what it is. I believe absolutely that I have seen the baby move.

As Peter Berger has said, "The fundamental religious impulse is not to theorize about transcendence, but to worship it." Staring at the image of the crèche that night, I felt something inscrutable. Though I didn't have a word for it at the time, I later understood that its name is "holy." Now I sometimes feel that force in the theater. By then, by the age of five or six, maybe I was already a goner, already lost to the fundamentalist cause.

It's dress rehearsal, the day after tech rehearsal, which lasted six hours because of the vast number of sound and light cues the script demands. We open tomorrow. The director is now jumpy. Being around him feels like crossing an intersection where eight roads come together. The Assistant Director needs information for the playbills. A reporter calls from the *Newark Star-Ledger* to schedule an interview. The light crew has lost a page of cues. The costume designer wants to take the skirt off an actress to shorten it. The set designer has, for some unfathomable reason, painted the proscenium again, and

Diary of a Rehearsal

everyone has to be careful lest the costumes and props get smeared with black paint. The actors take a full, deadly twenty seconds to change costumes and move furniture between two of the scenes. The director snarls at them, then leaves to take a phone call.

Meanwhile, I sit in the darkened theater listening and seething at the way one of the actors is giving a key speech. He is emphasizing the wrong words, clipping ones that need to be lengthened, drawing out ones that are insignificant. I want to lunge onto the stage and throttle him. I want to read the lines to him exactly as he should say them. I want to make him repeat them after me. I want to shout that I am the only one who knows what the play means and it doesn't mean that unless actors say the dialogue right.

I get up and go outside into the radiant fall sunshine. I look at the trees, which are going down in red and yellow flames. Seeing how the world goes on helps me to recover some equilibrium. You don't give line readings to good actors for the same reason that you don't write directions in the script for the actor to say a speech *sadly* or *with jealousy*. Actors and directors don't like adverbs that explain how to say the lines. Rote little instructions for the voice never illuminate character. Ultimately, actors have to find the meaning of every line in relationship to the whole script.

Kafka said that art is like an axe that chops through the frozen sea within us. Before a script can do that for an audience, the actors have to chop through their own frozen seas. They have to get past formulas. They have to understand not only *how* their character says the words, but *why*. That involves tracking the character, making his choices, taking his emotional steps. It is not something adverbs can explain. It's not something a playwright can explain.

I kick a few leaves, and then I go back to the rehearsal. I am already in the rowboat with these actors. We will either capsize or get somewhere together. They have given me the compliment of trusting the script. Tomorrow night, they will have nothing but my lines to offer the audience.

Then it dawns on me that the actor of whom I've felt so critical may be trying an interpretation. He may be hacking his way through a thicket of possibilities. Until he tries this wrong one, he may not be able to find his way to something that works. This seems like an error in the direction of charity, but I go with it. It would be counterproductive to start momentous script changes at dress rehearsal. And if there's one thing I know, it's that every performance in the theater—unlike the movies—is different. That if the actors are good, every performance tends to get better.

It's opening night, and the critics have come. I sit in the back row of the theater and watch the audience watching the play. No one moves. No one sniffles or coughs. The crowd is big, and it is interested. You can see them concentrating. When the curtain comes down at the end, the audience brings the actors back on with an avalanche of growing applause. It's clear that the play is a triumph. By the end of the run, it captures box office records. But we don't know that now. All I know—and I can tell by looking at the actors that they know—is that the first performance worked.

The actors have gone backstage to change. We are all invited to a party in the lobby with the audience and the critics. The audience is still clapping when the stage manager comes to me and says, "You have to go backstage. They want the playwright. The actors need to see you." I know I'll stumble around, perhaps trip over the props and sets back there, but I think the actors will forgive me, and so I go.

11

The Communion of Saints

ONE DAY IN THE FALL, I wake up alone. It's dark. There is an empty spot in the bed next to me, and I remember that my husband is working in another state. Through the window, I see a black shape tossing its leaves like the mane of a great tethered horse, as though it were trying to get away. The wind hisses. I smell wet earth. Seconds later, just after 7:00 a.m., our clock radio erupts with the news that there's a tornado watch. The storm might hit any time until two this afternoon. Feeling a smattering of rain blowing sideways into the open window, I get up, pull a hoodie over my nightgown, and tug at the window till it slams shut.

Rain is swilling down outside, splattering fatly into pools of standing water. I imagine the brown rabbit who lives in our backyard must be huddling under the rhododendrons. I envision my mother's grave, how she is lying in a tiny room under ground with rain pounding down, knocking, knocking. The untrustworthy body, the body that breaks down. I pray that is not the final, final end and try to imagine her in heaven, maybe sauntering with my father down a golden street or strolling by the river of life with her mother. But nope. I'm still here in our cold bedroom, which feels as lonely and primal as a cave.

Last night I made a list of chores I need to do today, but I can't remember where I put it. Dimly I remember that my husband is coming home this afternoon, and there's nothing in the house to eat, so I have to buy vegetables before I go to school to teach. Vegetables, I think, know about rain like this. They come from the earth. I flick the light switch, and suddenly I am looking at the jumble of last night's discarded clothes.

And then I am parking and walking toward Produce Junction. The rain has thinned to mist. The wind turns my umbrella inside out. Out of the corner of my eye, I notice a cardboard box flying through the air. Turning, I spot a semi filled with boxes of mushrooms. Apparently, the guy unloading his truck has stumbled and lost his footing, so hundreds and hundreds of button mushrooms are raining down all over the driveway and sidewalk. He curses vibrantly. Shoppers stop briefly to watch, snickering, then hurry on through the mist. He surveys the soggy mess, kneels to pick up the mushrooms, peers around at us, his audience, and grins. Some of us stop to help him. Hands of all sizes and shades and ages, mine among them, drop wet mushrooms into his box.

Produce Junction is a simple one-story shack slathered in dirty beige stucco. On its left stands an abandoned, rickety garage and to the right, an expanse of cracked sidewalk. As I juggle slippery mushrooms, I realize I've come here every day this week and I can't remember why. Not because I needed to buy food, I know. Although I can't afford the time to keep coming back, when I feel the call of the place, I come.

Inside the shack, a bank of dusty windows filters light, revealing how the main part of the building stretches back several hundred feet, thinning to a dim cave where workers drag and unload boxes. Above us, crude rafters are hung with light bulbs dangling from bare wires. I stand looking around until my eyes adjust to the dimness. There are about a dozen people cruising the fruit and vegetables.

A woman holds up a papaya. "What's this-here thang called?"

"You don't want them. They're overripe," a worker yells.

The place is filled with bins, and every bin is piled to tumbling with hunks and colors. The air in here smells like the earth and rocks and moss. None of the produce is labeled, either by name or with a price tag.

"These rutabagas is ugly as carp today!" an old Chinese lady complains to her husband.

A young mother barely misses me, sprinting for her toddler, who has dumped raspberries on the floor. She calls to her older daughter. "Samantha, will you get over here? And tell your sister to stop playing with the raspberries!"

Meanwhile, a tanned diva in dark glasses and toreador pants drifts from strawberries to the cantaloupe. She collides with a thin blond guy in a postal uniform who's just barreled in the front door. Outside someone blasts a horn, and I see the postman has double-parked his truck. As he brushes past Toreador Pants, he cheerfully calls back an apology. Then he seizes two cantaloupes from the bin, one in each hand like barbells, and goes to stand in line.

People are streaming around me, as if I were a statue of a woman, and I realize that I'm meditating in the doorway, that I need to move. When a worker walks by, carrying a cardboard box filled to the top with bright green dill, I follow him, or, rather, I follow the smell of the dill, which he is dumping into one of the bins. Running my hand over the wet, soft, ferny fronds, I pick up a bunch that's light as a handful of air. I take it over to the checkout line.

While we are standing in line, a worker in tall olive rubber boots appears from the back and orders us all to move to the left so he can hose down the floor. Someone has apparently just dropped a bunch of tomatoes, and they've been smashed to a bloody pulp by our feet. Like a chorus line, we obediently step to the left.

I didn't come for herbs. But for the rest of the day, my car is filled with the aroma of dill.

What I didn't understand at the time, what lay buried beneath a year of escalating visits to Produce Junction, was the fact that, six months earlier, I had lost my church.

We were gathering in the shabby, comfortable parish house, where a dozen of us vestry members had spent hundreds of hours considering furnace problems, worrying about our leaky nineteenth-century roof, poring over revisions in the liturgy, thinking of ways to get the Eucharist to shut-ins. I took pleasure in working through these problems because they brought us together, my friends, a group of warm, funny, smart parishioners.

One of them, still wearing her pea jacket, was passing around pictures of her gorgeous dark-haired children, and then another showed up with a big plate of brownies. I slipped out of my coat, draped it around a chair, and pulled up at the large table. Warmed by the smell of chocolate and surrounded by the sweet harmony of chatter, I studied the parish balance sheet, formidable tables and columns of numbers. The e-mail announcing this meeting had told us that we would be voting on a big budget question.

The meeting started with prayer. Then our priest explained that she felt we needed to hire an assistant. Unfortunately, however, the day-to-day expense of lighting and heat and salaries and shoveling the sidewalks was taking up our whole parish budget. And still, she said, she desperately needed someone to help her with her duties.

Our Finance Warden took over then saying that the main budget question was this: could we violate a trust agreement that had been set up fifty years ago? The trust, he said, had been made by an elderly couple who attended and supported the church for many years. In the 1950s, they gave a large bequest in exchange for a written and signed promise that none of the principal would ever be used to pay for day-to-day operating expenses. For over fifty years, the church had paid operating expenses from the trust's interest, but it had respected the terms of the agreement and never touched the principal.

Impatient with his long explanation, our priest stepped in and emphasized that she needed an assistant, she needed one badly, she said, and she wanted us to break the trust agreement.

The vestry sitting around the table became very quiet. We looked at our hands. After a few minutes of heavy silence, the priest told us she would go around the circle, one vestry member at a time, and each of us had to tell her how we would vote.

It made me feel panicky to be put on the spot in this way. A river of fear and resentment rose in my chest as one friend after another spoke, and the focus moved closer to me. I worried about some of my friends, too, who were more diffident than I.

The first three or four vestry members, one by one, agreed with our priest that she had a lot to do. And after all, none of us knew the couple who had bequeathed the money. Moreover, it was a long time ago. The first four members of the vestry said they felt it would be okay to violate the trust.

About the time our priest got to me, the river of anger inside me reached flood stage and was filling up my throat, so I spoke faintly. I didn't think we needed an assistant, I said, since we averaged fewer than a hundred people in church on Sunday mornings, though I confess I was also thinking of the fact that our priest had just enrolled in a graduate program that was sapping her time. I said I thought that before we hired an assistant, we should work on attracting more members, and then maybe we would be able to afford an assistant without breaking the trust.

Our priest fixed her eyes on me, her face reddening, and asked whether I didn't think I should have more faith. She waited for me to answer.

I didn't know what to say. I found myself looking at her awkwardly while the silence accumulated.

God's just testing us to see whether we have faith, she explained to me. The point is not some legal document. We need the funds now, and we *have* the funds. This trust belongs to us. God is faithful, she told me, and he'll replenish whatever we take out.

I said, if we had made a promise to the old couple, I thought God would honor us for keeping our promise.

It wasn't *us* who made the promise, she told me. That was fifty years ago. And when they signed that contract, they didn't realize we'd need the money now.

"The people who signed the contract," I said, "were the church then. And we're the church now. The *church* promised."

My friends on the vestry gazed out the window. The smell of the hyacinths in the vase on the table all of a sudden seemed to stain the air with overbearing scent. A door slammed loudly in the hall.

This is a dark time, the priest went on, like Good Friday. A dark time. Dark times are precisely when we need to trust God. She looked pointedly at me and asked whether I trusted God.

This time she didn't leave space for me to answer. It was several weeks after Easter. She was wearing her collar and revving up the decibels. She slipped into a sermonizing cadence and went on for a long time, while I looked around the room at the bright watercolor paintings by Sunday school children.

"What *you* need is Good Friday faith," she concluded, gazing directly at me. "If you don't have Good Friday faith, you shouldn't be on the vestry."

The priest paused, waiting for me to answer, but I felt claustrophobic and powerless to reply. I thought we were supposed to be having a discussion, airing different points of view about whether we needed an assistant and, if so, where to get money to hire one, but the issue, as she defined it, was whether I had faith. I felt so mortified by the way she had singled me out that I couldn't think of a way to respond. Maybe she's right, I thought. Maybe I shouldn't be on the vestry.

"I vote against breaking the trust," was all I could think of to say.

Her piercing black-eyed gaze dwelled on me briefly, then traveled on to the next vestry member. Five of us voted against breaking the trust, but there were a dozen of us altogether, so we went ahead and broke the couple's trust and took funds from their principal to place an ad for an assistant rector, and we paid him every month with the money the donors said we were legally barred from using.

Since our priest had told me so publicly that I didn't belong on the vestry, for several weeks I wrestled over whether I should resign, but that seemed unfair to the people who had elected me. So I finished my term.

After that, I didn't go back to church.

As I am walking toward Produce Junction, a guy driving an eighteen-wheeler leans out his window and bellows at me to get out of the way. He swings his rig onto the sidewalk, jumps down from his cab,

The Communion of Saints

and at the rear of the truck, leans his upper body on the lever to raise the heavy door. Then he begins unloading wooden crates marked EGGPLANT.

I can't remember what I came for. I don't even recall the drive over. I must have been listening to NPR, letting the car drive itself. I warn myself about how unsafe that is, and a cold wind blows through my heart. I plunge my hands into my jeans pocket to feel for my grocery list. Light bulbs, it says. Freezer bags. Cereal. Half and half. Nothing I can buy here.

I think about leaving, but instead I stand and watch.

"You know anything about this vegetable?" a young woman asks the clerk at the checkout counter.

"Kohlrabi."

"What do you do with kohlrabi?"

"You cook it, ma'am. Did you want these peppers?" The clerk holds up a plastic bag of red peppers. Sassy, glossy, exquisite.

I find myself stopping by the market regularly, four or five times a week now. It's almost winter. The workers are bundled in coats and brown cloth gloves, and some of them wear earmuffs as they dump boxes of carrots into tubs and sweep the cement floor. I shiver in the freezing draughts blowing through the windows and walls. Today the apple bins are full of fruit hardly bigger than golf balls. *That's what nature can do to you*, the management seems to be saying, so that's what I pick up. If I think about it the right way, I can imagine these stunted apples blew down in our own backyard.

Since there are no shopping carts or baskets, we hug the dirty produce in our arms. Stuff topples to the floor. I lose a bunch of grapes, squat gracefully, side saddle, and swipe at the floor, just missing them. My bag of apples tumbles to the ground. When I lean over to pick up my apples, the bananas and broccoli fall.

An Asian teenager with tattoos, long black hair, and an earflap hat stops, bends down, picks up my produce, and plunks things back in my arms. His tattooed hand sweeps against my hand.

"Thank you," I say in surprise.

"Hey, no problem," he replies, trotting off toward the flowers.

I cradle my fruit and vegetables, walking over to stand in line.

The lady in front of me turns. She's African American with ample hips, and she is wearing dark blue jeans with rolled-up cuffs, boots. Over it she has thrown a fake tiger cape.

"I'll never use all this zucchini," she says. "Take a few."

I'm a million miles away, thinking about something else. I can't remember a stranger ever asking me to split an order before this. I don't need zucchini, or I'd have picked some up. I want to help her out, but I'm worried that so many vegetables will rot in my refrigerator, and then I will be responsible for wasting food. Besides, I don't know the etiquette for transactions with other shoppers.

I balance my stuff, manage to pull a dollar out of my pocket, and offer it to the lady with the zucchini. She waves me off with long, graceful red fingernails. I ask her whether she'd like some yellow squash. She says thank you, but she doesn't need any. She lays three big zucchinis atop the produce in my arms, lifts her bags with poise, and walks out.

I stand holding my produce with her zucchini on top. I realize with a pang that I might not see her again, that I have accepted vegetables from her and will not have a chance to pay her back. I don't know whether I've won or lost, and then I am taken aback by my way of measuring the exchange. It feels so limited and competitive.

That night I think about the zucchini woman, and again the next morning, I remember her. I believe I've seen her at Produce Junction before, maybe more than once. I decide to look for her next time I'm there. Sometime after that, the truth dawns on me: it was when I stopped going to church that I started driving to Produce Junction almost every day.

My first reason for loving Produce Junction was because it's so cheap: five eggplants for a dollar, a box of raspberries for two dollars. Finding the place felt like discovering that Aladdin's lamp is really a garden and that we'll never go hungry. Like many children of Depression parents, I adore bargains. I come from a grandfather who once bought a thousand trailer hitches because he could get them for a nickel apiece. No wonder I was thrilled to get three bags of celery for a dollar. The fact that I had to buy three, if I bought any at all, didn't worry me. I took them home and stashed them in our refrigerator.

In a month or so, I had to carry two soft, blackening bunches of celery to the trash, because we just don't eat that much celery. One of the main differences between celery and trailer hitches, I realized, is that celery goes bad and trailer hitches don't. For five years, my grandfather sold trailer hitches, one by one, to filling station attendants across the state of Minnesota, and eventually he made a profit. But I began to live on fairly close terms with death. There was nearly always a vegetable or fruit in my refrigerator in some stage of decomposition—softening, molding, rotting into black liquid. This didn't represent a waste of money because they had been so cheap, but every time I had to clean a corrupting bunch of asparagus from our vegetable cooler, I felt a little sick.

I decided to take responsibility for the surplus. So I started to give vegetables and fruit to neighbors and to our grown children. I still do, feeling slightly apologetic as I hand the stuff over, but my victims bear my gifts of peaches or arugula or scallions with patience. They thank me and assure me it will be useful. Still, forcing vegetables on them feels slightly un-American, because America is about choice, and my friends don't get to choose what I give them. The fact is, what I bring home isn't exactly my choice either.

One day I walk into Produce Junction looking for russets. Not only is the market out of russets, they have two bins of brussels sprouts instead of any broccoli. The beets are scaly and misshapen and clotted with a little mud. It all makes me a bit irritable. I think of driving to Super Fresh. But I've already figured out that one of the reasons I return to this shack is that I rather like working around the seasons. I don't mind if some things aren't available. At least, I say that I *like* craving what's not there, looking forward to the first whiff of asparagus in the spring, anticipating the way it resists a fork, imagining its buttered taste. If I have to improvise meals around what's available, I feel in partnership with the earth. If I have to think about collaborating with nature, I remember I am not the creator; I am a creature.

After the vestry meeting where we voted to violate the elderly couple's trust, I didn't merely leave one church for another. I went on strike. One year with no church stretched to two. Sometimes I tried other churches, but just showing up and sitting in the pew would turn me into a lump of self-righteous, critical protoplasm without grace or charm or a sense of humor. When I am thinking of someone I can't forgive, I become the sort of person I hate. Many members of my old church scattered to other parishes, and we sometimes brooded together on the various offenses of the spirit that had occurred there. We felt excluded and violated. I had enough sense to know that after sharing the Eucharist with friends every week for decades, I'd feel lonely if I gave it up, but every time I got close to any church, misery shut me down.

Following the mushroom incident, as I drove to school through the rain, I thought maybe gathering mushrooms in that storm was so crucial to me because in my suburb there isn't much street life. The summer my husband and I first moved here from the city, I remember, we ate breakfast on the front porch, thinking we would get to know our neighbors that way. After three weeks, I realized the reason there are no people on the street is because when we leave our houses, we get into our cars in our backyards. And coming home, I pull into the back, as we all do. It's no wonder we don't see one another. True, we do have block parties and we meet over lawn mowers in the summer. We share an amiable mailman and ask our neighbors to feed our cat when we're on vacation, but we don't see one another frequently.

And beyond that, I realized there are very few places where Americans get to talk to people of other ages and races. Supermarkets are amphitheaters with nervous music and garish lights. When I'm there, I don't talk to neighbors; I feel mesmerized. I've read that the aisles are specifically designed to move us along because the store has only so many shopping carts, only so much space. Since I've been shopping at Produce Junction, I've noticed that the food in supermarkets is trimmed and injected with color, waxed and sealed under plastic. Supermarkets aren't about human connection or about a connection with nature. I don't remember ever having an opportunity for insight on a moral behavior in the supermarket.

A couple of days later I am driving to Produce Junction, imagining the pungent aroma of fresh lemons which are the *sine qua non* for our evening's dessert. We don't usually have dessert, but tonight we are celebrating the successful end of a big project. I walk directly to the fruit and discover the lemons are almost gone. I'm vaguely aware that an older woman with a soft, powdered face is circling the herbs. She's dressed as if for church or a concert, in a good quality, loopy black wool coat with a big flowered scarf tied at her neck. I lunge toward the last bag of lemons just as she floats to a stop in front of the bin. Our hands meet. We both withdraw. I'm moving faster, with more certainty, and I got there first. But she is older.

She gives me an appraising look.

"Go ahead," she says. "You were here before me."

Her expression is that of someone pleasant and eager to please. Maybe this trip is her outing for the day. Maybe she has gotten dressed just to come here. Maybe she is determined to have a good time, whatever happens.

But her voice conveys disapproval. I consider what to do. There's no time for another stop. It's these lemons or none. Nevertheless, I think I ought to let her have them. That will show her she's not a victim, which might be good for her, I think, with entirely too much self-righteousness.

The woman and I each politely urge the other to go first until the exchange feels embarrassing. I give in and grab the lemons. I take them home, and we have a splendid dinner. But I don't eat any of the lemon torte because I'm realizing what I could have done that might have made me happier than dessert. I should have picked the lemons up and put them in her hands.

That evening it dawns on me that what happens at Produce Junction is not unlike what happens at the Eucharistic table. Maybe that sounds blasphemous. But for me buying produce was by then tangled up with the mystery of being fed. Those of us who regularly come to Produce Junction come for food and for fellowship.

The first time I left a church, I was twenty. I'd been sitting in a pew in our Baptist church like a ventriloquist's dummy for months—no, for years, so many years that my mind and soul were full of sawdust. I no longer believed I would find anything holy there, so I didn't. The truth is, instead of encountering God, I tended to spend the time cataloguing everything that was wrong with the place. During one Sunday evening service, I found myself holding a list which I had scribbled in pencil on the service bulletin. It was numbered. It was a grudge list. When I realized that, the penny dropped.

I needed to be sorry so I could be forgiven. But I wasn't sorry. I felt I was right. It was a terrible, terrible church. But at least I realized that criticizing the church was getting me nowhere. Maybe it would be better to stop going to church at all than to go to a place where my main activity was to feel superior. Slumping there in the pew under the fluorescent lights, I decided that the next Sunday I would try St. Mark's Episcopal in the neighboring suburb. I had friends who loved that place.

Sitting in my Baptist church for the last time, I thought with irony that no one knew what I had just decided. The last time you perform some actions is marked and celebrated. There are little ceremonies, for instance, marking the last day of school, marking the day you stop being forty-nine years old. But leaving church doesn't get commemorated. It's unremarked, like the last time you see your mother. As I plotted to leave my fundamentalist people, they stood around me singing, *Let the Lower Lights Be Burning.* No one guessed my spot would be empty next week and the next and the next.

That week I felt like a weedy, vacant lot with the wind whistling through it. But I didn't go back on my decision. I just hedged a little. I would try St. Mark's, yes, fair enough, but I reserved the right to go back to my fundamentalist people if I couldn't deal with the new, strange religion I might find in the Episcopal church.

From the minute I passed through its red door, St. Mark's electrified me. At the end of the service, the priest yelled, *Thanks be to God!* and everyone shouted, *Thanks be to God. Alleluia. Alleluia!* I felt off balance and out of place and humble. I couldn't find the right pages in the prayer book. When I sipped the real alcoholic wine from the chalice, a disconcerting buzz filled my head, and I worried about catching a cold from the shared germs. During the entire first week afterward, I feared punishment from God, which my fundamentalist people said He visited on people who turned to false religion. But astonishingly, as I kept returning to St. Mark's, the language of the prayer book seemed to express exactly what I felt. I realized it was becoming *my* prayer book. I would catch my breath, close my eyes, and grip the back of the pew in front of me.

This is what I gave up when I gave up my church after the terrible vestry meeting. This is what I gave up: worshipping with friends I think of as the communion of saints.

I keep driving back to Produce Junction three or four times a week, even though I think my attraction to this place is preposterous. I have shopped at produce markets on the streets of Bogota and Paris and London and Barcelona. I have shopped at street markets in small Maine villages, in California, in Vancouver, and in Minnesota towns. Unlike many of them, Produce Junction isn't outdoors, and it isn't run by the people who grow the food and it's not organic, and I don't have any idea what the place pays its workers.

I have begun to think about the workers there the way I used to think about our neighborhood filling station attendants, not as friends, exactly, but as minor stars, revolving within my galaxy. Some look Eastern European. One Saturday two of them listened sympathetically to my inquiries about whether one of the plants was an annual or a perennial, then smiled and shrugged, meaning they'd answer if only they could understand the question. Some of the workers are teenagers who, I suspect, might more profitably be in school. Several of the women laugh and comment to one another in Spanish, probably about us shoppers. Or is it paranoid to imagine that?

I want to think the faces of the workers at Produce Junction are full of character, but I know I might be partly inventing that. One late middle-aged man with a theatrical, expressive face and sproingy curls said, each time he gave me change, *Make this a good day.* I never took this lightly, but then, suddenly, he disappeared, and where he's gone, I don't know.

These people must often be bored or tired, I think. In the winter they are probably cold and, in the summer, hot. The week before Christmas I bring them a tin of cookies. I would like to bake for them, but I don't, since I know that to the people who work there, I am The Public. They have to be suspicious. They need a seal they can break, so they know the cookies are not contaminated.

I don't recognize many shoppers at Produce Junction, and that doesn't matter. I don't mind coming and going as a stranger. When I'm there, I don't have to pretend to be more patient or reliable or smarter than I am. What I do will not affect my status or job. It will not shape the ongoing persona other people know as me. It's enough, I think, that the choices I make there frequently reveal me to myself. Sometimes I am decent, sometimes truly awful.

So I'm standing in the vegetable market, coming to terms with the fact that we aren't going to have russets for dinner tonight. Then I notice broccoli on the floor, stoop down, retrieve it, and replace it in the arms of the woman who just dropped it. She's wearing a Chanel-style jacket and a black hat with a black veil. It was the slender, tattooed Asian teenager who taught me to pick vegetables up from the floor and return them to their owner. As I put the broccoli into the woman's hands, the warmth of her hand reminds me of passing the peace.

The word *peace* passes through me like a radio wave.

And I know, suddenly I *know*, that I am no longer holding a grudge, that I can return to church. I stand for a minute in the middle of the people and vegetables, while foolish tears swim in my eyes. The bins blur until they shimmer like jewels.

The next Sunday I wait outside a simple old brick church in Philadelphia under a canopy of maples, surrounded by graves that date back to the sixteen-hundreds, and listen to the congregation sing *All Hail the Power of Jesus' Name*. I walk by a big maroon sandwich board welcoming visitors to enter through the large white doors, which are propped wide open. I'm feeling nervous, slightly nauseated. I don't know exactly why I am so afraid. When the last notes of the hymn fade, I gather my courage and step onto the stone floor of the church, feeling the air shift slightly to coolness. A man in a suit hands me a bulletin. I find a pew, pick up the prayer book, which feels in my hands like my own prayer book, and begin reciting the confession with the rest of the congregation.

12

Christmas: The View from Prison

BING CROSBY CROONS "I'll be home for Christmas," as I pull into a muddy space in the prison parking lot. I snap the sentimental song off and then run with my head down through the spitting sleet, my sneakers splashing. The front door is bolted, as usual, so I press the red button in the pelting ice, keep pressing it, until I hear a buzzer. I lunge for the door, but even my split-second dive doesn't catch it before it automatically locks again—as if the door itself were determined to keep the prisoners inside and everyone else out. The women here are not waiting for Christmas, I realize. They are waiting for their sentences to be served.

The waiting room, when I finally get in, gives no hint of Christmas. It's cheaply tiled in beige with dirty blond wooden chairs arranged in a small square. A heavy-set, uniformed female guard appraises me from behind her fortified desk, then growls, "Get that pocketbook outta here."

"Yes ma'am."

"Your keys, your books, and a pencil. That's it." Her voice is stern.

I thank her and step back into the freezing drizzle. I want to keep the guards happy. Prison rules don't allow me to go beyond the front desk unless I'm accompanied by a guard, and I have found that guards can easily make themselves unavailable.

Christmas: The View from Prison

Three years ago, I signed up to teach writing to the women at Baylor Women's Correctional Institution. As the first day approached, I began to fret, wondering what language the prisoners and I could speak to one another. I had never known a prisoner, had never stepped inside a prison. I promised to show up on a Friday afternoon in October for a meeting with the Volunteer Coordinator and one of my university faculty colleagues, who, I discovered, had also committed herself to teaching at Baylor. On the hot, moonless October night, before I was scheduled to drive to the prison, the air in Philadelphia was thick with humidity. I pitched and tossed in bed, flung the covers off, yanked them back, and finally fell asleep.

The training session for volunteers was run by a short, bald, uniformed African American officer, who warned us not to reveal our names or anything else about ourselves to the "offenders," as he called the women. We were not to invite them to talk about their personal lives, and we were not to reveal anything unless we wanted to find them stalking us years after they had been released. "These women are expert cons," he told us. "If they weren't when they got to prison, they've learned by now."

At that, a woman in a lovely blue silk scarf raised her hand. "What do you mean—cons?" she asked.

"They'll use you."

"Use us for what?" she asked politely.

"To bring in bullet."

She looked puzzled.

"That's what they call drugs."

"Or to angle for a jackrabbit parole." He went on to explain that they could dupe us easily, green as we were. "For example," he said, "you don't wear that scarf around your neck in here." He paused. "I shouldn't have to explain why."

Everyone chuckled grimly.

He went on. No jewelry. (I learned to slide my wedding rings onto the candle on our dinner table Friday mornings before I drove to Baylor.) No jeans, bright colors, or sleeveless shirts, no short skirts or tight pants, no coded clothing of any kind, not even red and green at Christmas. We were forbidden to bring the women presents or to offer them cookies or candy. Surprisingly, we were permitted to call them by their first names, though the staff called them by their last names, as in, "Nelson, what are you doing over there?" I thought about that with irony later when I got to know Jody, who was called by the name of the man she had married and—after years of abuse—had finally killed. She couldn't even get away from him in prison.

When I returned to the waiting room after sequestering my purse in the trunk of my car, my colleague, Deb, had arrived. We greeted one another formally and chatted as we waited for a guard. Before we were allowed to enter the cell area, the guard ordered us to give our keys and driver's licenses to the officer at the front desk. In return, we were given badges that clipped onto our collars, identifying us as visitors. As I handed over my keys and license, I was aware that I was giving away proof, not only of my identity—if I needed it—but also of my ability to drive away from the prison. The guards didn't know most of the volunteers. They didn't even know all the prisoners; they recognized the women mainly by their polyester uniforms, which were shapeless and color-coded by unit. If a prisoner locked one of us in a closet and donned our street clothes—as had happened two weeks earlier in the men's state prison—she might hope to slip out as a visitor. But for her to get away, in a car at least, the system required that she check in with the front desk for keys.

Soon Deb and I were called to enter the cell area. Two massive sides of an enormous iron floor-to-ceiling door slid apart. A burly guard in a gray uniform stood there with a holstered gun at his hip. He accompanied us down the walkway, as the eighteen-foot stockade door behind us sealed itself shut.

"What a day!" I said to the guard, who was looking straight ahead.

"Yes, ma'am."

"I hope it stops raining."

"Yes, ma'am."

"Have you-all had your lunch?" Deb inquired.

"Yes, ma'am."

"Thanks for walking us down."

"Yes, ma'am." He opened a door and held it while we entered the room.

Minutes later, fifteen women in loose-fitting maroon prison smocks and pants filed into the prison's cement block room to sit in front of us at cheap wooden desks. Some gazed at us coolly, some smiled, some stared defiantly, one slapped rhythm on the table with her hands, only to be hooted at and reprimanded by others sitting around her. Several intimate groups of two sat close and murmured to each other. The guard who had escorted Deb and me to the room left us sitting together at the front desk with the chattering women under the glaring fluorescent lights.

My colleague and I persuaded the women to get quiet, finally, then introduced ourselves. We handed them the composition books and pens and colorful folders I had bought for them. They eagerly jockeyed and scrambled to get their favorite colors. Then we handed out a syllabus for the first few weeks' lessons. They listened as each of us spent a couple of minutes explaining our vision for the class. We would give them Xeroxes of reading they could do during the week. We would talk and write about it together the following Friday. We explained with regret that we had no way of supplying them with books, and they informed us that they had no place to keep books anyway, a discussion which led to their long and passionate complaints that they had no privacy and no personal space. We could change that, one of them suggested. Yes, the others agreed. We should help them redefine the rules of the prison.

They didn't raise their hands, they shouted, sometimes over one another. We suggested that they talk one-at-a-time, which would require that they raise their hands. They booed and murmured disapproval. I worried that they must think we were turning out to be like all the other teachers they'd ever had, rule-driven and condescending. I felt disappointed; I had hoped that some of the women, at least, would be eager learners, happy finally to find a way to develop their skills. The chaos of that first session left me feeling swamped, engulfed, overwhelmed. Deborah and I left together, trying to grasp and understand what we had signed up for. We agreed as we walked to our cars that we would meet at the local Dunkin' Donuts at noon the next Friday to plan our hour-long session with the women.

When I got to Dunkin' Donuts the next Friday and stepped over the wet gray mop of a youngster who was cleaning the floor, I ordered coffee, black, from the sweet, skinny high school student behind the counter. Deb arrived a couple of minutes later, hugging her cardboard box of papers and pens, which she set down on a table. Although we barely knew one another, we greeted each other with the sort of affection we might have felt for a colleague with whom we were soon to face devouring lions. Then we began hammering out a syllabus for our one o'clock class.

At the second class, fewer women showed up. We handed out Xeroxes of short essays, explaining that to get into college or to apply for a job they would probably have to write short answers to employers' questions. To learn to write well, we argued, it would be helpful to read examples of good writing and use them as patterns.

A rap at the door interrupted us. I hollered, "Come in." The volunteer coordinator stepped in and called out names from his list. "Smith. Baxter. Johnson." Obediently several women rose, headed for the door, and disappeared. This happened every week with different women. It became clear that we could not establish a group of women who would be available to work with us every week to master one skill and then another and another.

As the months went on, my colleague and I pieced together the facts we were gleaning from the patchwork of conversation: that the women in our class lived in three or four different prison units and they were "in" for assorted offences—drug and alcohol crimes, shoplifting, embezzlement, assault, disorderly conduct and, of course, murder. We knew that serving time in prison, no matter how short, might destroy their chance of being hired for a good job in the future, but the record of their consistent attendance in a writing class might help them to prove their worthiness for future positions. In fact, steady attendance in the writing class even could have helped those who had

Christmas: The View from Prison

not yet been sentenced. It could document their good behavior to a judge who might have shortened their sentences.

But only four or five of the women showed up for class consistently. The following week, even these women dribbled in twenty minutes late, telling us they had been released late by guards from their different units. We didn't know: had they? Only three or four said they had done some of the reading, and maybe they had, but no matter how we tried, we couldn't convince them to talk about it. I suspect they didn't know how to participate in a discussion that appeared to them trivial compared to their daily drudgery and their shame at being incarcerated. As we encouraged them to participate, the women drummed their pencils on the table, they fussed with their hair. They made jokes about one another that flared into petty quarrels.

When I read their first three paragraph essays, I was struck by how many of them muddled verbs. Their mistakes were strangely different from those of freshman students at the university. Some of our women seemed to use, higgledy-piggledy, whatever verb tense came to mind. Others consistently employed past tense with baffling excursions into past perfect or future. *He drives. He drove. He is driving. He will drive. He's driven.* I began to realize that some of them, especially those serving long sentences, seemed to have come totally unmoored from our generally understood, seemingly "natural" system of verbs.

Verbs, of course, express actions that happen in the past or in the present or in the future. "Doing time" in prison apparently had messed with their ability to conceptualize time—not only on paper, but in their own lives. I wondered: if they can't tell themselves the stories of their own past, how can they understand themselves? How can they change? What a third grader could tell you in perfect sequence, these women could not.

Because of their writing, in spite of severe warnings during our volunteer orientation at Baylor not to engage in personal conversation, after almost four years with them, I know a little about who the ladies are: one is resigned to being treated by prison doctors for what she says she is sure is a brain tumor. She expects to die in her cell. Several claim they are about to be released. Most of them spend their days watching TV, and the shows are what they talk about the most. They laugh more easily than I do. Some of them seem motherly and have found another more vulnerable prisoner to take under their wings. (Prison literature suggests that these relationships are often gay. Whatever—they are real and deeply felt.) A few are smart alecks; several are sober and motivated students. Most of them are loveable.

Together, over years, they have formed a complex social and political status and relational system, which I have only begun to figure out. They are not allowed to own much: soap, a toothbrush, some snapshots. One of the women owns a Thesaurus, and when the others don't know what a word means, they pester her until she looks it up. One, whose daughter goes to junior college, asked me to bring the novels and poems her child was reading so she could read them at the same time; she reeled off titles and authors of obscure nineteenth-century British novels. I brought her the paperbacks she wanted from my own shelves.

Inevitably I met Barbara, a woman who wasn't in our class, a lifer, a slip of a woman with no teeth, her lips sunken, her face deeply lined and the color of a walnut shell. Barbara appeared to be seventy or so. She hung around in the computer room and offered to help some of our students who were having trouble logging on. On the Friday before Christmas, as I walked with a guard from the entrance to the classroom, I saw her watering a plant in the hall. She perked up and waved a smiling hello. When Barbara and I were stuck alone together during a lockdown for a couple of hours, she told me about the prison garden, which she had started years earlier. The kitchen was using lettuce from her garden for dinner that night, and she was babying tomato plants at windows inside to get them through the cold January into the spring so they could bear. I believed her, but now I am not so sure. She spoke with a Southern accent and confided that she was Jewish and that she was terribly worried about a cactus that had been overwatered and was getting brown. I asked if she wanted me to bring her a Christmas cactus, and she excitedly agreed.

Christmas: The View from Prison

So on Monday I called the Volunteer Coordinator to get permission to bring it in. No, he said. Absolutely Not.

Baylor isn't visible from the highway. The first day I tried to drive to the prison, my GPS couldn't locate it; it doesn't exist on my GPS map. That seems like an accurate metaphor for how we Americans think about our local prisons. The only hint of Baylor is a sign beside the turn-off from Route 13 which is so small that, although I was looking for it, I drove by it three times before I saw it. The turnoff leads to a paved road that curves through a mile of uncultivated woods to a clearing far behind Route 13. Any inmate who could escape from the prison would find it nearly impossible to cross the rough forest on foot, and if she did, she would find herself facing a fast four-lane divided highway.

It's Christmas now again, and I know that our women will not celebrate what for me is among the most holy days of the year. They will not be gathering to sing "Joy to the World." They will not be setting a table with Lenox or any other kind of china. They will not be roasting a turkey and mashing potatoes for their kids. They will not be opening presents; they will most certainly not be giving any. Visitation rules limit each of them to two adults and one child or one adult and two children per day, and they can have visitors for only one hour around noon. There is an increasing body of literature that argues prisons may help purge criminals from society, but at what cost? The American way of imprisonment leaves these women worse when they are discharged from prison than when they entered. They leave prison bereft of their families and work; they often revert to their old neighborhoods and their crime buddies.

Meanwhile, at Christmas the choir at St. Peter's here in Philadelphia this week will be singing "O Little Town of Bethlehem" and "Hark the Herald Angels Sing" and "Joy to the World." The music will thrust us into time-out-of-time, to celebrate the birth of the Holy Child into human history. As Frederick Buechner has written, "history itself falls in two at the star" that stood above the Christ Child in the manger. Our celebration of Christmas with its soaring music, its winsome clothes, its Christmas cards, its beautifully decorated trees, its feasts, its family gatherings, its vibrant creativity offers us every year a heavenly rest from what can sometimes seem, even to those of us outside prison, a daily slog. The church calls non-holy days "ordinary time." Once a year Christmas interrupts ordinary time, elevating us to a different sense of time—transcendence—as we celebrate God's coming to us from beyond time.

But the strict, rule-governed drudgery of prison makes transcendence seem impossible for its inmates. The prison building itself offers little to the women except routinized ugliness. If beauty can save the world, as Gregory Wolfe argues, what chance do these women have? Finally, the most horrible punishment the women at Baylor endure is to never be able to leave ordinary time. Prison makes many of them grimly aware that they will be putting in one dull, lonely, repetitive day after another, many of them for decades. I imagine they will spend the coming Christmas day in their cells, as usual. They tell me they have been forgotten by their people. Prison rules and staff vacations make it well-nigh impossible for the women to enjoy visits, even from their spouses and children, at Christmas.

Heading toward my fourth Christmas at Baylor, I know none of our women have written long enough or clearly enough for me to help them find a place to publish their work. Maybe they will never write their stories for publication. Instead, I have written this for them. I have a lot in common with these women. Many of us were raised as fundamentalists, and we have strayed from that path. We love our children. We are all "doing time" until we die, though I have been blessed with liberty and choices they can only dream of now. Ironically, getting to know inmates at Baylor Women's Correctional Institution has made the world a less frightening place for me than it might be if all I did was to drive by the prison and think of the women as Dangerous Others. My truest Christmas gift this year has been my discovery that words can sometimes connect me with the women at Baylor in love instead of fear.

13

Deeper than Memory

FAR AWAY, AS IF THROUGH mist, I hear my husband calling my name. Swimming up from a dream, I roll over, feeling tightness wrench my back as I open my eyes. He's leaning on one elbow in bed, facing me, softly repeating, *Jeanne, Jeanne, Jeanne, Jeanne.* In the milky gloom, I can barely make out his figure.

We're in a hotel in Paris. That much I remember.

"What?" I say, feeling annoyed. I don't get back to sleep easily.

"I think something's happened to your mother," he says.

Sitting bolt upright in the frigid dark, I quickly yank the duvet around my shoulders, watching as he rummages on the floor. I press the stem of my watch, illuminating the face, and see that it's 2:30 a.m.

My husband is mistaken, I think. How can he possibly know that something is wrong with my mother? She's in Dallas. He's just jumpy. We're both jumpy after so much bad news: my mother's been in a car accident; the Christian Care Center is moving her to the Alzheimer's unit; she has broken her hip; she needs hospice care.

My husband sits in bed pushing buttons on his cell phone, dialing, then pressing the phone against his ear. The curtains ripple. I can hear the monotonous, vengeful January wind whipping the trees outside.

"Hi Rich," my husband says.

Rich is my brother-in-law in Dallas.

Silence. Then my husband looks troubled.

He takes the phone away from his ear. "Your mother has died," he tells me.

I try to believe this news, but I don't really understand it. How did he know? How did he know? He holds out the phone.

I accept the receiver.

"We were with her," Rich tells me. "She was asleep. She didn't seem to be in any pain. She never woke up."

With Alzheimer's, I know, finally the brain and lungs shut down. But the rate at which the body shuts down varies so much with each victim that no one can predict what month or even what year the shutdown will happen. I thought, as the doctors did, that we had many months to go.

It is a cold January and outside, cracking sounds come from the bare treetops. I can see the eerie shadows of branches thrashing against the filmy curtains. The wind moves the drapes, and I hunch further down into the blankets. My hands feel numb, and I can't seem to make my mind work. Rich goes on talking calmly, a man who has been through many emergencies, offering me valuable facts in his calm voice, the equivalent of throwing a life preserver to a struggling swimmer.

"One of her favorite aides was there, and the hospice nurse," he says.

"I'm glad."

"You want to talk to Julie?" he offers.

"Yes."

After she takes the phone, Julie announces, "You don't have to come home."

"Oh, but I want to."

"Don't you have to teach over there for another week?"

I fumble, trying to think of an answer, while she waits patiently. My husband is pulling on his clothes. When he turns on the light, the massive ornate furniture rears up around us, a walnut dresser, the maroon duvet with a green and white paisley pattern. He is at the window, drawing back the curtains at one corner to look out.

"I *want* to come," I say.

"How many students do you have?"

"Twenty."

"You can't leave them in the middle of the program, can you?"

"I don't know what would happen."

"I can take care of things here," she says.

By *things*, she must mean the body. She means my mother's body has to be buried, the final thing we can do for her. My mother looked like a little hollowed-out canoe a month ago when I last saw her. She weighed barely a hundred pounds.

For six or seven years my sister and I together have taken care of our mother's clothes, her medicine, her friends, her housing. Julie does most of it because she lives in Dallas. But I fly there three or four times a year to go through her closet, buy her shoes with rubber soles, take her to lunch in a restaurant, encourage her friends to keep visiting her, bring candy to her nurses, stock her apartment with flowers, whatever I can think of. For years Julie and I have been writing one another long emails scheming about how to get her to stop driving, what might keep her occupied and challenged, what we can do to keep her place from smelling. Together we cluck and fuss over her, and, in the process, we are getting to know one another, coming to rely on one another.

I understand this, too, has now come to an end. I understand it better than I understand the fact that my mother is dead.

"Promise me something," I say to Julie.

"What?"

"That we'll still get together."

"Sure," Julie replies.

The wind rattles the glass in the windows. My husband is going through the receipts in his billfold, glancing over at me from time to time.

"Promise me we'll have family reunions every year," I say to my sister.

"Okay."

"The whole family."

"Yes."

"Really?"

"Yeah."

"Can I call you tomorrow?"

"Fine. And if you can't come home, we really are okay here."

It's a long night. Time slows down, lengthens, stretches out. We sleep fitfully, or rather, we don't sleep, lying in a semi-wakeful stupor of strange, distorted thoughts and images.

The next day, Sunday, charcoal clouds hang low over Paris, and the air is gray. While we drink coffee and eat croissants in a neighborhood hole-in-the-wall, we locate an internet cafe on a jaunty, brightly colored tourist map. Precisely at nine, when the cafe opens, we pull on our hats and coats and gloves and step out into the January wind to look for it. We need to email my office and call to tell our children about their grandmother.

The trouble is, I can't remember the names of streets. A few minutes after I see a name on the side of a building, it erases itself from my mind. I am supposed to be the navigator, but we wander like homeless people, finally realizing that we've looped past the same stores several times. We stop in a computer store so my husband can ask for directions in his elementary French, which is better than mine, and then we start out again, in the opposite direction, where the kind salesperson has told him, in French, to go. Following this route for a mile or so, we turn left and then right, but find no internet cafe. So my husband steps into a stationers' to ask again. Again, we set out. My feet are so icy by now that I can't use my toes for balance, and I feel as if any moment I may topple over. I open and shut my hands inside my gloves to get the blood going, and as we trudge, I begin to recognize buildings, and slowly realize that we are moving back toward the restaurant where we had breakfast. We have wandered for almost the whole day, it seems to me, though when I look at my watch, I discover that it's only eleven. We hone ourselves like zombies to find some internet cafe, because we are carrying news that we must tell. We must let people know that everything has changed, that nothing will ever again be the same.

Deeper than Memory

Around noon we are exhausted and frozen, and when we find ourselves close to Notre Dame Cathedral, we join a stream of worshippers flooding through the immense doors. In the dimness, it takes my eyes time to adjust. Daylight shines weakly through the splinters of stained glass in the great rose window, illuminating vivid points of ruby and gold and blue. I hang onto these pricks of light with my eyes as we settle in the nave, surrounded by French people, mainly, I think. They are stylish, even the shabby ones, with a hat or a distinctive tie pin or a black and white checked coat.

As the massive congregation of strangers stands and steers through the French liturgy, I think in a dazed way about my mother lying alone in a funeral parlor. Or rather, not my mother, but my mother's *body* lying in some Dallas funeral parlor, her hands, her mouth, her forehead. I try to imagine the room—maybe the room where my stepfather was laid out and then, even in my bewildered daze, listening to the French liturgy reminds me that her breath and spirit aren't in that room. Her spirit left her body less than twelve hours before, at least presumably. So recently! I think with some panic that I'd better consider what that means while the event is still new. It's like being at the scene of an automobile accident and needing to study the details. I wonder whether her spirit is floating somewhere between her body and heaven. I begin to worry about my mother, the way I worried about my first child the day I combed her hair and took her to her first kindergarten class. It was all so new to her, and she felt strange there. I wonder whether my mother is trying to make herself understood to the other spirits or trying to make friends on this first day after her death.

And I wonder how my husband knew when my mother's spirit was leaving her body, what made him wake up at the exact minute she died. He loved her, of course—or rather, not *of course*, because I suppose many sons-in-law and mothers-in-law do not love one another. Did he know she was dying because she told him, somehow? Did he understand her? But how?

And most oddly, most fundamentally, at some primitive level, I feel that my mother cannot be dead, because, very simply, she gave me life. How can I still exist when the person who caused my existence has died? I hold my hand out and stare at it, bedecked with its familiar jade ring. It trembles slightly. I fear that I am not doing well, that we have decisions to make, that I cannot afford to fall apart, that I need to do whatever people mean when they say they are pulling themselves together.

As the vast congregation gets to its feet and sings "Holy God, We Praise Thy Name," I try to recall the unfamiliar Catholic English words, singing as many of them as I can. The cathedral brightens slightly as the priest begins his homily, the way the sky opens when a cloud passes from the sun. In that moment, I sense my mother. I feel a little frightened and improbably happy. I don't know why her spirit has come back or how. I just know that I am in a French Catholic church the day after mother died and her presence, like light, falls across us through one of the windows. It seems odd that she would come here because she was an anti-Papist and she held no truck with the French. But even in the later stages of Alzheimer's, she always had a sense of humor.

The following day, when I speak with the administrator at my university, she offers me the condolences of the whole staff. They're thinking about me, she says. She tells me I should do whatever I feel I need to do. But no, unfortunately, each Study Abroad Program is unique, and no one will be able to take over my program. I can't think of what to do. I know that if I leave, my students' program will be over.

A day later, after we fly back from Paris, the students and I climb to our classroom on the fourth floor of a Russell Square walkup. Their faces radiate the adventure of their recent travel to Rome and Edinburgh and Dublin. They laugh and pass around pictures on their cell phones and laptops, and they tell jokes and exchange souvenirs, whooping and laughing, happy to be reunited. In a stupor I watch them, unable to move or talk.

Finally, I yell "Hey!" The room gets quiet. When the students turn their faces toward me, I think they look like a bunch of sunflowers swiveling toward light. In that moment, I cannot conceive of how to tell them that their London program is over, that they waited tables summers to earn ten thousand dollars which may go down the drain, that they will have to fly home immediately, and they may not get credit for this trip.

I know perfectly well that I have the right to leave. It's my mother, after all. But I can't imagine what would happen to my students. And besides, I think my mother would want—no, that my mother does, right now, want me to finish what I've started.

Didn't she always tell us to finish what we start? If I could ask her and she could answer me, she would say she doesn't need me in Dallas. She's gone to a better place. She's with my father. Those are the words she would use.

So I don't leave my students. The students never learn that my mother has died. On Tuesday, my mother is quietly buried in Dallas with no mourners at her grave while I am teaching a class in London.

The year I bought my first laptop, my mother's memory began to fail. She'd squint her brown eyes and leave a blank in her sentence, which my sister and I would leap to fill in, a word like *shoeshine* or *explicit* or *Harold*. Around the same time, my techie son took me to a computer show to find a bargain computer. We stepped out of the bedazzling sunshine into a gloomy airplane-hanger-sized building. Long tables were loaded with computers, monitors, manuals, and parts. Glimpsing the sign, *Memory Bought and Sold,* I grabbed a fistful of my son's shirt and said, "Let's buy memory for your grandmother!"

Watching my mother slowly lose her memory was like watching a character in a movie bleaching out of the picture, because in some ways my mother *was* memory, not collective, cultural memory, but a repository of fundamentalist hymns and stories and language and jokes that had been handed down from generation to generation. As she aged, she served as the control center for the faith of many people, her friends, her fellow parishioners, her Bible study circle, her relatives. She knew and told stories about her parents and their parents and about herself and my father, always with a moral. She narrated tales from the Bible. She quoted the King James. She could reel off a twenty-minute-long pastiche of fundamentalist phrases and clauses when she prayed out loud. She dropped dozens of adages into her everyday speech: *Prayer changes things. Too soon old and too late smart. Give thanks in all things.* She became famous as a kind of memory retrieval system. Then Alzheimer's slowly erased her memory. And eventually she died of Alzheimer's, which is, I suppose, tantamount to dying of memory loss, because in the end she not only forgot the religion and culture she embodied; her body, itself, forgot to breathe.

The awful subject of memory loss is ironically fitting for a memoir, particularly a memoir about fundamentalism. At the headwaters of the genre lies the fear that a history will be lost if it isn't recorded. So I wonder whether I am trying to put a wrestling hold on Alzheimer's by bearing witness to what it wiped out: here is my mother reading Shakespeare at the kitchen table, and here she is taking us to school, and here she is sitting in her office at Irving Junior High School, and here she is judging a flower show. By sketching my mother as a character, it's possible that I'm trying to avoid losing her. But I know full well that this isn't my mother, it's only my version of her, a version severely limited by what I happen to remember now. Later I'll remember something different or something more, and in any case my sister's version of this story might be very different from mine. Beyond that, I know that no amount of reading or writing will bring our mother back.

 I am not writing to defeat Alzheimer's so much as to sort out the odd mixture of joy and grief I felt during those final years of my mother's life. Remarkably enough, her final years were not relentlessly grim. The story is not an utter nightmare, not entirely about suffering, by no means a tale of unremitting loss, even though the stories and articles I have read about Alzheimer's are characterized by unmitigated horror.

 I beg to differ. Perhaps this account will make me appear insensitive, or maybe I will seem to be in denial. But I have to bear witness to what I saw. The fact is, my mother's Alzheimer's years were a tragicomedy, a dark story, shot through with beauty and grace.

Deeper than Memory

Memory loss is a roomy subject, one we Baby Boomers are beginning to step into cautiously, rummaging around, frequently with an Erma Bombeck kind of humor. When I was in my mid-forties, I wrote a poem from the point of view of a woman whose decades of child rearing have erased details from her memory. I had just become aware that I was forgetting words. I had to cast about, sometimes, for the reason I had walked into a room. I wrote the poem in the spirit of light comedy. Memory loss seemed only a potentially dangerous eventuality, like the possibility of a death plunge when a person is standing at the brink of the Grand Canyon. In my imagination, a sturdy railing prevented my fall. By the Sunday afternoon when I suggested to my son that we buy my mother some computer memory, I understood that Alzheimer's is not funny, that my mother's memory loss wasn't going to be prevented by anything.

Watching my mother drift into Alzheimer's reminds me of those terrifying tragicomedies where the characters can't remember who they are. In Shakespeare's *Twelfth Night,* Viola crawls out of the sea, half-drowned, after a shipwreck she believes has killed her brother. She finds herself alone on a strange shore in an unidentifiable country, and, aware that she's a defenseless woman, she worries that she might be murdered or raped. So she puts on men's clothes. After that, because the characters in the play see Viola as a man, they start making life-changing, potentially tragic mistakes. Except for Viola, all the characters in the play act like the Alzheimer's patients who lived on my mother's hall.

Twelfth Night is a comedy (however dark), which means it has a happy ending, but long before the ending, a comic spirit guides the events of the play. Even in the first scene of *Twelfth Night,* so much joy and love flash through the dialogue that only a pathetically tone-deaf playwright would end the play in tragedy. In the same way, flashes of tenderness and humor—even in my mother's Alzheimer's ward—left me aware of what I often feel when I am walking on the nature trail at Haverford: that in spite of great anguish, there is a force that orders our universe, and that force is not chance, not brutality, not evil, but goodness.

I see Albert, the white-haired gentleman in a snappy denim shirt, take Elsie's arm, and no matter how hard Elsie pulls away from him, Albert hangs on. Elsie is his new love, and he's thrilled. He's determined to court her. When coaxing her in his charming South Carolina accent doesn't convince her, he shyly slips her two unwrapped chocolate Hershey kisses which have been in his drawer so long they look chalky. When she pushes his hand aside, he croons a couple of lines of "You Are My Sunshine." He has a pretty good voice. She ducks her head and wheels her walker expertly away.

That afternoon, when aides gather the residents for what the aides call "Bragging Time," Elsie casts him a flirtatious look and plops down in the midst of the women—that old junior high school girl trick—so Albert can't sit beside her. He turns his cobalt eyes on her and grins mischievously from across the room. She smiles back. Then he falls asleep.

There's tragedy in this, of course. Albert has lost his wife. Elsie has lost her husband. If friends visit them, more than likely they won't remember the visit. But there is also daring and flirting and wit and chocolate in their story. Watching Albert and Elsie reminds me of watching teenagers in the spring who, upon shedding their winter garments, fall in love for the first time. The witnesses who understand this most clearly are the aides in the Alzheimer's unit. They revel in that love as it unfolds; they do not discriminate against Albert and Elsie for being old; they carve a place in the grief of Alzheimer's for the joy of the moment. After the terror of moving my mother there, to my astonishment, I discover that these women are more talented and generous than I could have imagined. They are responsible for creating flashes of mercy and beauty themselves.

Not long after my son and I went to the computer show, my mother forgot the name of the county where she was born. When the Latin names for flowers and bushes fled her memory, she claimed she didn't anymore care to be a flower show judge. She put away her academic books about flowers, keeping out only the books with lovely pictures. Then she forgot her address and lost track of how to get home from the grocery store. It took her the whole month of December to address her Christmas cards. The following year she pretended to work on them but never sent them. She told us she was tired of doing the same old thing every year. Beside her phone she kept a pad of sticky notes broadcasting in a jaunty typeface: *What I Forgot to Remember.*

My sister and I started taking over. We sent Christmas cards to her vast list, enclosing a letter we had ghost-written for her. Noticing that my mother dropped food when she ate, I wracked my brain to find a way to help her; she had always been so modest and clean. I bought and mailed her eight white blouses, but the next time I visited, I saw that she didn't remember to change her blouse when it was stained. I was the one suffering embarrassment; she wasn't, though I didn't see that at the time. I refused to adjust, to give in to the disease, to let go. The truth is, for years, my sister and I only very reluctantly admitted that she was failing. We struggled to hold back gravity.

We did this by trying to arrange for her the very same activities she had for decades arranged for herself. We set up lunches for her with her friends. We picked up mail from her box, which she forgot to check. On one visit, I realized I needed to buy her Depends. I hunted for them in the grocery store, for the first time, standing in that aisle with other children of the elderly. Unlike some of them, I wasn't yet hardened to the fact that we had to take care of my mother that way. I left the box tactfully in her bathroom, where I found it untouched the next time I came. Once a week during that period, my sister sneaked up the back way to her apartment to scrub the rugs and set dozens of deodorizers behind the curtains and under the furniture. Face to face with the blunt processes of the body, as we had not been since our childhood—or since our own children were infants—the two of us talked by phone and emailed and buoyed one another up.

As my mother lost control of one part of her life after another, she worried less about what else might be taken away, and she certainly didn't talk about it. For the first time in her life, my mother wore red skirts with orange blouses. She threw rules for harmonious design out the window and layered herself in polka dots with plaids and stripes. To combat this, my sister and I coordinated the clothes in her closet and left her notes about what to wear with what. I tied the hanger of each skirt with a twisty to its companion blouse. Then at one point, I began thinking, *Why shouldn't she wear what she wants?* I began to relish her random, impulsive, gaudy combinations as if they were statements of extravagant taste or quirky jokes, and I think now I was right.

Back home, every night as I fried the chicken and cooked rice, my husband dialed my mother. Sometimes he would disguise his voice.

"This is Igorrrr Stravinsky," he once droned laconically.

"Oh, hello," my mother said cheerfully

"I know you luffff museeek."

"I do. I love music."

" I vant to half you to my house for dinner."

"I'm sorry. *Who* is this?"

"I yam Igor Stravinsky. I yam inviting you for dinner."

"I don't think I know you."

"I yam a vamous composer!"

"Oh Daniel!" my mother laughed, "I know who you are!"

Then he passed the receiver to me. I clamped it between my shoulder and chin while I snipped parsley. We gossiped about the residents in her building, about family news, about the weather, about everything we'd gone over the day before. It was repetitive, yes, but it was my mother, and she was alive, and she wanted to talk to us, and her voice sounded lit up with happiness.

One night, when my mother was almost ninety, she announced that she had regretfully decided not to marry again. She didn't want to take care of any more men. Several months later, she confided that a man had phoned and asked to visit her. She said she told him she wasn't taking social calls. She hoped she hadn't hurt his feelings. A month after that, she mentioned that this suitor had knocked at her door and introduced himself.

I thought of phoning the desk to find out what was going on, but my mother was in Assisted Living then, and I didn't want them to focus on her because I knew she was on the borderline of being moved to the Alzheimer's unit. Several of her friends had been sent there already. Cards we addressed to them came back with *Addressee Unknown:* the country never heard from.

Eventually, my mother began losing syntax, that mother earth of grammar, or I should say, that life-giving tree. If the trunk and branches are gone, there's nothing to hang the words on. As whole limbs of syntax blanked from my mother's mind, she became ever more silent.

On the phone with my mother at night, my husband and I took over more and more of the conversation. He is a great monologist, but I am not. I tried to refrain from asking questions which my mother had trouble answering. But I wanted to persuade her to talk somehow, because when she talked, her voice sounded like her old self. Hearing her, I'd forget that she wasn't the same woman I grew up with, the one whose voice I recognized in the womb, who chattered as she washed the clothes and drove me to orchestra rehearsals, full of advice about babies and men.

Even at ninety she could be diabolically clever.

"What did you do today?" I asked her.

She considered this briefly in silence. "You guess!"

"You went to the grocery store."

"That's right!"

Or maybe I guessed that she visited her best friend, Olive, or took a walk on the Christian Care campus. No matter what I said, she agreed with me in the festive voice of a game show host, successfully avoiding the dangerous shoals of language where her ship might flounder.

Once she admitted that she'd had back pain all day.

"We should do something about that," I told her.

"About what?" she demanded.

"Your back pain. Let's find you a doctor."

"Who said anything about back pain?"

So I pushed on. "Who are you voting for? I mean for President."

"Oh, honey, if I thought about stuff like that, I'd have no room in my head to think about important things."

I changed the subject. "Tell me more about learning to drive the Model A." She was narrating new and vivid stories about the past, stories that sounded authentic.

"It was a Model T."

"Okay. Tell me about learning to drive your Model T."

"Who said they let me drive it?"

Even then, I recognized that my mother was a comic, and I think she knew it too, and now I believe the woman who had been a loving wife and loyal mother and a respectful daughter and responsible employee for so many years might have enjoyed playing the droll grande dame. Perhaps she relaxed into irresponsibility with pleasure.

When my sister and I were finally forced to move my mother to the Alzheimer's unit, we were told we could not bring valuables, even her rings. So we took her to the local fire station in Mesquite, which, as a public service, saws off rings that won't slip off with soaping. I sat in the car with my mother while my sister went to find the fireman. Because mother was ninety, he brought his equipment outside rather than making her walk in. He was the age of her grandchildren. He knelt in the parking lot beside her like a Boy Scout. "Tell me if this hurts, ma'am," he said. "I don't want to hurt you." The way he held her veiny old hand was so courtly that my eyes misted over. We put her diamond rings in a lock box in her name so no one could steal them and bought her two rings with very large glass stones which she admired.

Without a backward glance, my mother shed the objects of a lifetime. She forgot her eighty-year-old china doll with the milk glass eyes named Marianne and the mink collars she scissored off her coats to save. She no longer remembered the genuine wool red blanket my father bought her on their honeymoon in Sault St. Marie. Once they slipped from her attention, all her alluring things grew lifeless. It turns out that her love was what electrified them. I didn't understand that until I went through her cedar chest.

During the week we moved her to the Alzheimer's unit, I sat cross-legged, alone in my sister's cold garage in front of that chest. The key made a metallic click as it spun in the lock. In the shadowy light, I couldn't make out why the lock wouldn't open, and I half believed the chest was forbidding me to touch it. She had bought that trunk with her first paycheck as a nurse, and no one ever opened it but her. She would summon us before she inserted the key in the lock, and I would lean forward to watch as she pulled out the magic objects. She would permit me to touch each one briefly.

She had the knack of limiting her possessions to the number she could really use, maybe because she was a teenager during the Depression. Even later, after my father's death and after she had married my stepfather, when she could afford what she wanted, she would buy a dress and hoard it in her closet as it accumulated glamour for several months before she wore it. So in the cold garage, when I finally got her cedar chest open and unfolded the careful tissue paper wrappings, I was flabbergasted to see that the sweaters were pilled and the long, white leather gloves had stiffened with age. All the mystery had dissipated from her things when she stopped holding them in her attention. Sitting on a shelf in my daughter's house, her doll Marianne looks like any other antique doll.

I could go on about my mother's objects. To see her marked-up King James Bibles in my house rather than at her bedside is to see matter out of place. As her old Bible filled up with notes, she kept buying new Bibles and jotting notes in them with red ink and black ink and blue ink and different kinds of pencil. The notes were always in her perfect, Palmer-method handwriting. They cross-referenced Biblical texts, recorded her insights, documented concordance-like information.

In one of her steel boxes, I found the letters I wrote to her in 1968 when I was first married. I took them home because I couldn't bring myself to throw them out, but I don't know what to do with them. They were half-truths, concocted with bravado to make her happy, and they make no sense without her. Her teacup collection, her Lenox dishes, her tablecloths—when she cared about them, their value transcended their worth as mere objects. I have discovered that none of them work as a retrieval system to remember her by.

But in fact, this melancholy litany of objects I have recited is a list of my own losses, not a catalogue of my mother's. When I lost her, I lost her objects, which ceased to hold the same allure for me. I am not sure, as I write this, that my mother objected to losing her objects. What if she experienced that offloading as a lightening, a lifting, a freeing?

So I try to recall details. I bring whatever I can to the surface of my memory.

She perches on her chair looking lady-like at her quarterly check-up. Dr. Roberts asks my mother how she's feeling.

"How do you think an old lady like me is feeling?" she demands.

I am shocked at her lip, but she's smiling. She's not about to list her aches and pains for a doctor. She spent thirty years working as a nurse. She knows no mere doctor can fix what's wrong with her. Besides, to list her troubles would be trivialize them. It would be to move them out of the permanent, immutable, Platonic realm, where they rightfully belong, onto a medical chart.

As her dark eyes grew vacant, my mother lapsed into bemused tolerance toward everyone and everything. She smiled easily. She became sweetly agreeable. When the aides gathered the old people in the lounge to see the Animal Lady, whose pet of the month was a ferret, my mother tried to get into the spirit. Although she never even liked our own dogs, when the ferret came around, crawling on the arm of the Lady, my mother valiantly reached out her hand and petted it. When one of the aides got up and danced with the Animal Lady, she giggled. She answered two questions during the quiz at the end of the show. Then she joined the procession of residents as they lined up their walkers like ancient elephants and took the elevator upstairs to their hall. She was game. She trusted the aides. She had long forgotten the details of her fundamentalist beliefs. The creed meant absolutely nothing to her. But she hung onto her faith, which must have been deeper than memory. She always preferred perennials, the flowers that wither in the fall and come back to life in spring. She was a specialist in hope.

So I was surprised when a well-dressed older woman accosted me as I stepped off the elevator on my mother's floor of the Alzheimer's unit. I was lugging a huge cardboard box full of stuff, and sweating, and my hair was sticking to my head, and I was aware the woman must find me rather disgusting. But she strolled alongside me, past the front desk, by the large fish tank. When I got to my mother's apartment, I stuffed the awkward box through the door, and it landed with a thud on the beige carpet. My companion waited beside me, smiling. I turned to her, wondering what she had to tell me—about my mother, about her medications, about her visitors and her doctors.

"You won't find her," the woman said.

"Why not?" I asked.

"She hides."

"Who hides?"

"You don't know me, so I don't have to tell you."

I felt depressed by the realization that this woman was not a health care worker but a sick resident. I was tired. Several months earlier, my sister and I had lost our fight to keep mother out of this place. I couldn't imagine what lay ahead for her. I felt we were sliding into a nightmare, that the world might be, indeed, governed by chance, by darkness, or by nothing at all.

I looked toward the desk, hoping to be rescued. The aides were gathering residents for dinner down the hall, which I could hear being set out, the tick of ceramic plates on tables. There was not an aide in sight, so I was on my own in the strange country of this woman's mind, where the walls were not perpendicular and the logic seemed arbitrary. I didn't know the social rules. I knew that whatever I said, in five minutes she would forget. But to pander to her seemed condescending.

"I'm sorry. I don't understand you," I said, and I set off to find my mother.

The woman followed me. "Are you looking for her?"

"I think she's at dinner," I replied.

Then I noticed that my mother was snoozing in one of the Queen Anne chairs by the desk. I stepped over, scrunched down, and put my arm around her. She woke up and looked at me without recognition. Then her eyes cleared. "Well, look who's here!" she said brightly. She never called me "darling" anymore. She couldn't afford to be that revealing. But she knew who I was, and she loved me long after she had forgotten almost everything else.

The woman persisted. "I told her not to, and she went ahead anyway."

"Not to do what?"

I glanced at my mother. She shrugged, grinned at me, and circled her finger by her ear. I realized that my mother, who was deep into Alzheimer's, was blissfully identifying herself with me and other sane, rational people of the world.

Aha! I realized. This must be the woman who answered my mother's phone, when my husband called from Philadelphia one night. The phone rang. A strange voice picked up and told my husband that my mother wasn't there, that my mother had moved. He was confused. He asked when.

"Six weeks ago."

"She's moved?"

"Yeah, out of here."

"Am I talking to an aide?" my husband asked.

"Yes."

This woman, my mother's neighbor, must have hoped that my mother would leave. Maybe my mother reminded her of someone. Or maybe my mother was moving into the apartment of her best friend, who had been shifted to nursing care, or who had died.

As I grabbed my mother's bony hand and walked slowly with her to dinner, the smell of mashed potatoes and hamburgers rising around us, it was getting hard for me to tell the difference between my own thoughts and the madness around me. Sitting down across from my mother and feeding her with a spoon, I tried to freeze the moment. Someday, I thought, as a way to stay sane, maybe I will write about this. What I remember of that moment now, which registered then as nothing but overwhelming loss, is my mother's courtesy, amusement, and love.

Habit is the memory of the body. For sixty years, I was accustomed to seeing my mother and hearing her voice. I even got used to flying to Dallas to take care of her. No wonder for these two years since her death, under my dreaming and waking, I have been listening for her the way I listened for my children.

After the phone call in which Rich told us about my mother's death, I phoned my sister from London to plan her memorial service. Then I finished the program with my students and flew with my husband to Dallas. There we commemorated my mother's spirit with eulogies and flowers and food and hymns and readings from the Bible.

But the body cries out to escort a loved one back to the earth. To believe in my mother's death, I probably needed to see her dead, distorted face, to throw clods on her coffin and hear the resounding thud. The fact is, I did not understand this when I was deciding whether or not to fly to Dallas to bury her. I chose not to leave my students. It was a difficult choice, but it was mine, and I am not altogether sorry. The students needed me. But the truth is, I have paid for that decision. I have trouble sustaining any image of my mother in heaven. Maybe that's not because I lack faith, but because I don't yet entirely believe she's dead. Perhaps it's a failure not of belief, but of my own imagination, and I hope someday to correct it.

The fact that I can't imagine my mother in heaven doesn't mean there is no heaven. She lived beyond the time when she could remember any creed, but I have learned that there is something deeper than either memory or imagination, and that is faith. My mother never lost her faith, and I suspect she did not find her slide into Alzheimer's as distressing as I did. Faith is the conviction that this world is not tragic but comic. Maybe it gives a person the ability to see whatever joy and beauty and wit flickers in the disorienting darkness. Or maybe it is the result of noticing those flickers. I don't know. And how can we know for sure that the flickers are clues to how the story will end? We can't know for sure. Nevertheless, most mornings I wake up believing that we are perennials not annuals—a feeling that itself is a gift. Surely what dies will spring back to life. I suspect it was my mother who taught me that faith—good and true flower show judge that she was.

Acknowledgments

Though the actions and people in this book are not invented, the names are sometimes fictional. When I am talking about a close family member, I usually just refer, for example, to "my brother" or "my mother." Some familiar ministers and teachers, for example, are called by their actual names. But in the case of neighbors, students, and friends, the names are either fictional or missing—that is, referred to as "her" or "him."

Chapter five of this book was previously published in *The Geography of Memory*.

Portions of this book were originally published in *Image*, *Prairie Schooner*, *Shenandoah*, and *The Other Journal*.

Thanks to Julie and Rich Thomas, whose detailed memories have added immeasurably to some of these stories.

I wish I could adequately thank my two writing workshop partners, Deborah Burnham and Elaine Terranova, themselves distinguished writers. For almost half a century I have been meeting with each of them nearly weekly to drink (usually) tea and share manuscripts.

Thanks to E. Daniel Larkin, my husband and reader at many early stages of everything I write. He remains perpetually patient, smart, good natured, and supportive. Without his encouragement, I would be lost.

Finally, thanks to Gregory Wolfe, whose rigor as an editor and whose kindness as a friend mean the world to me.

This book was set in Sabon, designed by the German typographer and book designer, Jan Tschichold, and released in 1967. Tschichold was inspired to design Sabon after encountering a sixteenth-century specimen sheet produced by the legendary printer and typographer, Claude Garamond (1480–1561). The typeface is named after one of Garamond's students and colleagues, Jacques Sabon (1535–ca. 1580–90).

This book was designed by Shannon Carter, Ian Creeger, and Gregory Wolfe. It was published in hardcover, paperback, and electronic formats by Slant Books, Seattle, Washington.

Cover photograph: Dmitry Daltonik via Pexels.

www.ingramcontent.com/pod-product-compliance
Lightning Source LLC
Chambersburg PA
CBHW030853170426
43193CB00009BA/598